LA PARISIENNE IN CINEMA

Manchester University Press

La Parisienne in cinema

Between art and life

FELICITY CHAPLIN

Manchester University Press

Copyright © Felicity Chaplin 2017

The right of Felicity Chaplin to be identified as the author of this work has been asserted by her in accordance with the Copyright, Designs and Patents Act 1988.

Published by Manchester University Press
Altrincham Street, Manchester M1 7JA, UK
www.manchesteruniversitypress.co.uk

British Library Cataloguing-in-Publication Data is available

ISBN 978 1 5261 0953 8 *hardback*
ISBN 978 1 5261 3953 5 *paperback*

First published by Manchester University Press in hardback 2017

This edition first published 2019

The publisher has no responsibility for the persistence or accuracy of URLs for any external or third-party internet websites referred to in this book, and does not guarantee that any content on such websites is, or will remain, accurate or appropriate.

For Gigi

Contents

		page
	Acknowledgements	ix
	Introduction: 'What's she like?'	1
1	Muse	18
2	Cosmopolite	47
3	Icon of fashion	71
4	Femme fatale	95
5	Courtesan	120
6	Star	150
	Conclusion: 'Look, let's start all over again. What's she like?'	180
	Films cited	185
	References	190
	Index	203

Acknowledgements

This book would not have been possible without the intellectual and moral support of many people. In particular, I would like to thank Philip Anderson, Adrian Martin, Deane Williams, Sarah McDonald and Benjamin Andréo, who each brought to the project a different and enriching perspective. My thanks go to staff and students of French Studies and Film and Screen Studies at Monash University. I would also like to acknowledge the support received from the Monash University Postgraduate Publications Award. On a personal note, I would like to thank Elizabeth, John, Annelies and Catherine Chaplin, Miriam Saward, Belinda Glynn, Anna Parry and David Jack.

Introduction: 'What's she like?'

There is a scene in Vincente Minnelli's *An American in Paris* (1951) in which two friends, Adam (Oscar Levant) and Henri (Georges Guétary), discuss the various merits of Parisienne Lise Bouvier (Leslie Caron). The attempt to describe, and in a way to categorise, the 19-year-old perfume-shop clerk begins when, over coffee and brioches at the Café Huguette, Adam asks Henri: 'What's she like?'

> HENRI: Well, she has great vitality and joie de vivre. She loves to go out, have fun and dance. She could dance all night!
> ADAM: Sounds tiresome. Kind of a wild kid, huh?
> HENRI Wild? Whatever gave you that idea? No, she is very simple. She works all day at the Maison Nicole, the perfume shop.

The camera pans away from Adam and Henri and rests on a large gilt-framed mirror in which they are now reflected, and Henri continues: 'She's an enchanting girl, Adam. Not really beautiful, and yet she has great beauty.' This shot dissolves to reveal Lise framed in the mirror. The camera tracks forward, obscuring the frame, and Lise, in a pale pink Romantic tutu with satin bodice, small wing-like sleeves, tulle-lined skirt and a matching pill-box hat, performs a graceful dance in the classical ballet style. As the dance ends, Lise looks into the camera with a beaming smile. As this fantasy interlude concludes, we return to a shot of the two men, and Adam remarks: 'A very spiritual type, huh?', to which Henri replies: 'Not at all. She's an exciting girl.' The shot again dissolves to Lise, poised seductively on a balloon-back chair, dressed in a tight-fitting purple dress split up both thighs to expose her long, sheer-stockinged legs. A sultry jazz score with a wailing saxophone accompanies the scene. Fade back to the café, and Adam remarks: 'She seems to be a lusty young lady.' Henri insists, however, that 'she's sweet and shy'. The camera dissolves to a shot of Lise in a canary-yellow dress, holding a small posy of flowers and tentatively dancing to the accompaniment of a light orchestrated ballet score. The sequence ends with a slow, carefully developed arabesque. 'An old-fashioned girl, huh?', Adam concludes, to which Henri replies: 'Of course not, she's vivacious and modern.' We then dissolve to a shot of Lise in a white 1920s style flapper dress, dancing the Charleston against a bold red background. 'Always yakking it up, hey?', Adam remarks; to which Henri replies: 'Don't be silly! She reads incessantly!' The shot dissolves to a scene accompanied by sombre baroque music in which Lise, in simple black leggings and a black long-sleeved T-shirt with white collar and cuffs, performs a series of splits and arabesques while completely absorbed in a book. Adam asks: 'Doesn't all that reading make her moody?' to which Henri replies: 'Never! She's the gayest girl in the world.' Dissolve again to a shot of Lise in a vibrant blue Classical tutu performing a series of frenzied pirouettes to lively, carnivalesque music. The music continues as one by one the previous manifestations of Lise are superimposed onto this final image. As each image appears, Lise looks toward each incarnation of herself, demonstrating an awareness of the various representations of her. The five 'Lises' then wave coquettishly to Adam and Henri and, by extension, to the audience. As this collage shot dissolves finally to the café, Adam turns to Henri and says: 'Look. Let's start all over again. What's she like?'

The back-and-forth volleying between the two men, set off by Adam's outwardly simple question and giving rise to a series of vignettes depicting Lise in various guises, suggests the impossibility of answering the question in any definitive way, or arriving at a conclusive definition of Lise. Further, once any kind of consensus is reached concerning Lise, Henri abruptly changes tack. Rather than becoming exasperated by this process, Henri simply accepts that Lise is all these things at once. Indeed, the whole opening sequence proceeds by way of thesis/antithesis, without ever arriving at a synthesis; the 'true' Lise, her 'essential' identity, remains ambiguous and elusive. As Louis Octave Uzanne remarks in his study on *la Parisienne*: 'On a peint ou décrit des femmes à l'infini; *la Femme* n'a jamais été strictement synthétisée' (*The Modern Parisienne* 45; original emphasis) (Women have been painted or described ad infinitum; Woman has never been strictly synthesised). This scene from Minnelli's film is significant too in that the fantasy sequence constitutes our first encounter with Lise. We are introduced to her through an imagined collage of images, generated by Henri's descriptions and Adam's imagination. Thus her first 'real' appearance on screen, that is, her entry into the 'real world' of the film's diegesis, is anticipated by this fantasy sequence. In a certain sense, this is how any Parisienne first appears to us, pre-empted or prefigured by the proliferation of images and (re)presentations which precede her.

Who or what is *la Parisienne*? Some definitions

La Parisienne has been defined as a myth or dogma, a stereotype, a cliché and a cultural icon. Ruth E. Iskin argues that the 'historical conditions for the rise of the chic Parisienne were a convergence of mass-production, consumption and the spread of a visual culture promoting consumption' (223). The origins of the term *la Parisienne* are difficult to trace: while it was in use in the late eighteenth century, it only came into frequent use in the mid-nineteenth century to describe 'a specific type of urban woman whose garments declare a self-fashioned image of position and desire' (Mancoff 145). Despite the uncertainty of the origin of the term, Debra Mancoff does provide the following definition: 'a contemporary type of frivolous, fashion-minded young woman, middle- or working-class, who used her looks as capital in an upwardly mobile society' (44). This definition touches on two essential features of the Parisienne type: fashion and social mobility. Indeed, fashionability appears as the dominant idea with which the Parisienne type is associated. Françoise Tétart-Vittu describes *la Parisienne* alternately as 'synonymous with fashion' (80), 'a woman of fashion' and 'a woman of the world' (78). Sidsel Maria Søndergaard claims the 'designation, Parisienne, was a blanket term for the well-dressed women of the metropolis, applied to both the elegant ladies of the bourgeoisie and the chic *demimonde*' and that the chic *Parisienne* 'became an *icon* for metropolitan femininity and an integral part of the visual *culture* of Modernity' (39). Jean-Christophe Ferrari refers to her as 'an aesthetic figure' and a model 'in the pictorial sense of the word' (71), while Iskin claims the type 'played a central role in the shift from academic to modern painting led by Manet and the Impressionists, replacing nude or draped figures with modern Parisiennes in contemporary fashions' (198).

The term *la Parisienne* denotes far more than simply a female inhabitant of Paris. She is a figure of French modernity, and this can be taken in two senses, the technical/industrial and the cultural. The technical or industrial sense refers to the modernisation of Paris and its transformation into the capital of the modern world. This process included the reconstruction of Paris by Baron Haussmann and the widening of the boulevards, the extensive use of iron and glass in the construction of the arcades, the expansion of the railway system, the revolution in printing technology, the rise of the department store, the new system of capitalism and consumer culture, and increased leisure activity amongst the city's inhabitants. In the days before Haussmann, 'it was impossible to stroll about everywhere in the city. Before Haussmann, wide pavements were rare; the narrow ones afforded little protection from vehicles. Flânerie could hardly have assumed the importance it did without the arcades' (Benjamin, *Illuminations* 68). Anne Friedberg traces the appearance of the *flâneuse* to the emerging consumer culture and development of department stores in late nineteenth-century Paris which afforded women a legitimate reason to occupy public space: 'The female flâneur, the flâneuse, was not possible until she was free to roam the city on her own. And this was equated with the privilege of shopping on her own' (36).[1] With the boulevards and arcades, as well as the construction of extensive parks and gardens, women could for the first time be seen in public, on display, without being considered *filles publiques* or prostitutes.

Fashion, too, dictated the redesigning of Paris: in *The Arcades Project* Walter Benjamin writes that 'the widening of the streets, it was said, was necessitated by the crinoline' (133). This remark indicates a close relationship between the creation of the boulevards and fashionable women in their abundant crinoline dresses, parading down the wide streets of Paris, participating in the spectacle of modern life. This was the era when women began to stroll publicly in the city streets, their emergence facilitated by the arcades and department stores which legitimated their temporary leave of the interior or private sphere and their entry into the public sphere as consumers. The expansion of the railway network, from a few disparate strands totalling 1,931 km in 1850 to an intricate network of 17,400 km in 1870, opened up Parisian industry and commerce to interregional and international competition (Harvey 109). David Harvey sums up the effect of this expansion in the following way: 'it was not only goods that moved. Tourists flooded in from all over the world ... , shoppers poured in from the suburbs, and the Parisian labour market spread its tentacles into ever remoter regions in order to satisfy burgeoning demand for labor power' (111). The ease with which provincials and foreigners could now travel to Paris was also formative for *la Parisienne* who, according to Georges Montorgueil, 'est de partout, mais ... ne devient qu'à Paris la Parisienne' (v) (is from everywhere but ... only *becomes* the Parisienne in Paris).

A further important development in the creation of the Parisienne type was the revolution in printing technology in the nineteenth century. This resulted in both a dramatic decrease in the production cost of print media and the considerable increase in the availability of visual material, which in turn saw not only the proliferation of illustrated journals, particularly fashion journals, but their dissemination across a wider readership, including both the working and lower-middle classes (Menon, *Evil* 7). For the first time, women across a much broader social spectrum were exposed to a single homogenising image of the fashionable woman. Iskin writes that women were able to 'acquire a certain amount of information on how to look like a chic Parisienne by reading fashion magazines, illustrated journals and ordering from department store catalogues' (192).

This revolution in printing technology took place contemporaneously with the rise of haute couture and the development of the department stores and prêt-à-porter clothing. In 1872 there were 684 couturiers in Paris compared to only 158 in 1850; by 1895 the number had increased to 1,636 (Iskin 190). Tamar Garb writes that the 'department stores and shopping arcades proffered an unprecedented array of goods aimed at seducing women and creating in them the desire to consume luxury goods indispensable to their identity as women' ('Painting' 98).

Brian Nelson argues that shopping facilitated a woman's entry into and occupation of the public sphere (xvii). This reflected a more general tendency in Paris of the nineteenth century, resulting in increased visibility and mobility in the modern city: 'The newly revitalized city gave rise to a new culture. Life became more public' (Mancoff 8). According to Nancy Rose Marshall, it was in 'the new urban spaces in which the concept of the *Parisienne* was formed' (154).

In a cultural sense, *la Parisienne* is a figure of French modernity in that she was a feature of the visual arts, literature, physiognomies and popular culture of nineteenth-century France. She appears in the novels of Balzac, Flaubert and Zola; in the short stories of Maupassant; in Henry Becque's 1885 play *La Parisienne*; and in the poems of Baudelaire. She was also the subject of many studies and physiologies, including Taxile Delord's *Physiologie de la Parisienne* (1841), Théodore de Banville's *Les Parisiennes de Paris* (1866), Arsène Houssaye's *Les Parisiennes* (1869), Georges Montorgueil's *La Parisienne* (1897), and Louis Octave Uzanne's *Parisiennes de ce temps en leurs divers milieux, états et conditions* (1910), an expanded edition of the original 1894 version, which appeared in an English-language edition entitled *The Modern Parisienne* (1912). There have also been numerous paintings, lithographs, etchings and pastels of Parisiennes: Tissot, Morisot, Stevens, Renoir, Helleu, Cassatt and Toulouse-Lautrec, among others, all sought to capture the type in their work. Visual artists, too, explicitly titled their studies *la Parisienne* or included the descriptor 'Parisienne' in the title. According to Marie Simon, the proliferation of paintings featuring *la Parisienne* demonstrates 'the individual being replaced by the abstract. Artists no longer painted a woman but a human type, a quality' (199).

The attempt to capture the Parisienne type visually continued into the twentieth and twenty-first centuries in photography. Three photographic monographs in particular took the type as their primary subject matter: André Maurois's *Femmes de Paris* (1954), featuring photographs by Nico Jesse; *Parisiennes: A Celebration of French Women* (2007), a collection of photographs of Parisian women taken by celebrated as well as anonymous photographers; and Baudouin's *75 Parisiennes* (2013), which puts into play various pre-existing themes or motifs, revealing the vitality and currency of the Parisienne type.

Baudouin draws on an already existing iconography of *la Parisienne* in composing his photographs, focusing on the repetition of familiar motifs such as the Eiffel Tower, the little black dress, the feather boa, the *chevelure*, the fashion journal and the cat. The iconography of *la Parisienne* that Baudouin draws on is largely informed by nineteenth-century visual and literary representations of the type. Baudouin also provides each sitter's profession and Metro station, which serves to indicate the meta-sociological aspect of the Parisienne type, a type not restricted by economics, class, nationality, ethnicity or status, but rather transcending these limits.

While there is significant scholarship on *la Parisienne* in the fields of art history, fashion theory and culture and cultural histories of Paris, there is little written on the (re)appearance and function of the type in cinema. In part, this is because her presence in cinema is not always immediately discernible and frequently forms or creates a subtext to the films. The goal of this book is to outline a 'cycle' of Parisienne films; however this cycle, like the type itself, is never complete and is always in the process of evolving, due both to the plasticity of the type and to the myriad possible ways of representing her. The films under consideration are limited to narrative feature films, which is not to deny the presence of the Parisienne type in short films, documentary or experimental films.

An iconographical approach

Erwin Panofsky's theory of iconography was first developed in relation to Renaissance art and later applied to cinema. His theory of the iconographical type was developed in relation to silent cinema, and later applied to sound cinema by Stanley Cavell and Jean-Loup Bourget. *La Parisienne* constitutes what Panofsky calls a 'type' because it possesses both a fixed and fluid iconography, the fixed aspects being those necessary for any preliminary identification of the type, the fluid referring to the variations the type undergoes during its development. In his essay 'Style and Medium in the Motion Pictures', Panofsky argues that in early silent cinema we find the introduction of 'a fixed iconography which from the outset informed the spectator about the basic facts and characters .... There arose, identifiable by standardised appearance, behaviour, and attributes, the well-remembered types ... . The conduct of characters was predetermined accordingly' (254). The introduction of types into silent film was necessary in order to help the audience confronted with the new medium 'understand the meaning of the speechless action in a moving picture' (253).

For Panofsky, the 'readability' of these types 'depend on pre- or extra-cinematic knowledge' (Levin 34). The idea of the pre- and extra-cinematic is particularly pertinent to this study, which seeks to demonstrate how pre-cinematic knowledge (nineteenth-century art, literature and mass culture) and extra-cinematic knowledge (stars and intertexts) inform the Parisienne type in cinema. *La Parisienne* may not initially be a recognisable type, particularly when compared with the more easily recognisable types of the silent era such as the villain, the gangster, the vamp or the 'good woman', due in part to the moral ambiguity of the Parisienne type and to the fact that she seldom resembles herself. Thus built into the Parisienne type is an elusiveness or multiplicity which makes easy recognition more difficult than it is with the more generic types originally considered by Panofsky. Yet, *la Parisienne* is a type nonetheless and she does possess certain motifs which make her recognisable, provided these motifs are thoroughly and accurately identified.

Panofsky argues that the introduction of a fixed iconography became less important once the cinemagoing public was acclimatised to the different typological signifiers and that these signifiers were 'virtually abolished by the invention of the talking film' (254). In spite of this, however, there survives 'the remnants of a "fixed attitude and attribute"' (254) by which types can be recognised. While Cavell and Bourget agree that cinema introduces a fixed iconography, both have challenged Panofsky's claim that sound cinema effectively abolished the need for typology. Bourget remarks that he is struck by the persistence of iconography after the silent era (39). In a similar vein, Cavell writes that 'such devices persist as long as there are still Westerns and gangster films and comedies and musicals and romances. *Which* specific iconography the Villain is given will alter with the times, but that his iconography remains specific (i.e., operates according to a "fixed attitude and attribute" principle) seems undeniable' (314; original emphasis). Cavell further argues that cinema 'created new types, or combinations or ironic reversals of types; but there they were, and stayed' (314), as well as for the 'continuing validity of a Panofskian iconographic program for the study of film' (Levin 40). In *Studies in Iconology: Humanistic Themes in the Art of the Renaissance*, Panofsky proposed a model for the analysis of Renaissance painting which corresponds to three levels or strata of meaning. The first, or pre-iconographical, level of a work of art is made up of motifs, pure forms which are the 'carriers of *primary and natural meanings*' (Panofsky 5; original emphasis). The second level involves the identification and description of the images; that is, the secondary or conventional meanings conveyed by the motifs. '*Motifs* thus recognized as carriers of a *secondary* or *conventional* meaning may be called *images*' (Panofsky 6; original emphasis). This is the stage of iconographical analysis proper. The third level consists of an iconological interpretation, that is, the interpretation of the images and their 'intrinsic meaning and content' (Panofsky 7).

Bourget argues that Panofsky's three-stratum model can be applied to cinema. For Bourget, an analysis of cinema which draws on models or methods from art history is highly productive, primarily because it restores an imbalance in film studies, which has often focused on questions of narrative or plot derived from the history of literature, often neglecting the image or figure (38). Bourget also considers a reference to art history in the analysis of cinema fruitful in that films will often cite motifs, either intentionally or unintentionally, which come directly from the history of painting (40). For Bourget, nothing assures that the reference to painting is completely intentional, while at other times the reference is manifestly intended (40–1).

In 'Style and Medium in the Motion Pictures', Panofsky raises the idea of medium specificity to found cinema as an art form in its own right, distinct from other art forms in terms of its technicality. Yet in terms of iconography, cinema can be subjected to the same type of analysis as painting. Having established cinema as a distinct art form through its medium specificity, Panofsky emphasises not the kinetic but the photographic aspect of cinema. He de-emphasises the technical specificity of the medium in favour of its origins in pictorial rather than narrative art: cinema originally not as 'filmed theatre' but literally as 'moving pictures' (254).

In 1982, Bourget adapted Panofsky's iconographical model for cinema; however Panofsky's iconographic approach had already been used in film studies by Lawrence Alloway. Steve Neale writes that while Panofsky himself considered the application of the terms iconography and iconology to an analysis of films, it was Alloway 'who sought to apply them in a systematic way to the analysis of genres and cycles' (13). In a 1963 article for the film journal *Movie*, Alloway argues for the application of Panofsky's method to cinema: 'The meaning of a single movie is inseparable from the larger pattern of content-analysis of other movies' (17). For Alloway, iconography provides a way of 'charting the flow and the evanescence' of films which belong to a popular art which does not possess 'an unchanging significance' but is rather in a constant state of flux (18).

For Alloway, the natural subject matter of Panofsky's first stratum when applied to cinema 'consists of the physical reality of the photographed world' which includes the actor and thus relates to the star system: 'The star whose personality and status are created as a product, is, when photographed, continually present in a more powerful form than the individual roles he or she may be playing ... . Thus, even the "primary or natural subject matter" is not without its iconographical potential' (16). For Alloway, the realm of iconography begins, unlike in Panofsky's tripartite model, at the first level or stratum. Alloway's reworking of Panofsky for cinema deals primarily with motifs and images and less with interpretation (Neale 14–15). What Alloway was most interested in was founding a 'descriptive aesthetic' (qtd in Whiteley 276).

Ed Buscombe's synonym for iconography is 'visual conventions' (Neale 15). While there is some merit in this definition, the term is too narrow because iconography often encompasses more than just the visual, extending to more literary motifs such as narrative and character. Furthermore, these conventions are subject to historical variability. The limits of visual conventions can be seen in the following example: in the nineteenth century the Parisienne type wears a crinoline and carries a parasol, whereas in Jean-Luc Godard's À *bout de souffle* (1960) she wears cropped trousers and has a 'pixie' haircut. The particulars change but the general – that is, the notion or concept of fashionability and style – remains the same.

Alloway extended iconography to include cycles of films: a film cycle 'explores a basic situation repeatedly, but from different angles and with accumulating references' (16), and 'provides the audience with a flexible, continuing convention and a body of expectations and knowledge on which the filmmaker can count' (18). Motifs appear repeatedly throughout certain films in different ways or from varied perspectives, each (re)appearance adding to the growing iconography of a type. When discussing cycles of films, Alloway is not interested in judgements of quality. Nor is he interested in an auteurist approach, arguing that 'treating movies as personal expression and autographic testament has led to the neglect of the iconographical approach' (16). Alloway gives the example of a cycle of films starring Frank Sinatra to demonstrate the 'necessity for considering movies in groups not necessarily dependent upon directors', and writes of Sinatra's 'iconographical profile' (17). These ideas are central when considering, for example, Jeanne Moreau's successive appearances in a number of Parisienne films which build an iconographical profile both for the actress and the characters she plays.

In adopting an iconographical approach to cinema, Alloway does not privilege only those films created by an auteur and considered masterpieces of cinema by some critics; rather, his selection of films is more encompassing and wide-ranging. Andrew Sarris, a proponent of auteur theory, criticised Alloway's approach, remarking that 'he transforms what is too frequently a dismal fact into a visionary ideal. Badness and banality become sociological virtues; familiarity breeds contentment' (69). Sarris attacked Alloway for implicitly endorsing 'bad' films. However, Alloway wanted to avoid evaluation because he wanted to found his descriptive aesthetic not so much on quality as on repetition or enumeration. Discussing the debate between Sarris and Alloway, Nigel Whiteley remarks that far from privileging only so-called 'bad' films at the expense of quality cinema, Alloway 'took a far wider view of creativity', seeing culture as a continuum which 'ranged from individual masterworks to depersonalized, expendable, commercial products of consumer society' (276). In Alloway's judgement, Sarris 'mistook one end of the continuum as its only edifice' (Whiteley 276). The films set for discussion in this book are chosen from this continuum, ranging from celebrated masterpieces by auteurs like Carné and Godard, to more 'lightweight' films like Jules Dassin's *Reunion in France* (1942) and Michel Boisrond's's *Une Parisienne* (1957), and lesser-known French romantic comedies such as Yvan Attal's *Ma Femme est une actrice* (2001). Critical reception is of less interest than the way these films employ certain motifs. Taking the notion of cultural continuum into account, there then appears a vast cycle of Parisienne films and a limited space in which to discuss them. Chance and availability have played their part in the selection process as well, and there are certainly films which might take their place in the cycle of Parisienne films which receive no mention in this study.

While this book confines itself to an iconographical approach to the Parisienne type, the relevance of critical approaches such as feminism and feminist film theory must also be noted. While a sustained feminist engagement is outside the scope of this book, such engagement seems an obvious omission from any detailed consideration of the type. There are two reasons, however, why this is not the place for such an engagement. First, this book, intended as an introduction to *la Parisienne* and her iconography in cinema, deals predominantly with visual and narrative conventions, derived primarily from nineteenth-century art, literature and visual culture. Thus it lays the groundwork for further scholarship which may take into account concepts such as gender, race and ethnicity, all of which are relevant to the study of the Parisienne type. Secondly, a feminist or gender studies approach may appear too polemical for a work intended as an introduction or overview.

Beyond the iconographical approach, however, the Parisienne type in cinema could and should be critically examined through an engagement with feminist film theory, reception studies and theories of spectatorship. Laura Mulvey's seminal essay 'Visual pleasure and narrative cinema' (1989), for example, might be a useful starting point for a discussion of identification and spectatorship practices in relation to the Parisienne type in cinema. In particular, Mulvey's claim that the visual pleasure in cinema is 'split between active/male and passive/female' (19) appears relevant to the films discussed here. Indeed, the following lines appear to describe well the way this heterosexual matrix functions, particularly in mainstream films featuring *la Parisienne*:

Traditionally, the woman displayed has functioned on two levels: as erotic object for the characters within the screen story, and as erotic object for the spectator within the auditorium, with a shifting tension between the looks on either side of the screen. For instance, the device of the showgirl allows the two looks to be unified technically without any apparent break in the diegesis. A woman performs within the narrative, the gaze of the spectator and that of the male characters in the film are neatly combined without breaking narrative verisimilitude (19).

While it can certainly be argued that Parisienne films, particularly those of 1950s Hollywood, conform to this notion of what Mulvey calls "neatly combined spectacle and narrative" (19), there are certain traits of the Parisienne type which in fact work against this. As we shall see, the self-fashioning aspect of *la Parisienne*, alongside her role as active rather than merely passive muse, in some ways undermines the description of her as a purely male fantasy. In the representation of *la Parisienne*, one also frequently finds the comingling of life and art, the presence of 'real-life' women behind, or blended with, fictional characters. This is the case whether it is a historical personage overdetermining the representation, or the actress herself. Thus it is argued here that feminist critiques of *la Parisienne* would have limited purchase, in spite of the visual pleasure and spectacle these films offer. *La Parisienne* is a fascinating figure precisely because she continually escapes representation, and as we shall see, more than one theorist of *la Parisienne* has noted the difficulty of capturing her essence.[2]

In the nineteenth century in particular (and continuing in cinema with a few exceptions), *la Parisienne* remains in part at least a male construction, but in part only. If, as Janet Wolff has argued, the "literature of modernity describes the experiences of men" (37), women must appear coloured by this experience, as objects rather than subjects of the modern world. Deborah L. Parsons, however, questions the notion that Baudelaire's depiction of women occurs within what Wolff calls a "classic misogynist duality" (cited in Parsons 24). Rather, according to Parsons, Baudelaire's poetry in particular raises the question of 'the place of women in the city and art of modernity that goes beyond personal prejudice' (24). Of particular interest for Parsons is the woman who appears fleetingly in the poem 'À une passante', the 'unknown woman who cannot be easily defined and thus controlled' (24). Parsons also notes that 'all the women common to Baudelaire's work are observers, and through them it is possible to question the assumption of the masculinity of public space and to formulate the beginnings of the conceptual idea of a *flâneuse*' (24). Indeed, the figure of *la Parisienne* was one of the first *flâneuses* in a time when women were liberated from the interior space of the home, primarily through changes in the configuration of social space through the introduction of arcades, parks and gardens. The image of the *flâneuse*, first captured in Baudelaire's poetry, is that of the liberated, autonomous woman. A more contemporary example of the way *la Parisienne* might circumvent the standard feminist critique of male fantasy is in the figure of Brigitte Bardot. According to Ginette Vincendeau, Simone de Beauvoir praised Bardot's new form of sexuality in *Et Dieu ... créa la femme* as 'progressive' and a 'welcome change from what she saw as the passivity of the *femme fatale*' (94). Vincendeau herself notes a 'tension between the Bardot character [in *Et Dieu*] as subject (agent) of the narrative, initiating action and expressing her own desire without guilt, and as object, both of male desire and the camera' (94). However, elsewhere she admits a 'paradox' which makes Bardot fascinating: 'rather than being either pure male fantasy, or affirmation of women's desire, she is both. The force of her star persona is to reconcile these two antagonistic aspects' ('Brigitte Bardot' 115).

In confining this study to the development of a descriptive aesthetics and establishing the Parisienne as a type in cinema through developing an iconography of the Parisienne type based on the recognition of various motifs, the foundations are laid for future scholarship that will deploy other approaches to the subject such as feminism, gender studies, or indeed, other more critical or evaluative approaches, such as ethno-criticism, that could not be pursued here. Indeed, the Parisienne type contains a kind of in-built critique of ethnic/national identities, and is supposed to transcend national/ethnic borders towards a more cosmopolitan identity. It is important to remember that *la Parisienne* is not a stereotype (e.g. white, middle class, European) but a type in the iconographical sense; that is, recognisable through certain recurring motifs, yet also constantly being reinvented. That *la Parisienne* is 'from anywhere and everywhere' is one of the main arguments put forward in this book. This definition leaves room for Parisiennes from any number of national or ethnic backgrounds, as such films as Céline Sciamma's *Bande de filles* (2014) demonstrate. Indeed, the main character of Sciamma's film, Vic (Karidja Touré), rather than presenting a challenge to the Parisienne as a type, may actually reinforce it, by demonstrating both its fixed and mutable nature. Further, contemporary popular images of *la Parisienne* such as one finds in recent style guides or magazines like *Vogue*, as well as in photography such as in Baudouin's work, go well beyond any Eurocentric stereotype.

Iconography of *la Parisienne*

The iconography of *la Parisienne* can be categorised according to the following concepts: visibility and mobility (both social and spatial); style and fashionability, including self-fashioning; artist and muse; cosmopolitanism; prostitution; danger; consumption (the consumer and the consumed); and transformation. Central to the iconography is the city of Paris, its streets and monuments, and its overall signification as the capital of modernity. The nature of the project, however, is such that it is constantly expanding, shifting ground and overlapping, and indeed one of the main problems is the question of containment, of how to set limits and bring content under complete control of the proposed form. This is partly due to the nature of *la Parisienne* as a type, a figure who never resembles herself. What constitutes a chapter of this book, then, is really a limit set on the Parisienne type itself, a limit that is continuously exceeded. This excess will take the form of an overflow from one chapter to the next; however it is difficult to avoid damming the flow with definitive statements. Thus a more openended approach is taken, bringing the categories to bear on the films only to indicate certain fixed attributes or motifs while at the same time allowing the more mutable aspects of the type to emerge.

The six chapters set down in this book reflect the notions or categories associated with the Parisienne type and explore each of them in turn, building up an overall iconography from the motifs associated with them. The titles of the chapters take not the categories themselves, but their associated figuration (not 'Cosmopolitanism' but

'Cosmopolite'; not 'Danger' but 'Femme fatale'), to shift the emphasis away from concepts which tend to fix the Parisienne toward the figure itself, which is far more mutable. The precondition for *la Parisienne* as a type is that she generally fulfils all the categories at once, but some more prominently than others within the films set for discussion. How she appears in each film also sets the tone and focus of the discussion in each chapter. Often visual considerations are paramount, while at other times the narrative function of the type is more evident. At other times again it might be a question of reference, of the relation between cinema and other media such as painting, literature or advertising.

Chapter 1 argues that *la Parisienne* is a type which exists between art and life, and who exists on the boundary between representation and reality. The figure that emerges from this blurring of art and life is *la Parisienne* as muse. Chapter 2 considers the cosmopolitanism of the Parisienne type, in the sense of 'anyone' and 'anywhere', and argues that *la Parisienne* was conceived not only as a figure of French femininity but of femininity as such. Chapter 3 explores the relationship between *la Parisienne*, fashion and film. Chapter 4 looks at *la Parisienne* as femme fatale within the context of French film noir. Tracing her development in nineteenth-century art and literature, Chapter 5 examines the way the Parisienne as courtesan is (re)presented in cinema. Finally, Chapter 6 investigates the contribution particular actresses' star personae have made to the Parisienne type in cinema and, reciprocally, how the type has inscribed itself on the personae of these stars.

Geographically speaking, the films come primarily from France and America because the Parisienne type is most ubiquitous in these national cinemas. Of particular interest for the development of the Parisienne type is what Vanessa Schwartz in *It's So French!* describes as the transatlantic cultural exchange between French and American cinema in the 1950s and 1960s. Indeed, the development of the Parisienne type owes much to the rapport between French and American cinema of this period, because in order for *la Parisienne* to develop as a type, or even a stereotype, a global or cosmopolitan perspective was necessary. Indeed, this transatlantic cultural exchange figures as the culmination point in the development of the Parisienne type and it is therefore not surprising to find a concentration of films featuring *la Parisienne* made by Hollywood during the 1950s and 1960s. There are earlier cinematic incarnations, including silent cinema, but they have become more recognisable in light of this cycle of so-called Hollywood 'Frenchness' films. Thus, when approaching the Parisienne type in cinema (and this is something that can be said of any type in an iconographical sense), there is frequently a retrospective elaboration at work, insofar as much of what leads to recognising the type in earlier films derives from exposure to later films, particularly from what Schwartz calls the cycle of 'Frenchness films' (*It's So French!* 19). Chronology is not a necessary consideration for charting the iconography of a type.

The films included in this book were chosen for both for their affirmation and interesting treatment of the Parisienne type. There is certainly no claim to exhaustiveness in coverage of the field, nor does this book offer a comprehensive portrait or visual history of *la Parisienne* in cinema. Attempts to include a large number of examples in order to demonstrate the ubiquity of the type in cinema, as well as the richness of variations of the type, have been tempered by the desire to provide more meaningful and sustained engagement with individual films.

A final note

Lastly, I want to briefly draw attention to the slippage in the terms 'she' and 'it', and 'her' and 'its' when referring to the Parisienne type. This slippage is due to *la Parisienne* being at once a concept and a material reality; an idea and – at least for the films discussed in this book – a woman; and both the subject and object of narrative and discourse. All translations from the French, unless otherwise stated, are my own.

Notes

1 Indeed, the figure of *la Parisienne* as flâneuse appears frequently in cinema, for example Cléo (Corinne Marchand) in Agnès Varda's *Cléo de 5 à 7* (1962).
2 It must be noted that Mulvey herself revised her essay some years later to consider both the 'women in the audience issue' and the issue of 'how the text and its attendant identifications are affected by a *female* character occupying the centre of the narrative arena' (68).

I
Muse

Paris est la ville artiste et poète par excellence; mais les plus grandes artistes et les plus grandes poètes de Paris, ce sont les Parisiennes. Pourquoi? Parce que les Parisiennes imaginent, achèvent, complètent à chaque instant une œuvre réelle et vivante, car elles se créant elles-mêmes. (Théodore de Banville, 'Le Génie des Parisiennes')

(Paris is the artist and poet city par excellence; but the greatest artists and the greatest poets of Paris are the Parisiennes. Why? Because the Parisiennes imagine, finish, complete at each moment a real and living masterpiece, because they create themselves.)

Life imitates Art far more than Art imitates Life. (Oscar Wilde, 'The Decay of Lying')

Elena (Ingrid Bergman) pins a marguerite to her bodice, a talisman at the ready to offer her men. Enchanted by his latest muse, Klimt (John Malkovich) sketches from memory Léa de Castro (Saffron Burrows) performing her Cambodian dance. Already a muse to writers and artists in 1920s Paris, Adriana (Marion Cotillard) captures the attention of Degas, Gauguin and Toulouse-Lautrec at the Moulin Rouge. Jean Renoir's *Elena et les hommes* (1956), Raúl Ruiz's *Klimt* (2006) and Woody Allen's *Midnight in Paris* (2011) all feature *la Parisienne* as muse and depict the complicated relationship between art and life.

Even where historical or 'real-life' Parisiennes are concerned, it is often difficult to discern where real life ends and representation begins. Joanna Richardson highlights this ambiguity in her discussion of Blanche d'Antigny, a Second Empire courtesan and stage actress who was also the inspiration for the title character of Zola's *Nana*:

Zola's *L'Assommoir* inspired Edouard Manet to paint *Nana*, and Manet's painting in turn inspired Zola to write the sequel to the novel, in which Nana played the principal part. But when Zola talked to a bon viveur of the Second Empire, when he took notes on courtesans of the imperial age, Blanche d'Antigny and Nana became identified in his imagination. They became merged in a single creature, the prototype of the *cocotte*. (9)

The figure that emerges from this blurring of art and life is *la Parisienne* as muse. Many Parisiennes are described as muses not only to painters, poets and writers, but also fashion designers, musicians and filmmakers. Madame Sabatier, known as La Présidente, is perhaps the quintessential Parisienne muse of the nineteenth century and 'directly responsible for some of the finest poems in the French language' (Richardson 171). She was the inspiration for the courtesan Rosanette Bron, alias 'The Marshal', in Gustave Flaubert's *L'Education sentimentale*.

The blurring of art and life is integral to the type *la Parisienne*, an enigmatic figure whose existence is as much determined by art as art is a re-presentation of her material existence. Yet the real life or material existence of *la Parisienne* is already highly constructed or artificial. Tamar Garb argues that artifice is in fact the hallmark of *la Parisienne*, describing her as 'the sophisticated product of modern tailoring, grooming and cosmetics' ('Painting' 115). *La Parisienne* thus became an ideal woman for nineteenth-century artists who demonstrated a preference for the artificial over the natural. In 'The Painter of Modern Life', for example, Charles Baudelaire writes: 'All things that adorn woman, all the things that go to enhance her beauty, are part of her self .... When he describes the pleasure caused by the sight of a beautiful woman, what poet would dare to distinguish between her and her apparel?' (424). Baudelaire goes on to refute the popular Romantic idea that 'nature embellishes beauty' (424), claiming that everything natural is ugly and that beauty is found solely in artifice. *La Parisienne* emerged as the quintessential aesthetic archetype in the nineteenth century during a time in which there was a preoccupation with anti-nature and artifice. Oscar Wilde remarks: 'Life and Nature may sometimes be used as part of Art's rough material, but before they are of any real service to Art they must be translated into artistic conventions'

(239). The difference here is not between life and art in the sense of what is natural and what is artificial but rather between two different types of art, that of *la Parisienne* and that of her representation. It is the woman's artifice and not her nature which inspires the artist.

In cinema, there are two further senses of this idea of between art and life by which the figure of *la Parisienne* can be considered: the intra-filmic and the extra-filmic. The intra-filmic deals with considerations pertaining to the film's diegesis, but also with whether the Parisienne character exists on the same ontological level as other characters in a film (as she does in *Elena et les hommes*), or, on the contrary, if she exists in an interstitial space either as fantasy or hallucination or figment attributable to another character (as in *Midnight in Paris* and *Klimt*). The extra-filmic deals with considerations falling outside the film's diegesis, which belong properly to the creation and production process, including the various sources, inspirations and texts which inform the creation of character. The extra-filmic is concerned with whether these Parisiennes are based on or inspired by real life or historical personages, as is the case in *Klimt* and *Elena*; or wholly fictional, or not based on anyone immediately identifiable, as is the case in *Midnight in Paris*. Both *Midnight in Paris* and *Klimt* represent the blurring of art and life quite literally. Allen does this temporally through the use of a fantasy sequence in which the hero Gil Pender (Owen Wilson) is transported from the Paris of around 2010 back to Paris in the 1920s, the era of the so-called Lost Generation. It is here that he first encounters the Parisienne Adriana. Ruiz uses different media within the cinematic medium (painting, mirrors, sketches, shadow play, cinematograph) to achieve this effect.

In any Parisienne film there are three possible categories for the origin of the Parisienne character: directly based on a real-life Parisienne (the protagonist of a biopic or a minor character in a historical drama); loosely based on or inspired by one or more historical Parisiennes; or wholly fictitious yet having prefigurations in history, art and literature and the conscious or unconscious, intentional or unintentional, creation of the writer/director. This latter category makes up the bulk of films featuring the Parisienne type, primarily because every Parisienne character draws on an iconography derived from a diversity of sources, including history, art, literature, mass culture and cinema.

In iconographical terms, there are three motifs associated with *la Parisienne* as muse: she is depicted as inhabiting an artistic milieu; she is the subject of portraiture; and she is *sui generis* or self-fashioning. In her essay on Édouard Manet's *The Parisienne*, Françoise Tétart-Vittu writes: 'From Nina de Callias ... to Valtesse de La Bigne and Méry Laurent, Parisiennes were fashionable, chic, and beautiful women who moved freely in the artistic circles of Paris' (78). According to Vincent Cronin, during the Belle Époque Parisian women 'played an influential role in intellectual, literary and artistic life' (287). *La Parisienne* is also often found in an artistic milieu in literature and the visual arts. The protagonist of Colette's novel *La Vagabonde*, Renée Néré, is the former wife and model of portrait artist Adolphe Taillandy who finds herself on the music-hall stage in the company of acrobats, mimes and dancers. In Flaubert's *L'Éducation sentimentale* Rosanette Bron has her portrait painted by Pellerain:

> Il engagea donc Rosanette à se faire peindre, pour offrir son visage à son cher Arnoux. Elle accepta, car elle se voyait au milieu du Grand Salon, à la place d'honneur, avec une foule devant elle, et les journaux en parleraient, ce qui 'la lancerait' tout à coup. (171)

> He accordingly urged Rosanette to have her portrait painted, so that she could present her likeness to her beloved Arnoux. She agreed, for she saw herself in the middle of the grand salon, in the place of honour, with a crowd in front of her and the newspapers talking about her, something which would immediately 'launch her'. (Baldick 154)

In the visual arts, *la Parisienne* is depicted in such settings as the café-concert or the music hall, particularly in the works of Toulouse-Lautrec and Degas, in the salon or artist's studio, as in Vuillard's painting *Jeune Femme en rose dans le salon rue de Calais* (1920), and in the theatre as in Mary Cassatt's paintings *In the Loge* (1878) and *Woman with a Pearl Necklace in a Loge* (1879). The very concept of the portrait implies the association of *la Parisienne* with painters and her presence in the studio, and many Parisiennes were artists' models. For Julie Johnson, modelling was 'not just a rite of passage for would-be artists but was also a serious profession for many

Parisian women. The woman artist-as-model became a pervasive and provocative cultural image in the late nineteenth century, one that was discussed and described in the popular literature and fiction of the day' (234). Indeed, an 1897 illustrated book, *Autour d'elles*, features Henri Boutet's sketches of the artist's model in Paris. Marie Lathers writes how in his Preface to the book Georges Montorgueil 'revealed the interchangeability of the *Parisienne* and the model' when he suggested that one of Boutet's chapter titles 'The Model in the Studio' could become 'The *Parisienne* in the Studio' (40). Montorgueil writes:

> How interesting it would be to follow, in their misleading movements, these Parisian models! Not a one who resembles another in this amiable flock; each has her type and story. Whereas the Trasteverine, statue in the flesh, earthly bronze, is one and indivisible, they are multiple in appearance, figure, sentiment, intellect, these girls of Paris who have come to Art as its eternal source of Beauty, brought by the most capricious twists of fate. (qtd in Lathers 40)

In the films discussed below, the protagonists are all depicted inhabiting an artistic milieu. In *Midnight in Paris* our introduction to Adriana takes place at Gertrude Stein's apartment at 27 rue de Fleurus Montparnasse, an open house for writers and artists which functioned 'as a kind of literary American embassy' (Hussey 336). Adriana is depicted in the company of Ernest Hemingway, Pablo Picasso and Stein, as well as fictional American writer Gil Pender. In the 1920s Montparnasse replaced Montmartre as 'the latest outpost for the avant-garde' (Wiser 38). During the decade Paris was a 'veritable palace of modernism', with Montparnasse at the heart of artistic activity (Hussey 336). During the scene in Stein's apartment, Adriana remarks to Gil that Paris is a 'wonderful city for writers, artists'. She is shown attending a Surrealist wedding and, later in the film, at the Moulin Rouge in the company of Toulouse-Lautrec, Degas and Gauguin. After enumerating her various liaisons with Braque, Modigliani and Picasso, Gil exclaims: 'My God, you take art groupie to a whole new level!'

Elena et les hommes opens with an establishing shot of Elena seated at a piano beside an emerging young composer. As the camera pulls back, we see the walls of her apartment adorned with paintings, which, given Elena's poverty, suggest they were gifts from painter friends. Susan Hayward writes: 'That she has some contemporary canvasses surrounding her points to her aesthetic acumen or her desire to support artists' ('Design' 101). In *Klimt*, Léa de Castro is found in the company of Georges Méliès, Klimt and James Abbott McNeill Whistler.

The second motif in the iconography of the Parisienne as muse is *la Parisienne* as the subject of portraiture. By the late nineteenth century *la Parisienne* had become the subject of many paintings, drawings and etchings. As well as portraits of the generic type, there are also many portraits of real-life Parisiennes, including Georges Clairin's *Sarah Bernhardt* (1876), Giovanni Boldini's *Cléo de Mérode* (1901), Jacques-Émile Blanche's *Colette* (1905), Pierre Bonnard's *Misia* (1908), Moise Kisling's *Arletty* (1933) and Kees Van Dongen's *Bardot* (1964). In *Klimt*, Léa de Castro has her portrait painted by both Whistler and Klimt. In *Midnight in Paris*, Picasso paints a portrait of Adriana which becomes a focal point of discussion in the film, particularly around the question of representation. While Elena is not a subject of a portrait in *Elena et les hommes*, the film as a whole can be considered a cinematic portrait of a complex or composite subject.

The third motif in the iconography of the Parisienne type as muse is *la Parisienne* as *sui generis* or self-fashioning. Lisa Tiersten remarks that 'fashion and decorating were themselves art forms and the chic Parisienne an artistic creator in her own right' (121). In *Parisiennes de ce temps*, Uzanne remarks that '[l]a toilette pour la femme moderne est le premier des arts, celui qui les contient tous. C'est, nous l'avons dit, son style caractéristique, c'est aussi sa palette harmonieuse, sa poésie rythmique, sa mise en scène élégante, son chant de triomphe, son apothéose en un mot' (57–8) (the toilette is for the modern woman the highest of the arts, that which contains all others. It is, as we have said, her characteristic style; it is also her harmonious palette, her rhythmic poetry, her elegant *mise en scène*, her song of triumph, her apotheosis in a word). One of the defining features of *la Parisienne* is her desire to create an appearance. This self-fashioning motif often finds expression in depictions of the Parisienne at her toilette, or contemplating her image in a mirror. The term 'toilette' originates from the piece of fabric or *toile* upon which the accoutrements of the toilette were arranged. Joan DeJean traces the emergence of the toilette as an art form and spectacle back to the reign of Louis XIV and the Versailles era when 'many aristocrats began to stage la toilette as still another scene in their highly theatricalised lives' (252). By the end of the eighteenth century the dressing table and dressing room had been invented, as it was conceded that the ritual of the toilette warranted its very own space (DeJean 253). *La Parisienne* is often depicted in paintings of the late nineteenth and early twentieth centuries composing her toilette: Auguste Toulmouche's *Vanity* (1890), Alfred Stevens's *La Parisienne japonaise* (1872), Manet's *Nana* (1877), Kees Van Dongen's *Woman before a mirror* (1908), Mary Cassatt's *Woman at her toilette* (1909), Degas's *Woman combing her hair before a mirror* (c. 1887), Jacques-Émile Blanche's *Désirée Manfred face à son Miroir* (c. 1905) and Toulmouche's *La Toilette* (1890).

In her discussion of Georges Seurat's *Young Woman Powdering Herself* (1890), Garb remarks that the 'application of make-up, itself a kind of painting, became the subject of high art and popular imagery alike' (*Bodies* 115). Tiersten remarks that many writers 'described the Parisienne as a combination of the artwork and the artist' (144). Depicting *la Parisienne* before her mirror reinforces her self-fashioning aspect. Marie Double remarks that a woman is 'the artist of her own beauty, composing her toilette as a painter colors his canvas, perfecting the details, arranging the nuances, high-lighting a feature, concealing a flaw ... Woman, the Parisienne above all, has made herself her own creator' (qtd in Tiersten 144–5). In a similar vein, Simon remarks that the 'issue of make-up crystallized the movement which was tending to turn woman into an artist' (132), a movement which finds its clearest expression in Théophile Gautier's *De La Mode* (1858) and Baudelaire's *L'Éloge du maquillage* (1863).

Elena, Adriana and Léa de Castro are all depicted as self-fashioning. Elena is shown seated at her toilette before a mirror, fixing her hair with the help of her maid. The shot, the position of the two women before the mirror (Elena seated and her maid standing behind her leaning in), evokes nineteenth-century paintings of Parisiennes at their toilette, particularly, in terms of composition, Eva Gonzalès's *Le Petit Lever* (1875). In *Klimt*, this idea of self-fashioning is derived less from the character of Léa de Castro than from her real-life Parisienne inspiration Cléo de Mérode, whose greatest gift 'lay in the art of self-fashioning' (Garval 4). In Ruiz's film the idea of self-fashioning is taken up more along the lines of Léa de Castro's awareness of herself as an image and in the way that she partakes in the play of appearances. In *Midnight in Paris*, Adriana is depicted as self-fashioning through a self-conscious affectation of gesture. What underlines the fact that we are watching a performance rather than something natural is the innocent naivety of Allen's hero Gil Pender and the juxtaposition of Adriana's affectation with Gil's childlike astonishment. The first shot we see of Adriana is preceded by a remark of Gertrude Stein's addressed to Gil and thus implicitly to the audience: 'What is your first impression of Adriana?' We then cut to a medium close-up shot of Adriana, leaning nonchalantly against a doorframe, holding a cigarette with exaggerated insouciance. The doorframe creates the impression of a painting or portrait. What strikes the viewer most about Adriana's demeanour is her obvious awareness of being looked at. We then cut to a shot of a captivated Gil who replies: 'Exceptionally lovely.' What is important in the sequence is the movement from the contemplation of Picasso's portrait to a shot which is set up like a portrait. This reinforces the idea we are not shifting from representation to life but rather from representation to representation.

The self-fashioning aspect of *la Parisienne* leads to a problem at the heart of the concept of the muse: the movement between activity and passivity. In *Refiguring the Muse*, Gayle A. Levy begins her analysis of the term 'muse' with the distinction between the classical or ancient conception of the muse as active purveyor of inspiration, and the Romantic muse as the passive object of the poet's imagination. The Romantic muse, according to Levy, is generally an objectified, feminine figure, but also 'refers to poetic art in general, or any poetic inspiration with particular reference to the genius of each poet' (19). The Romantic muse is, for Levy, the modern or contemporary muse. Traditionally, despite being described as a modern muse, *la Parisienne* has been depicted as more active and closer to the classical conception of the muse, which Levy describes as 'an exterior force that stimulated the poet to sing his verse' (19). In spite of addressing *la Parisienne* as a modern muse, Theodore de Banville, in his study *Les Parisiennes de Paris* (1866), in fact goes on to describe *la Parisienne* as muse in a more classical or active sense:

> O Muses modernes! vous dont les chapeaux tout petits sont des merveilles de caprice et dont les robes effrénées semblent vouloir engloutir l'univers sous des flots d'étoffes de soie aux mille couleurs, inspirez-moi ! .... Donc, cher lecteur, regarde passer, au bruit du satin qu'on froisse et au bruit de l'or pudiques et amoureuses, et insolentes et souverainement maîtresses des élégances, les Parisiennes de Paris, ces femmes mystérieuses dont les toutes petites mains déplacent des montagnes. (1)
>
> (O modern muses! You whose tiny hats are the marvels of caprice, and whose dresses appear to want to swallow the universe under the flood of multicoloured silk material, inspire me! .... Thus, dear reader, watch pass, to the sound of creasing satin and of gold, discreet and sexual, and insolent and sovereignly mistresses of elegance, the Parisiennes of Paris, these mysterious women whose little hands move mountains.)

This description, although written during the era of the modern or Romantic muse, describes a Parisienne active in the creation of her own image.

The muse and her men: Elena in *Elena et les hommes*

> No doubt the beautiful Elena is merely a provincial Muse – but a Muse in search of the absolute. (Jean-Luc Godard)

In *Elena et les hommes*, Elena's status as Parisienne and muse is overdetermined by real-life nineteenth-century Parisiennes upon whom her character is based. The main inspiration for Elena Sorokowska is Parisienne Misia Godebska, a Polish émigré living in Paris during the late nineteenth and early twentieth centuries. Raymond Durgnat suggests one of the reasons Elena is 'a Polish princess, rather than a French one' is because she 'seems to have had a Polish original' (320). Durgnat is referring to Godebska, whom Renoir encountered as a young boy, and who appears in the filmmaker's biography of his painter father (356). These pages reveal that the young Renoir was much impressed by Godebska.

Elena is not a depiction of the real-life Misia; rather, Misia herself was already an aesthetic construct, not only through her self-fashioning but through the various representations through which she passed on her way to Elena. Thus Misia was a muse, not only to Renoir, but also to the painters and writers who depicted her before him, including Cocteau, Proust, Vuillard, Bonnard, Toulouse-Lautrec and Renoir *père*. Nor is Misia the only inspiration for the character of Elena, who is also partly inspired by two other prominent Parisiennes, Marguerite de Bonnemains and Marguerite Bellanger. Renoir's film constructs a portrait of *la Parisienne* from these diverse origins, incorporating the various motifs associated with these real-life women.

Misia Godebska is a Belle Époque Parisienne whose biography resembles closely that of Elena; that is, a woman whose persona conforms to the various visual and narrative conventions of the Parisienne type, such as cosmopolitanism, mobility or classlessness, fashionability, sexual availability and muse to men. In his biography of his father, Jean Renoir writes:

> Another of his models who stirred my imagination was Misia Godebska. At the time of her portrait she was Misia Edwards … . She was the daughter of a noble Polish family who had lost their fortune. She had grown up in a palace where, although the servants were rarely paid, royalty, great artists and millionaires would come to hear her play on one of her thirty pianos … . She had been so poor that she had slept on benches in public parks; and so rich that she could not begin to count her wealth. (356)

Misia's poverty is reproduced by Renoir in Elena's own financial situation. A penniless Polish princess living in Paris, Elena displays the classlessness and cosmopolitanism associated with *la Parisienne*. Like many Parisiennes, it is impossible to discern her social and economic status from her appearance. In nineteenth-century literature too, class ambiguity was a feature of the Parisienne type. Guy de Maupassant's 'La Parure', for example, describes how Parisienne Mathilde Loisel, wife of a low-ranking bureaucrat, puts herself together on limited means to attend a soirée held by the Ministry of Education. That she becomes the 'belle of the ball' in spite of her cheap dress and imitation jewellery indicates a charm that transcends class distinction and cannot be reduced to mere accoutrements: 'les femmes n'ont point de caste ni de race, leur beauté, leur grâce et leur charme leur servant de naissance et de famille. Leur finesse native, leur instinct d'élégance, leur souplesse d'esprit sont leur seule hiérarchie, et font des filles du peuple les égales des plus grandes dames' (1198) (women neither have caste or race, their beauty, gracefulness and charm serve as their birthright and heritage. Their native finesse, instinct for elegance, and suppleness of spirit are their only hierarchy, and make the women of the people the equals of the greatest ladies.)

In *Fashion in Impressionist Paris*, Mancoff also notes the way Parisiennes possess the art of making a virtue of necessity where their appearance is concerned. Commenting on Renoir's painting *La Parisienne*, Mancoff writes: 'The title of the painting, *La Parisienne*, refers to a contemporary type of frivolous, fashion-minded young woman, middle- or working-class, who used her looks as capital in an upwardly mobile society' (44). While Elena may not be described as frivolous, she is nonetheless obviously aware of the importance of appearances. Susan Hayward remarks that 'the décor of Elena's apartment tells us that while she is a woman of scant means, she is, nonetheless a cultivated woman ...and a patron of the contemporary arts' ('Design' 89). Having lost her fortune, Elena intends to use her charms to secure a marriage with wealthy entrepreneur Martin-Michaud (Pierre Bertin), and her typically Parisienne status of kept woman is not lost on her: 'Plus de perles', she remarks to herself at her dressing table; 'Je n'avais plus rien à vendre que moi-même' (No more pearls ... I had nothing left to sell but myself). It is Elena's poverty which leads her to consider a marriage of convenience. This does not, however, prevent her from pursuing amorous flirtations with Général Rollan (Jean Marais) and the aristocratic dilettante Henri de Chevincourt (Mel Ferrer). This *ménage à quatre* constitutes another Parisienne trope and one that Ronald Bergan identifies as one of Renoir's 'pet themes' (188).

Misia was both a muse and patron to artists; however she was also considered a talented pianist in her own right. As a young girl Misia had 'learned the piano on the knees of Franz Liszt, who marvelled at her talent', and later took lessons in Paris with composer Gabriel Fauré (Vezin and Vezin 213). It is no surprise, then, that in Renoir's film we first encounter Elena seated at the piano, her hair, like Misia's in the many depictions of her, 'piled up like a brioche' (Fizdale and Gold 29). Indeed, Bonnard, Toulouse-Lautrec and Vuillard all painted Misia seated at the piano in this fashion. Renoir's film begins with a mid-shot of Elena at the piano. Behind her, to the right of the screen, is an unframed canvas mounted on an easel, visually establishing the connection between the character of Elena and the arts. The camera pulls back to reveal that she is seated beside a young composer, most likely based on French composer Maurice Ravel. Later, when the young composer receives the news that his opera *Heloïse et Abélard* (a reference to Ravel's *Daphnis and Chloë*) will be performed at La Scala, Elena replies she knew it, because she gave him a daisy. When he asks Elena when they are to be married, she evades the question, insisting that now his success is assured he no longer needs her and her mission has been accomplished. Elena's demeanour at the piano in the opening sequence suggests more an indulgence toward the young composer's music than any real interest in it. She stifles a yawn and quickly becomes distracted by the sounds of the approaching Bastille Day parade outside. The parade will bring with it Général Rollan in whom Elena will find her next mission as muse: to help Rollan reach his political goals. That same day, she meets aristocratic dilettante Henri de Chevincourt, whose goal in life is to do absolutely nothing, and who Elena also inspires in this direction. In her role as muse, Elena recalls the following remark by Uzanne:

> Magicienne omnipotente, la Parisienne fait, pour ainsi dire, mouvoir dans son axe cette grande usine bourdonnante de cerveaux. C'est à elle que tout se rapporte indirectement dans cette terrible bataille quotidienne des devoirs et des intérêts ... car cette véritable instigatrice des ambitions et de la fortune est comparable à la Reine des abeilles, qui domine, conduit et anime l'activité générale dans l'immense et bruissante ruche en travail. (24)
>
> The Parisienne is an all-powerful enchantress: she is, so to speak, the motive power of the great factory whose humming wheels are human brains. Indirectly all duties and interests in the great daily battle come back to her ... . It is she who is the instigator of ambitions and the source of fortunes, and, like the queen bee,

she rules, guides, and stimulates activity in her immense and busy hive. (*The Modern Parisienne* 4)

Misia was herself a muse to many men. She was married three times: first, to Thadée Natanson, who founded the periodical *La Revue blanche*; then to newspaper tycoon Alfred Edwards; and later to Spanish painter José-María Sert. She was a close friend of Coco Chanel, and of Serge Diaghilev, whose Ballets Russes she generously patronised. Describing Misia as the 'muse to end all muses', Mitchell Owens remarks: 'Renoir, Toulouse-Lautrec and Bonnard painted her; Proust and Cocteau transformed her into fiction; and in her honor, Mallarmé wrote poems, Ravel composed music and Diaghilev staged ballets' (37). In their study of Misia as muse to Vuillard, Annette and Luc Vezin remark:

> Marcel Proust gave the nickname of 'the patroness' to Madame Verdurin, the great socialite who loved to live surrounded by artists and dreamed of being the inspiration for their creativity. Neither a wife nor a mistress, the "patroness muse" is more like the guardian figure who creates a working environment for the painter or the musician. And so it was for Misia Sert, married to the founder of *La Revue blanche*, who fascinated her weepy unrequited lover, the painter Édouard Vuillard. (194–5)

In their biography of Misia, Fizdale and Gold remark that Misia 'became not only a patron of the arts but a muse, an inspiration to artists' (3). Misia was a friend of Lautrec, who 'in allusion to her swift grace called her "The Lark"', and of Renoir *père* who in 'seven different portraits had depicted her eager, wide-eyed cat face' (V. Cronin 34). A 'glittering portrait' of Misia appears in Marcel Proust's *À la recherche du temps perdu*: 'Proust described Misia, transforming her into the "Princess Yourbeletieff, the youthful sponsor of all these new great men," who appeared in her box at the ballet "bearing on her head an immense, quivering aigrette, unknown to the women of Paris, which they all sought to copy' (Fizdale and Gold 3). In *Elena et les hommes*, Renoir too makes Misia a princess. Like Proust, he also depicts Misia as Elena in her box at the opera, the aigrette replaced by a bodice ostentatiously trimmed with feathers. The composition of this shot also recalls nineteenth-century depictions of *la Parisienne* in her box, including Eva Gonzalès's *A Loge in the Théâtre des Italiens* (1874), Renoir's *The Theater Box* (1874) and Mary Cassatt's *The Loge* (1882). Later in the film, Elena does appear wearing an aigrette on her head, as in Proust's depiction of Misia. Jean Cocteau, too, cast Misia in the role of princess, making her the heroine of his novel *Thomas l'imposteur* (1923).

Elena is a muse because she inspires the men around her. The symbol of this inspiration is the daisy Elena presents to the men who are drawn to her: the young pianist, the bohemian aristocrat and Général Rollan. Each of these men achieves their respective ambitions with help from Elena. The marguerite talisman, however, provides a key to two other Parisiennes who haunt the character of Elena: Marguerite de Bonnemains and Marguerite Bellanger. De Bonnemains was the mistress of General Georges Boulanger on whom Renoir based the character of General François Rollan. Bergan writes how Renoir had initially intended to make a satire about General Boulanger, 'who led a brief authoritarian movement to topple the Third Republic in the 1880s. The General committed suicide in Brussels over the grave of his mistress Marguerite de Bonnemains' (304). De Bonnemain's favourite flower was said to be a red carnation, which Boulanger wore and insisted his men do the same. Marguerite Bellanger was the adopted pseudonym of a nineteenth-century courtesan and mistress to Napoleon III, Julie Marie Leboeuf, whose emblem was the daisy or marguerite (Richardson 116–17). Indeed, there is a photograph of Bellanger in male attire with a daisy brooch pinned to her jacket, and another photograph depicts her crowned with marguerites. It is said that Bellanger's writing-paper was 'embossed with a marguerite, and the motto: "All things come to those who wait"' (Richardson 128). This, too, becomes the motto or moral of Renoir's film.

There is, however, a fourth historical precursor to Elena, Marguerite Charpentier (née Lemonnier), a patron of the arts who often wore a daisy pinned to her dress. Renoir *père* painted her in her salon in 1878, and Renoir *fils* was familiar with her both by reputation and through his father's work. In his biography of his father, Renoir writes of Madame Charpentier: 'Her "salon" was celebrated: and deservedly so, for she was indeed a great lady, and had succeeded in reviving the atmosphere of the famous salons of the past' (126). Renoir's painting, *Madame Georges Charpentier and her Children* (1878), depicts Charpentier with a daisy brooch pinned to her dress.

Interestingly, as Bergan points out, Renoir's film 'was originally to be called *The Red Carnation*, but was changed to *Elena et les hommes* to highlight the principal character' (304). The changing of the flower to a daisy or marguerite connects Elena to the three aforementioned Marguerites but also gives the exchange between Elena and her men a distinctly, although diegetically suppressed, sexual overtone. The term or phrase *effeuiller la marguerite* (literally, to pluck or pick the petals from a daisy) is idiomatic for 'to strip', in the sense of performing a striptease. Originally, *effeuiller la marguerite* referred to the children's and lovers' pastime of literally picking the petals off the daisy while chanting 's/he loves me, s/he loves me not' (Hérail and Lovatt 193). The phrase *effeuiller la marguerite* is also a euphemism for 'an amorous activity taking place outdoors' (Lamy 41). The change of title also shifts the emphasis from the Rollan/Boulanger plot to the character of Elena. Renoir remarked of the character General Rollan: 'He's a very weak man. He is the selfish, rich man who likes any kind of adventure under one condition: that it can't harm him. He's too careful to get into anything serious. The real hero of Elena is Elena herself' (qtd in Braudy 8).

The character of Elena is also overdetermined by actress Ingrid Bergman, for whom Renoir claimed he made the film in the first place: 'The only reason for Elena is: Woman ... represented by Ingrid Bergman' (qtd in Durgnat 315). Similarly, Claude-Jean Philippe writes: 'L'inspiration initiale tient au désir de "faire quelque chose de gai avec Ingrid Bergman"' (421). (The initial inspiration came from the desire 'to make something gay with Ingrid Bergman'). Jean Renoir remarks that *Elena et les hommes* 'owes its unity entirely to a certain spirit that I maintained throughout the film, by clinging to the main character. That's the glue, the cement that joins it all' (qtd in Bergan 305).

Bergman's own Parisienne profile, derived in part from her film roles and in part from her biography, is used in Renoir's film to further blur the boundaries of life and art. Bergman's Parisienne roles include Ilsa Lund in Michael Curtiz's *Casablanca* (1942), Joan Madou in Lewis

Milestone's *Arch of Triumph* (1948), and Paula Tessier in Anatole Litvak's *Goodbye, Again* (1961).[1] The cosmopolitanism of Bergman's own life – Swedish born and working in Hollywood as well as French and Italian cinema – also infects the character of Elena. Critics too have noted that Bergman both sets the tone of the film and forms its visual core. Bergan writes that Renoir's film 'opens with Ingrid Bergman, who has seldom been more beguiling, sitting at a piano, looking ravishing in a white lace dress, and smiling. It is she who sets the joyous tone of the operetta-like comedy as she flits from one man to another' (306). Similarly, Sue Harris remarks that while *Elena et les hommes* is seemingly a political tale, the 'visual core of the film is Ingrid Bergman as a foreign princess in *belle époque* Paris, surrounded by a world of Parisian gaiety: street singers, uniformed officers, open air dance halls' (97).

In terms of treatment, Renoir employs a painterly aesthetic to create his portrait of *la Parisienne* in *Elena*. Bergan identifies several sources of this painterly aesthetic: popular nineteenth-century prints and paintings; the paintings of Renoir *père*, particularly *Le Moulin de la Galette*; a 'Dufy-like array of tricolours and Chinese lanterns'; and, in the final scene of the film in which Juliette Greco sings 'O Nuit', 'blue-period Picasso painting' (307). Similarly, Harris remarks that the influence of Caillebotte is evident, particularly in the opening scenes when Elena surveys the passing parade in the streets below from her balcony (97). For Harris, the 'ornate mise en scène' demonstrates an engagement with Paris as a city mediated through painting, and the 'heavy reliance on iconography in the film's first act confirms Renoir's stated passion for artifice, and signals' (97).

Elena et les hommes depicts the figure of *la Parisienne* as muse in two main ways: historically, through reference to the lives of three real-life Parisiennes, and visually through the use of a painterly aesthetic. The real muse of the film is not, however, Misia Godebska, but Ingrid Bergman herself. Indeed, while Misia may have been the original inspiration for Elena, the film was conceived for Bergman, and during the film's production a subtle transition takes place from Misia to Bergman, such that, in a certain sense, the latter became for Renoir *fils* what the former was to Renoir *père*. Unlike other cinematic treatments of *la Parisienne* which use painting diegetically – usually as part of the *mise en scène* in the form of a portrait (*Midnight in Paris*, *Klimt*) thus confining the notion of muse to the dramatis personae – Renoir effectively 'paints' a cinematic portrait of Bergman as Elena, with the celluloid canvas as colourful and overstuffed as the impressionistic canvases of his father. As Renoir himself remarked: 'I like films or books which give me the feeling of a frame too narrow for the content' (qtd in Braudy 65).

'But an image of an image': Léa de Castro in *Klimt*

In Ruiz's *Klimt*, the space *la Parisienne* occupies between art and life forms the actual subject matter of the film. This is achieved through the mixing of reality, art, memory and hallucination, primarily mediated through the character of Klimt. In his 'Note d'intention' accompanying the press-release dossier in 2006, Ruiz himself remarks:

> Il s'agit bien d'une fantaisie, ... d'une fresque de personnages réels et imaginaires qui tournent autour d'un seul point: le peintre Klimt. On peut même dire que c'est lui la caméra. Donc, d'une certaine manière, on verra les images du film comme si c'était Klimt lui-même qui les voyait. Ou plutôt qui les rêvait. Car ce film sera une rêverie: exubérance de couleurs, distorsion de l'espace, extrême complexité des mouvements de caméra. (2006)

> (It is really a fantasy ... a fresco of real and imagined characters who turn around a single point: the painter Klimt. One could even say he is the camera. Thus, in a certain manner, one sees the images of the film as if it was Klimt himself seeing them. Or rather he dreams them. Because the film will be a reverie: exuberance of colours, distortion of space, extreme complexity of camera movements.)

Léa de Castro is introduced into the film subjectively through Klimt. Her character is based loosely on the real-life dancer and Parisienne Cléo de Mérode. Michael Garval remarks that 'so much about Léa – as courtesan, enticing performer, exotic temptress, nude model, or proto film star – stands in for the legend of Mérode's life and career' (212). The daughter of a Viennese baroness and an unknown father,

Cléopâtre-Diane de Mérode was born in Paris in 1875. Garval writes of how de Mérode 'entered the Paris Opera *corps de ballet* at seven, rose through the ranks, and began to attract attention, less for dancing than for her great beauty, and a distinctive, ear-hiding hairdo' (2). Her reputation went beyond the Opera by the mid-1890s when photographs of de Mérode were widely disseminated in France and abroad. She attracted further publicity when rumours circulated that she was the mistress of Belgian King Leopold II and modelled for a publicly exhibited nude statue (Garval 2). The name Léa de Castro is significant in that it is a blurring of the names Cléo de Mérode and Laetitia Casta, the French actress who was originally set to play Léa in Ruiz's film. By incorporating Casta's name into the character, Ruiz further blurs the line between the character and the actress incarnating the role. The significance of the name is eventually diminished with the casting of Burrows; however, as Garval remarks, the name Léa de Castro is 'a palimpsest retaining traces of the role's first designation' and recalls 'names of other Mérode doubles' (210).

In *Klimt*, Léa is always only an apparition, a shadow, a double – in short, an *image* – and the hallucinatory nature of Ruiz's film creates an interstitial space for *la Parisienne* between art and life. Ruiz's film is itself framed by the drugged reveries and hallucinations of an anesthetised Klimt on his deathbed, and Léa is called into the film through Klimt's memories of her. Janet Stewart writes that the opening scene of *Klimt*, set in 'the sterile, if rather surreal, environment of a clinic' depicting Egon Schiele visiting Klimt on his deathbed, 'provides the framing narrative for the series of loosely connected memories that transport the viewer back to early-twentieth-century Vienna' (54). Instead of a straightforward narrative trajectory, Ruiz links Klimt's memories 'visually through the double trope of mirror and water, which offer a set of "memory-images"' (Stewart 54). The film's episodes are, according to Stewart, 'framed through a number of devices that question the boundary between the real and the imaginary' (54). This framing device already assures that Léa de Castro will never be a fully realised character but rather an apparition, a memory; or to keep the analogy of art and drawing, a sketch or a trace.

In terms of treatment, *la Parisienne* appears in Ruiz's film across different media. Interestingly, she first appears to Klimt in a film-within-a-film, a short piece produced by Georges Méliès depicting Léa performing a Cambodian dance, the signature dance of Cléo de Mérode at the 1900 Paris World's Fair. This world's fair featured Mérode's 'much-admired, much-parodied "Cambodian" dances, which became her premier number, and broadened her international appeal' (Garval 3). Thus Klimt first encounters Léa at a time in which de Mérode's image was at its most reproduced. It is fitting, too, that Klimt should encounter her at the same world's fair which featured *la Parisienne* as its mascot. However, it is not the real Léa dancing on screen but rather an actress interpreting Léa. Ruiz films the encounter as a shot reverse shot, showing the cinematic Léa and then cutting to a close-up of Klimt enchanted by her image. To further complicate their initial encounter, Klimt himself appears on screen with Léa. He introduces himself and then begins to paint her portrait, establishing their relationship as artist and muse. This cinematic meeting prefigures their actual meeting. Stewart remarks: 'Méliès's film apparently offers evidence of Klimt's liaison with a beautiful young woman, only for it to become clear that the copy precedes the event; the relationship exists first on screen and is consummated only after the film has been viewed' (65). Following the screening of the film, Klimt is introduced to Méliès and to the woman whom he believes to be the real Léa. When she asks Klimt to paint her portrait the following dialogue ensues:

MÉLIÈS: Tell me, what do you think of Léa?
KLIMT: She could charm the trees themselves.
LÉA: If you like this one you'll like the real Léa even better.
KLIMT: Pardon?
MÉLIÈS: Don't worry Monsieur Klimt; the real one is not nearly
    as real as the false one.

From the first meeting between Klimt and Léa, Ruiz introduces the complication between art and life, image and double, real and fake, and the relationship between artist and muse. While Klimt is immediately enchanted by Léa, it is Léa herself who complicates the active artist/passive muse relationship by *asking* Klimt to paint *her* portrait.

Not only is Léa an artist's model and muse, she is also an artist herself: the real Léa is a world-famous demimondaine and dancer, while the 'false' Léa is an actress whose art lies in mimesis and illusion. Léa's role as artist also extends to her self-fashioning, both in terms of her toilette and interior decorating. Indeed, interiors are an extension of the affected beauty of *la Parisienne*. Uzanne remarks how the Parisienne uses interior decorating as an extension of her own elegance:

Rien ne choque dans l'ordonnance des logis que se font nos mondaines pour rehausser leur fine élégance. — Elles y apparaissent vêtues de négligés exquisément vaporeux, de robes de satin ou de crêpe du Japon, de *tea gowns* de pongis indiens ou de velours orientaux, sur le tissu desquels volent des théories d'oiseaux ou de chimères fantastiques. (27)

There are no defects in the home surroundings which the lady of society chooses to set off her elegance and beauty. She is to be found there in exquisitely vaporous undress, in charming satin or Japanese *crêpe* tea-gowns, or Indian silk or Oriental velvet on which are embroidered processions of birds or fantastic dragons. (*The Modern Parisienne* 6)

This aspect of Léa's art comes to the fore in the scene at her apartment. The interior is typical of a chic apartment of the era displaying a predilection for Japonisme and orientalism in vogue at the turn of the century. Paris in the second half of the nineteenth century saw a rise not only in Japonisme but also exoticism more generally, its primary sources being the East, Spain and Japan. Military conquests and the Expositions Universelles of 1855, 1867, 1878 and 1889 all contributed to this rise (Simon 109). Léa's apartment is rich in the design details which epitomise the exoticism style. The vogue for Japonisme can be traced back to 1855 when several Parisian stores specialising in Japanese kimonos, engravings, teas and curios opened, following the first commercial treaties between Japan and the West (Simon 115). There are many portraits from this period depicting Parisian women in Japanese dress or contemplating Japanese objects, including Tissot's *La Japonaise* (1864) and *Young Ladies Looking at Japanese Objects* (1869), and Monet's *La Japonaise Portrait de Camille* (1868). While Japonisme had a significant impact on painting and the decorative arts, its influence on fashion was restricted mainly to the wearing of the kimono as a peignoir (Simon 118). Léa wears a kimono in the apartment scene, highlighting her fashionability, but as this item of clothing is also erotically charged it therefore connotes sensuality and sexual availability. Marie Simon notes that to paint a woman in her peignoir in the nineteenth century was a bold move:

> In painting, it was audacious to depict this sphere of feminine intimacy. To depict a woman in her nightdress, while washing or dressing, or less bluntly, in her morning house-coat, showed either a desire to ignore social rules by moving towards realism (as in Manet, Caillebotte, Morisot, Lautrec), or to be deliberately provocative by harking back to the seductions of the previous century (as in Stevens, Tissot, Madraxo y Garreta). The peignoir ... was one of the items of dress most heavily charged with meaning for painters. (22)

Significantly, for his portrait of Léa, Klimt chooses to depict her in a kimono.

The overall aesthetic of Ruiz's film is clearly modelled on Klimt's work. Ruiz remarks how his film uses 'the prevailing beauty, excess of colour, spatial distortion and complex angles [in the artist's work] to bring to life and illuminate one of the richest, most contradictory and eerie epochs in modern history' (qtd in Macnab 32). Ruiz's film features 'a dazzling array of gold leaf' which mirrors Klimt's painting (Macnab 32). However, the aesthetic of the scene at Léa's apartment more closely resembles the paintings of George Hendrik Breitner. Léa's long limbs, red kimono and her hair worn back from her face, as well as the rich tapestries and opulent furnishings of her apartment, all recall Breitner's paintings *Girl in Red Kimono* (c. 1893) and *Girl in Red Kimono* (1893–95). During the scene at her apartment, Klimt discovers Léa has already had her portrait painted by Whistler. The fictional painting of Léa is based on Whistler's painting *Symphony in White, No. 1: The White Girl* (1862), which serves as another intertext for Ruiz's film. *Symphony in White, No. 1: The White Girl* is a portrait of Whistler's Irish mistress and model Jo Hiffernan, who later, while in France, became the mistress of Gustave Courbet (King 180). Hiffernan was the subject of Courbet's painting *La belle Irlandaise [Portrait of Jo]*

(1865–66) as well as one of the models for his painting *The Sleepers* (1865). Hiffernan, herself a Parisienne muse, haunts the character of Léa de Castro through the presence of Whistler's painting of Léa. From their very first encounter, Léa is already cinematic vision and double. Léa appears three more times to Klimt throughout the film: as a shadow on the wall conjured up by Méliès is his studio, as a ghost in limbo, and in the scene at her apartment which features doubles, mirrors and painted portraits. These all work together to create the effect of Léa as a Parisienne who is only ever an image of an image, where the lines between real life and artifice are in a constant state of flux. As Garval writes: 'In Ruiz's strange, ambiguous, but compelling universe, nothing is quite what it appears, and the film's persistent play with lenses, frames, screens, mirrors, and pictures reflects upon reality and illusion, vision and representation, and the movie-making art in particular' (210). In *Klimt*, the figure of the Parisienne muse is depicted through a deliberate blurring of art and life, such that from the artist's first encounter with his muse he is uncertain which is the real and which the representation. Klimt desires the real Léa, but must settle for her image. Stewart remarks: 'In *Klimt*, Ruiz explores the idea that every image is already but an image of an image through the technique of film filming film itself. The film of Klimt that Méliès presents for the edification of the assembled guests at the Paris exhibition is offered to the viewer in the form of an image of an image, a film of a film' (65). Stewart further suggests that beginning Klimt and Léa's relationship as a projection (in both the physical sense of cinematic projection and in the more psychological sense) 'allows Ruiz to suggest the primacy of surface over depth' (59). However it also demonstrates the way *la Parisienne* is never who she appears to be, is always only an image of herself, and remains an infinite series of potential representations or projections in painting and in cinema.

Midnight muse: Adriana in *Midnight in Paris*

> La Parisienne est une noctambule. Elle ne commence bien à vivre que le soir. A minuit, elle resplendit.
>
> *La Parisienne is a night owl. She only really begins to live at night. At midnight, she sparkles.* (Arsène Houssaye, Les Parisiennes)

A promotional poster for Woody Allen's *Midnight in Paris* features the film's hero, Gil Pender (Owen Wilson), strolling by the Seine against a backdrop of Paris rendered in the recognisable swirls of a Van Gogh painting. That the figure of the hero is reduced to such a small scale indicates that Allen's film is more about the city of Paris than about any single protagonist. The painterly aesthetic used in the poster further indicates that for Allen, as for his hero Gil Pender, Paris is a city mediated through art. Indeed, the opening scene of *Midnight in Paris* is set in Monet's garden at Giverny, where an enthusiastic Pender announces to his fiancée his intentions to move to Paris to write novels. The film also includes scenes shot at the Rodin and Marmottan museums, as well as in the maison-salon of Gertrude Stein and Alice B. Toklas. The film is full of artistic and cultural references, and features a cast including the who's who of the Lost Generation and their artistic milieu, as well as prominent painters of the Belle Époque. While *Midnight in Paris* is ostensibly a film about Gil Pender's decision to give up his conventional life as a Hollywood scriptwriter and pursue the life of a novelist, its narrative centrepiece is the beautiful and enigmatic Parisienne Adriana, muse not only to Picasso, Braque, Modigliani and Hemingway, but also to Pender.

Unlike Léa de Castro in *Klimt* and Elena in *Elena et les hommes*, Adriana is not directly inspired by any single, recognisable historical personage; rather, she is inspired by art itself, by the various depictions of *la Parisienne* in art and literature of the nineteenth and early twentieth centuries. Adriana embodies many of the characteristics of the Parisienne type: she is fashionable, elusive, sexually available, self-fashioning, a muse to various painters and writers, inhabits an artistic milieu, and is both historically situated and temporally mobile. Indeed, she could easily be a figment of Pender's imagination, a composite image constructed through the various depictions of Parisienne women Pender has read about or seen (however, one scene in the film where Pender discovers her memoirs at a bookstall by the Seine disrupts this reading). Nonetheless, Adriana is not on the same ontological plane as the other characters inhabiting Pender's 1920s Paris, including Hemingway, Scott and Zelda Fitzgerald, Cole Porter, Josephine Baker, Gertrude Stein and T.S. Eliot, among others, and she cannot be said to 'exist' in the same way as these personages existed.

At the outset, Adriana is depicted as belonging to her time, and is recognisably Parisienne through her beauty, mystery and fashionability. Her hair is bobbed in the 1920s style and her costumes throughout the film conform to the fashionable 1920s silhouette which flourished following the establishment of Coco Chanel's fashion house on the Rue Cambon: 'Paris s'habitue à cette nouvelle silhouette d'une femme svelte, sans hanche ni poitrine, qui montre ses jambes, qui fume et teinte ses lèvres de rouge vif' (Denuelle 55) (Paris accustomed itself to this new silhouette of a svelte woman, without hips or chest, who showed her legs, who smoked and painted her lips vivid red). Adriana's dresses made of comfortable, new, fluid fabrics fall just below the knee, the standard fashionable hemline of the 1920s, and feature waistlines which drop towards the hips. Pierre Sicard captures this popular 1920s 'look' in his painting *Cabaret Le Pigall's* (1925), and this painting is evoked in the Fitzgerald's party scene in *Midnight in Paris*.

The first shot of Adriana shows her wearing a little black dress, a garment made famous by Chanel, who did not strictly 'invent' it, but rather claimed it as her own (Mackenzie 75). A symbol not only of Paris but also of modernity, the little black dress was almost industrial in its functionality and design. Peter Wollen writes:

> Coco Chanel's black crêpe-de-chine sheath of 1926 was seen by *Vogue* as analogous to Henry Ford's Model T – functional, impersonal, with design and ornamentation reduced to an absolute minimum. Every Model T was identical. They were available only in black. Chanel was seen as implementing the modernist program, the elimination of waste and excess, the demand for reason and simplicity, within the world of fashion itself, apparently the most privileged realm of fantastic opulence and decorative display. (Wollen et al. 25)

In the popular fashion press too, the little black dress is considered the epitome of Parisian chic and has become a perennial favourite amongst stylists and fashion-magazine editors. Recent style guides released around the same time as Allen's film feature the little black dress. In *Paris Street Style: A Guide to Effortless Chic*, Isabelle Thomas and Frédérique Veysset refer to the little black dress as 'the ultimate symbol of refinement in 1926, thanks to Coco Chanel' (128), and in the same book couturier Alexandre Vauthier calls it 'part of the established code of elegance' and representative of Paris (qtd in Thomas and Veysset 134). In *Parisian Chic*, Inès de la Fressange includes the little black dress in her list of the 'brilliant basics' which constitute the '"made in Paris" look' (23). De la Fressange also claims that the little black dress 'is not simply an item of clothing, it's a concept' (32). This comment highlights how the dress is no longer simply a dress but also a signifier of Paris and Parisian chic and elegance. To have Adriana first appear in the little black dress is to distil a whole range of connotations – elegance, chic, refinement and Parisienne-ness – into our first impression of her. It is the first of the mythological conventions or clichés Allen employs in *Midnight in Paris* in his construction of the Parisienne type. The association between Adriana and fashion is further strengthened in the film by her having come to Paris from the provinces to work with Chanel. Two other dresses Adriana wears also conform to a fashionable 1920s silhouette. At a wedding party at Deyrolles Adriana wears a chemise dress hung from the shoulders to create a straight silhouette. The dress is a soft, pale, golden yellow and features intricate beading both vertically down the bodice and in scalloped shapes around the skirt. The light, fluid structure and fabric of the dress made it ideal for dancing the Charleston, a popular pastime for the Parisienne of the 1920s (Denuelle 155). Later Adriana wears a simple white sheath, featuring cap sleeves and a sailor collar with pink and white detailing.

In addition to her fashionability and style, Adriana is also Parisienne through her provincial origins and her cosmopolitanism. She conforms to the prototype Parisienne of Jean de Préchac's 1679 novel, *L'Illustre Parisienne, histoire galante et véritable*, whom Ellen Welch describes as possessing an 'innate cosmopolitanism that makes her comfortable with foreign individuals, cultures, and languages' (69). Adriana speaks English and consorts with many foreigners in Paris, including the American Hemingway, the Italian Modigliani and the Spanish Picasso, among others. That Adriana came to Paris from the provinces is another popular Parisienne trope. Taxile Delord dedicates his *Physiology de la Parisienne* to the women of the provinces and reveals that the Parisienne is, first and foremost, a provincial. Provincial women, according to Delord, have grace and spirit provided solely that they do not live in the provinces (13). Adriana's frankness, demeanour and actions suggest she is open to sexual encounters, another hallmark of the Parisienne type. After having met Gil only moments earlier, Adriana speaks openly to him about her life as a mistress to Picasso, Braque and Modigliani. In a later scene where Gil and Adriana observe the streetwalkers lining the streets of Montmartre, she recounts how, when at her Catholic school, she and a roommate paid a girl from Pigalle to teach them 'all her tricks'.

Work in the fashion industry often saw Parisiennes, many of them from the provinces, moving in artistic circles. As Tétart-Vittu writes:

> In Paris it was the most natural thing in the world for a young woman who worked during the week, went dancing at public balls on Sunday, and relaxed with students and painters on the banks of the Seine in the summer to become first a model and then a companion for an artist. Norbert Goeneutte, Claude Monet, Renoir, and Rops all married couturiers. (80)

Adriana's function in Allen's film is primarily that of artist's companion and muse. Costume designer for *Midnight in Paris*, Sonia Grande, remarks: 'Adriana is romantic, idealistic, feminine and a dreamer, but also exquisite. She's a delicate muse to artists and intellectuals in the '20s' (qtd in Godley and Hemphill). When Gil meets Adriana for the first time, she is involved with Picasso and had previously been the lover of both Modigliani and Braque. Later in the film, when Gil and Adriana travel back in time to the Belle Époque, she is enlisted by Degas and Gauguin to design ballet costumes for Diaghilev's Ballets Russes and it is evident she is soon to become the muse and lover of Gauguin, who is immediately enchanted by her. That no single man can possess Adriana is figurative in the film both for the elusiveness of *la Parisienne* and for the impossibility of capturing her essence in art. As Arsène Houssaye remarks: 'Qui pourrait bien peindre la Parisienne? Son grand art est de ne jamais se ressembler à elle-même' (273) (Who could accurately render *la Parisienne*? Her great art is to never resemble herself). In a key scene Gertrude Stein (Kathy Bates) discusses Picasso's portrait of Adriana. Stein argues that Adriana's appeal is 'plus subtile' and that Picasso has failed to capture this in his painting. She accuses him of being too reductive in his attempt and of having 'made a creature of Place Pigalle, a whore with volcanic appetites ...'. It is not so much that Picasso is wrong in his depiction, but that he has emphasised one aspect of the Parisienne mythology – prostitution – at the expense of others.

Unlike Renoir and Ruiz, Allen does not use a strictly painterly aesthetic in depicting the Parisienne Adriana, although certain framing techniques are suggestive of portraiture. Rather, he uses a meticulously reconstructed Paris of the 1920s and, later, of the Belle Époque, and a modernist conception of time. Principally, the temporality in the film is derived from three sources, each cited more or less directly in the film. The first is the appearance of T.S. Eliot, to whom Pender remarks: 'Prufrock is, like, my mantra.' However, Eliot's sense of the contemporaneousness of all time is best exemplified in lines from 'Burnt Norton' from *Four Quartets*:

> Time present and time past
> Are both perhaps present in time future,
> And time future contained in time past.
> If all time is eternally present
> All time is unredeemable. (177)

The second source of the film's modernist temporality is a line taken from William Faulkner's experimental novel *Requiem for a Nun* (1951), which Gil cites in the film: 'The past is not dead. It's not even past' (92). The third source is Surrealism, and in a scene where Gil presents his dilemma to Dalí, Buñuel and Man Ray, Man Ray replies: 'Exactly correct! You slide through time!' They find the idea of 'a man in love with a woman from a different era' perfectly acceptable, an idea which the more 'normal' Gil finds difficult to accept: 'Well, yeah, you're Surrealists, but I'm a normal guy.' *Midnight in Paris* moves between three presents – Paris *c*. 2010, in the 1920s and during the Belle Époque – each connected by Allen's Orpheus-like hero who moves between them. As Vanessa Schwartz remarks:

Although the American protagonist is propelled repeatedly backward into the world of the inter-war Lost Generation of his fellow Americans in Paris, his French fantasy woman insists on returning to the Moulin Rouge – Toulouse-Lautrec's, Vincente Minnelli's, John Huston's, Baz Luhrmann's, and the audience's Moulin Rouge – where Paris always is: 1900. ('Paris' 127)

As a Parisienne, Adriana finds her spiritual homeland in Belle Époque Paris, with all the visual conventions associated with it, leaving Gil to return to his present, Paris in 2010. The film's ultimate message echoes T.S. Eliot's idea that no matter where it takes us, time always returns us to the present. It is a present that contains the past, like the modern-day launderette which was once the bar that was the haunt of Hemingway and Scott Fitzgerald. Adriana is returned to history, but her place is taken by another Parisienne, from Gil's own present, Gabrielle (Léa Séydoux), who Gil first meets at a nostalgia shop in the Marché aux Puces de Saint-Ouen. That the novel Gil is working on is also set in a nostalgia shop adds to the overall feeling of fantasy and nostalgia in the film. Indeed, Maroussia Dubreuil claims that *Midnight in Paris* 'associates the French capital with nighttime and dreams' and cites Allen's remark that 'the city lends itself to this kind of reverie' (248).

In spite of her contemporaneity, however, Gabrielle is no less a fantasy figure than Adriana, and may in fact be more so: she too appears before Gil at the stroke of midnight on the famous Pont Alexandre III. These two Parisiennes, Adriana and Gabrielle, represent the two different conceptions of the muse outlined by Levy. Adriana, as self-fashioning and active, corresponds to the ancient conception of the muse, placing the poet, Gil, in the position of passivity; she is the muse who chooses the men she inspires, and exhibits volition independent of Gil's desire. In this way she is unsuitable for any satisfactory closure for the film. Gabrielle, on the other hand, corresponds more to the passive, Romantic muse, and appears in Allen's film as the extension of Gil's narcissism: like Gil, Gabrielle loves Cole Porter and enjoys walking the Parisian streets in the rain. In this sense, Gabrielle does not *inspire* Gil in the ancient sense, but is rather *inspired by* Gil's own ideas about what constitutes the perfect Parisienne.

Midnight in Paris, *Klimt* and *Elena et les hommes* offer different treatments of the Parisienne type as muse, demonstrating the way the type inhabits an interstitial space between art and life. As Parisiennes, Elena, Léa and Adriana share recognisable iconographical motifs. They are fashionable, elusive (insofar as they are not able to be possessed by any man nor adequately rendered by any artist) and self-fashioning (they take charge of their own image and can never be reduced to another's desire). This self-fashioning aspect means these Parisiennes cannot be reduced to the modern or Romantic conception of the muse as passive object of male desire or artistic construction. Rather, they conform more to the classical ideal of the muse as active, in relation to the artist as passive receptor of inspiration.

A further motif discernible in these three Parisiennes not discussed in detail in this chapter is cosmopolitanism, communicated diegetically (Adriana recounts the story of her arrival from the provinces; Elena is Polish but living in Paris) or extra-diegetically (the actress incarnating the Parisienne is not French: English-born Burrows and Swedish-born Bergman). *Midnight in Paris*, *Klimt* and *Elena et les hommes* are set in Paris, giving the impression that cosmopolitan Parisiennes only inhabit Paris, having come to the city from other places (the provinces or abroad). However, this only represents one side of the cosmopolitanism of the Parisienne type, which has the broader sense of *anyone* and *anywhere*. The following chapter will take up these two aspects of the cosmopolitan Parisienne by looking at films set outside, or partially in, Paris.

Note

1   The character of Ilsa fits the profile of the Parisienne in the following ways: her identity is in part shaped by a sojourn in Paris, shown in the flashback sequence in *Casablanca*; she is cosmopolitan in the sense of her mobility across borders and the ease with which she takes her place in foreign cities; she is involved in a *ménage a trois*; there is the ambiguity surrounding her motives and the suggestion of courtesanship (does she *love* Rick, or does she renew their liaison in order to gain important papers?); she is dangerous, in the sense that her actions/decisions drive the narrative in a way that threatens the male characters (she also threatens to shoot Rick if he does not hand over the papers); and she is fashionable.

2

Cosmopolite

Il est bien entendu, n'est-ce pas, que par toute la terre et partout où l'homme a bâti des villes, une femme réellement belle, riche, élégante et spirituelle est une Parisienne.

It is well-known, isn't it, that across all the Earth where man has built cities, a truly beautiful, rich, elegant and spiritual woman is a Parisienne. (Théodore de Banville)

In 2009, French fashion house Yves Saint Laurent chose British model Kate Moss to be the face of its perfume 'Parisienne'. The advertising campaign accompanying the perfume's release featured Moss, dressed in a structured black leather bustier and holding a pink rose, strolling through the Paris streets at dawn. The most famous of Parisian signifiers, the Eiffel Tower, is prominent in the background. The product description on YSL's American website reads: 'The new fragrance by Yves Saint Laurent is a sensuous bouquet to the woman whose heart belongs to Paris ... even if home is elsewhere' (yslbeautyus.com). Claire Humphrey remarks that the use of Moss in the advertising campaign demonstrates that 'the identity of la Parisienne can extend internationally' (257). The Yves Saint Laurent claim that 'any woman anywhere can be a Parisienne' echoes an aphorism of Uzanne written more than a century earlier: 'On peut naître d'instinct et de goûts Parisienne sur tous les points du territoire, voire même en différentes villes ou contrées du globe' (18), 'A woman may be Parisian by taste and instinct anywhere on French soil, and indeed in any town or country in the world' (*The Modern Parisienne* 1). Nevertheless, the cosmopolitanism of *la Parisienne* is inextricably linked to Paris as a cosmopolitan city, the nineteenth-century capital of the modern world.

Paris has from the nineteenth century onwards been 'long-celebrated and decried as "cosmopolitan"' (Rearick 193) and perceived as 'the ultimate Cosmopolitan capital' (Steele, *Paris Fashion* 74). As a personification of the city, *la Parisienne* was necessarily cosmopolitan and, since the nineteenth century, has been the figure of not only French femininity but femininity as such. As Uzanne remarks: 'les Parisiennes sont ... astreintes à poser en modèles devant l'univers' (59), 'Parisiennes are compelled to pose as models to the universe' (*The Modern Parisienne* 23). Thus *la Parisienne* is a figure whose national particularity was always already international or global at its conception. In 1900, the cosmopolitanism of *la Parisienne* was solidified when she appeared as a symbol or mascot for the world's fair held in Paris that year. Ruth E. Iskin claims that the 'choice of the *Parisienne* monument for the most prominent location in the exposition suited her role as a symbol of the nation' (222). There are, however, precedents for *la Parisienne cosmopolite* which pre-date the nineteenth century; for example, Jean de Préchac's 1679 novel *L'Illustre Parisienne, histoire galante et véritable*, which Ellen Welch describes as follows:

> The novel's heroine, the 'Parisienne' of its title, embodies the charms of the metropolis, possessing beauty, intelligence, perfect 'French' manners, and an innate cosmopolitanism that makes her comfortable with foreign individuals, cultures, and languages. She also becomes the human object of desire for foreign characters in love with her home city. (69)

As part of the mythology of *la Parisienne*, cosmopolitanism has the sense of anyone and anywhere: 'Les femmes de Paris ne sont pas pour un tiers Parisiennes par droit de naissance' (Uzanne 17), 'Scarcely a third of the women in Paris are Parisiennes by right of birth' (*The Modern Parisienne* 1). The potential for any woman anywhere to become *la Parisienne* is not, however, absolute. Taxile Delord has qualified this potential by grounding it in something more intangible: a stay in Paris is considered necessary to complete the transformation, but even this is no guarantee. Delord claims that to be Parisienne it is not enough to be merely Parisian by birth or to simply have spent time in Paris; he uses the metaphor of the uncarved block to demonstrate how a woman becomes *la Parisienne*:

Le monde lui envoie des blocs de marbre; il en fait des statues.
Paris est une artiste. Statuaire infatigable, Paris équarrit sans
cesse avec le marteau de l'esprit. Chaque année, plus de trente
mille ébauches passent sous son ciseau; à peine un tiers est-il
reçu à l'exposition. La capitale est un paradis où il y a beaucoup
d'appelées et peu d'élues. (14)

(The world sends Paris blocks of marble; Paris makes statues
out of them. Paris is an artist. Tireless statuary, Paris ceaselessly
squares off with the hammer of the mind. Each year, more than
thirty thousand unpolished blocks pass under the chisel; barely
a third are accepted at the exposition. The capital is a paradise
where there are many conscripts and few elect.)

If it is possible that anyone anywhere can be *la Parisienne* provided they possess that unknowable something, that *je ne sais quoi* irrespective of time and place, then this universal essence is, paradoxically it seems, the only thing that cannot be bought and sold in the marketplace. The essence of *la Parisienne* lies, it would seem, somewhere outside the economy of exchange, production and consumption. Indeed, Susan Ossman argues that a woman becomes Parisienne not by possessing some innate or indefinable essence but rather by assuming an identity based on a principle 'tethered to a specific ground through multiple mediations' (25). This ground is the city of Paris itself; however a woman may be tethered to Paris from anywhere in the world. What is important for Ossman is that a woman 'be willing to work with a particular understanding of the city, of culture, and self-cultivation' (25), independent of location or habitus. Indeed, Ossman writes, the Parisienne 'could be considered a critical demonstration of the determination to break with the idea that a person is simply a product of an unconsciously transmitted *habitus*, a singular emanation of some natural cultural context' (25–6). Ossman further describes the Parisienne as 'a highly gendered figure of a type of woman who has learned to take a certain distance from the idea that a person is simply a product of a natural or social milieu' (25). This suggests not only a figure which exists outside national borders but also apart from class divisions. Richard Bernstein claims that to be Parisian "is to have an identity that transcends social class, economic distinction; it is to belong to a world apart, to an intellectual and moral category, not of class, race and gender, but from a qualitative difference from the rest, an essential worldliness' (73). For both Ossman and Bernstein, then, to be Parisienne is more than the mere transmission of a particular *habitus* or milieu. What defines *la Parisienne* is in fact her ability not to be delimited in this way, by maintaining an essential connection to Paris without necessarily being confined to the city geographically.

These foregoing remarks deal with the relationship between figure and place. In terms of the cosmopolitan Parisienne in cinema, in the case studies that follow, this might be expressed as the relationship between character and setting. Generally speaking, there are three possibilities for the setting of a film featuring the Parisienne type and two possibilities for the origin of the type in any given film. The films may be set in Paris, outside Paris, or partially in Paris (usually to depict the necessary sojourn). The Parisienne of the film may be from Paris or from outside Paris (either from the provinces or abroad). In general terms, any combination of protagonist and setting is possible.

'Une Paris portative': Gaby in *Pépé le Moko*

While hiding out in the Casbah, the Arab quarter of Algiers, notorious gangster Pépé (Jean Gabin) meets the beautiful Parisienne Gaby (Mireille Balin), a demimondaine holidaying in Algiers in the company of a wealthy Champagne magnate. For Pépé, not only is Gaby a reminder of the Paris he fled, she *is* Paris itself, 'une Paris portative', to use Janette Bayles's term, a portable Paris. Pépé's encounter with Gaby inflames his nostalgia for Paris which, in turn, leads to his downfall. In this way, the Parisienne of Duvivier's film functions as metonymy of Paris. This idea is unique neither to cinema nor to twentieth-century discourse on the type. During the Second Empire *la Parisienne* 'personified the joyous, sophisticated city that outdistanced all its rivals as the high-society playground of the world' (Berlanstein 117).

As *la Parisienne*, Gaby is associated with fashion, prostitution, consumption, social mobility, cosmopolitanism and danger. These condense down to two interconnected elements associated with, not only the Parisienne type, but with modernity and modernisation itself: visibility and mobility. In his study of nineteenth-century Paris, Walter

Benjamin identifies these two motifs as typical of the modern city and of modernity as such. Gaby exemplifies mobility in three ways. First, she is transnationally mobile, travelling between Paris and North Africa, presumably by train and then steamship, a prominent symbol of Art Deco and modernity. Secondly, she is mobile in terms of class, moving from working-class origins to the inner circle of wealthy businessman Kleep and back again in the company of Pépé. Thirdly, she is spatially mobile, moving freely between the European quarter of Algiers and the Casbah. This latter mobility is one not afforded other characters in the film: Pépé is trapped in the Casbah and unable to descend into the European quarter, while the French police are unable to penetrate the Casbah, and Kleep is unable to tolerate it. Gaby is the only character capable of moving freely and easily between the two spaces, with the exception of the hybrid figure of Slimane, a native working for the French colonial police whose deliberately feminine appearance and manners make him the evil 'double' of Gaby. Unlike Pépé, who must remain invisible and stationary, Gaby's mobility is not hindered by her visibility.

To the spatial dimension of Gaby's mobility is added a temporal dimension. In temporal terms, Gaby is situated at a turning point that both recalls the past and points towards the future. This ambiguity is played out on two levels: on the one hand, through Pépé's vision of Gaby as representing a lost Paris; and on the other, through her appearance, predominantly her wardrobe, which speaks of everything forward-looking and modern, and her attitude, revealed in those scenes played out in Pépé's absence, to which we can give the name modern in juxtaposition to Pépé's Romantic or old-fashioned ideas.

Gaby is a kept woman, as she reminds Kleep during an argument at the hotel; a high-class prostitute like *les grandes horizontales* of Second Empire France. She is, in other words, an object of consumption. But she is also the consumer *par excellence*, in particular of expensive jewellery and haute couture. When Pépé asks Gaby what she did before she had the jewels, Gaby replies that she desired them. Gaby is a social climber of humble origins, hailing from the same working-class Parisian neighbourhood as Pépé, and it is her status as a demimondaine which affords Gaby social mobility. Like Pépé, she has escaped her working-class origins through socially dubious means, and this, in a way, unites them. Indeed, there is a distinctly narcissistic element to their association. Sartorially, too, Gaby mirrors Pépé, her black-and-white polka-dot scarf matching his tie. For Gaby, however, Pépé is little more than a novelty, the famous gangster, and one of the attractions the Casbah has to offer the wealthy tourist. For Pépé, however, Gaby is a Beatrice-like figure come to lead him out of the Purgatory of his present and into the Paradise of his lost Paris. Gaby stands in, not only for Paris and its stereotypes, but also for Pépé's investment in them.

For Ginette Vincendeau, Gaby is 'the epitome of the elegant Parisienne whose plucked eyebrows denote the beauty salon, and who wears a different, carefully chosen couture outfit for each occasion' (*Pépé* 50–1). While these outfits obey the dress codes of 1930s women's fashion, they exude an impractical opulence which distinguishes Gaby from the inhabitants of the Casbah. Throughout the film, Gaby radiates whiteness; an effect achieved both sartorially and through the use of lighting. This is best exemplified in the scene in which Gaby, dressed in an evening gown of white satin and adorned with diamonds and pearls, first encounters Pépé. The scene comprises a series of close-ups: her brilliant jewels, the soft milky complexion of her face, her shining eyes and finally a smile which reveals her gleaming white teeth. In each shot Gaby appears bathed in a luminous white light. According to Dudley Andrew, *Pépé le Moko* produces

> a fatal feeling of helplessness when a strong male from an older tradition ... becomes obsessed by a French woman wearing white, and bearing the look of the modern. The distance between the sexes amounts to a distance between two styles, one coded as authentic but out of date, the other as attractive but empty, or unreachable. Poetic Realism saw women and modernity in just this way. (*Mists* 274–5)

Andrew remarks that poetic realist films are generally 'sombre in tone' apart from the appearance of a beautiful and compelling woman dressed in white, both the colour of Hollywood deco and the coloniser (*Mists* 275). The woman in white is, however, not only the embodiment of the white coloniser of oriental nations; she is also a precursor to another coloniser, the American ideal of the white, gleaming bodies that a dirty post-war France was to aspire to.

The scene which best encapsulates Gaby's metonymic function occurs 40 minutes into the film. Contemplating Gaby's face after they have just made love, Pépé remarks:

> Tu me plais, tu sais, t'es belle. Et puis avec toi, c'est comme si j'étais à Paris. Avec toi, je m'évade, tu saisis? Tu me changes de paysage. Tiens tout à l'heure, je faisais semblant de dormir. On ne parlait pas, hein? Je me laissais glisser ... Eh bien, sais-tu ce que j'entendais? Le métro! Tu te rends compte, le métro! T'as des bijoux ... t'es tout en soie, t'es pleine d'or et tu m'fais penser au métro, à des cornets de frites et à des cafés-crèmes à la terrasse.

> (I like you, you know, you're beautiful. And with you, it's as if I was in Paris. With you, I escape, you know? You change my landscape. Like just now, I pretended to sleep. There was no talk, eh? I let myself slip ... Well, you know what I heard? The Metro! Do you realise, the Metro! You've jewellery ... you're all in silk, you're full of gold and you remind me of the metro, cones of French fries and *cafés-crème* at the pavement cafés.)

The working-class Paris Gaby signifies is, for Pépé, condensed into distinct and clichéd images: the Metro, cups of *café-crème* and *cornets de frites*. This image of Paris is reiterated in a song, occurring later in the film, in which reference is made to 'mon bistrot du coin' (my corner bistro). This song is performed in the film by Fréhel, a real life exponent of the *chanson réaliste*, a strain of popular music performed in the café-concerts during the Belle Époque. A Parisienne past her prime, an older, fatter and altogether more tragic Fréhel made a comeback in the 1920s and had a modest film career in the 1930s, usually in singing cameos. Vincendeau remarks that the 'elegiac words of "Où est-il donc?", ostensibly about a vanishing Paris, are also about Fréhel's earlier career, familiar to the 1937 spectator' (*Pépé* 24). Another cosmopolitan Parisienne, Fréhel came to Paris as a child from Brittany and took her stage name from the region's Cap Fréhel. She initially worked as a street-singer before making a name for herself in the music halls of the day (Hussey xx–xxi). Andrew Hussey describes

'Où est-il donc?' as a 'haunting and nostalgic lament for the Old Paris of the Place Blanche, an imaginary Paris that Fréhel can never return to' (xxi). A tragic figure, her career ended in poverty and alcoholism. The tragedy of the scene is indicative of Fréhel's mythical function in the film's narrative: her song is a Siren's song which prompts Pépé to leave the Casbah and follow Gaby to Paris. It is, however, a Paris that no longer exists, if in fact it ever *did* exist. It is a Paris, which like Gaby herself, has been reduced to a collection of stereotypical images.

Fréhel's singular narrative function is to express in song Pépé's longing for this lost Paris. Her song finished, her function is fulfilled. This is Fréhel's last hour, and her impending death mirrors the passing of a whole era. Her song represents not only Pépé's longing for a lost Paris, but cinema's nostalgia for its own past, its origins in the café-concert (*caf' conc'*) and the music hall. Although ultimately superseded first by the music hall and then by cinema, the *caf' conc'* was, according to Andrew and Ungar, 'explicitly recognized as the incubator and nourisher of virtually every form of popular French entertainment up to the Second World War' (201). Cinema's nostalgia for the *caf'conc'* is cinema's nostalgia for its own youth. However, any attempt by cinema to reanimate its past is doomed to failure. Fréhel can only signify the bloated decadence of this nostalgia when compared with the sleek, youthful and ultimately mass-reproducible lines of the modern Parisienne represented in the figure of Gaby. The motifs of whiteness, modernity and metonymy also find expression in another film featuring a cosmopolitan Parisienne: Jacques Demy's *Model Shop* (1969).

Lola in Los Angeles

On a sunny day in central Los Angeles a woman walks across the grey asphalt of an inner-city car park to collect her vehicle. Her appearance is revealed gradually. The camera frames, in close-up, tanned legs, black sling-back high-heeled shoes, a white hem skimming tanned knees, a hand clutching a black leather bag. As the figure moves towards the left of the frame, the camera pans up to reveal hips and upper body swathed in white chiffon. The camera continues to pan up, and comes to rest on a close-up which recalls a bust from classical sculpture. The mystery woman is dressed in a sleeveless V-neck white sheath dress with black leaf detail; a voluminous white scarf is draped loosely around her head and neck, and her eyes are hidden behind oversized sunglasses. Mysterious and majestic, despite being far from Paris she is straight out of a poem by Baudelaire: a *grande taciturne* poised to capture the attention of a modern-day poet. This is our introduction to Cécile/Lola (Anouk Aimée) in Jacques Demy's *Model Shop* (1969).

Model Shop is a distant sequel to Demy's 1961 film *Lola*, also starring Aimée as Lola, a Parisienne outside Paris, living and working as a taxi girl in the seaport of Nantes. The plot of *Model Shop* turns around Cécile/Lola's chance encounter with a young drifter, George (Gary Lockwood), which leads to a brief and troubled affair. Cécile/Lola continues to make her living by socially dubious means, the eponymous model shop where men pay to photograph beautiful women being a more contemporary euphemism for a brothel. Alexander Horwath remarks: 'It is typical of Demy's sensitivity that he does not show the usual forms of prostitution, and instead chooses a nice metaphor for it' (90). In addition to her line of work, which links her to the Parisiennes of the demimonde who sell their bodies for sex, Lola incarnates *la Parisienne* in two other main ways: through her enigmatic and chic appearance, and through her prefiguration in nineteenth-century French literature.

In *Les Parisiennes de Paris* (1886), Théodore de Banville identifies elegance and mystery as key features of the Parisienne type. Indeed, for *la Parisienne*, appearance conceals as much as it reveals. For Cécile/Lola, her mode of dress and gestures allow her to appear wealthier and more 'respectable' than she is, in the same way Gaby's stylish outfits in *Pépé le Moko* hide her working-class origins. When George follows Cécile/Lola to a mansion in Beverly Hills he assumes she belongs there. His presumptions about her wealth are, however, quickly dispelled when he later follows her into the model shop. After buying 15 minutes of her time, he tells her: 'I didn't expect *you* to walk into this *slut factory*.' Lola's appearance deceives George, making it difficult for him to determine both her socio-economic status and sexual availability. George's hostility toward Cécile/Lola in the aforementioned scene may be read as an expression of his anxiety at not being able to tell a virtuous woman from a 'slut'. This can be traced back to what Iskin calls the 'standardization of women's fashions' in nineteenth-century Paris which 'elicited some misogynist and class-biased observations, revealing a certain masculine anxiety over the difficulty in telling the difference between women of virtue and women who employed their fashionability to further their trade' (194).

The inability to categorise or fix *la Parisienne* in terms of nationality or class contributes, in part, to her mystery and her possession of a certain ontological *je ne sais quoi*. This may have much to do with the notion of ambiguity, both as a general feature of the historical period of modernity and as a particular feature of fashion (Benjamin *Arcades* 10). With the advent of standardised fashion in the nineteenth century, which replaced 'the coded hierarchy of dress fabrics, styles and colors in place in the eighteenth century, which had been legally maintained by sumptuary laws' (De Young Women in Black' 36), it became difficult to discern a woman's occupation, class and virtue:

> Central to the efficacy of the stereotype of the chic Parisienne was its appeal across class lines. The seemingly class-transcendent myth of the Parisienne appealed to a wide range of social levels, from upper-class moneyed women to middle-class women and working-class women of modest means. Women of the lower middle class and some working women could pursue the fashionability of the Parisienne by shopping in less expensive stores and in the bargain areas in front of upscale department stores. (Iskin 193)

Fashion became increasingly democratised as women gained access to the same widely disseminated newspapers, journals and periodicals which featured clothing and couturier advertisements as well as depictions of fashionable women. These images, primarily intended to arouse the desire to acquire the latest fashions, were addressed to women of all socio-economic groups. Consequently clothing 'became unreliable as an indication of social status or class, and frustrated police could no longer distinguish a prostitute from the bourgeoisie by dress alone' (Menon, *Evil* 44).

In her discussion of Baudelaire's 'À une passante', Beryl Schlossman remarks:

In Second Empire Paris, the anonymity of prostitutes offered to the desiring gaze of observers aroused bourgeois masculine indignation and fear: the controversy around Manet's 'Olympia' gives substantial journalistic evidence of these emotions, especially in connection with the 'honest women'—bourgeois wives and daughters—who could no longer be visually distinguished from the 'fallen' daughters of Eve on city streets. (1021)

For Schlossman, the appearance of the *passante* is ambiguous and raises the question as to whether she presents 'the image of an idol, an offering, or a commodity' (1022). Steele argues that 'the ideal of the Parisienne potentially embraced women across the social spectrum (from the lady to the milliner)' (*Paris Fashion* 75); while Garb claims that the Parisienne 'became the generic term for describing the essence of a particularly modern, peculiarly French form of femininity, which could, ostensibly, encompass women of all classes by a shared "je ne sais quoi"' ('Painting' 98). Fashion allowed the possibility of eradicating notions of class, because women from across all socio-economic groups had access to the same images of the fashionable woman and could seek to fashion themselves after the same image.

As an ambiguous presence, Cécile/Lola is prefigured by the heroine of Baudelaire's poem. Benjamin notes that it was Proust who first named this nameless *passante* of Baudelaire's poem 'la Parisienne' (*Illuminations* 169–70). When Cécile/Lola first appears in *Model Shop* she immediately captures the imagination of the younger George, representing for him another world and another time. His fleeting encounter with this mysterious, statuesque beauty recalls the following lines from Baudelaire:

> La rue assourdissante autour de moi hurlait.
> Longue, mince, en grand deuil, douleur majestueuse,
> Une femme passa, d'une main fastueuse
> Soulevant, balançant le feston et l'ourlet;
>
> Agile et noble, avec sa jambe de statue.
> Moi, je buvais, crispé comme un extravagant,
> Dans son œil, ciel livide où germe l'ouragan,
> La douceur qui fascine et le plaisir qui tue. (101)

(The deafening street screamed all around me.
Tall, slender, in great mourning, majestic pain,
A woman passed by, with a sumptuous hand
Lifting and swinging her festoon and hem;

Agile and noble, with a statue's leg.
I drank, like a twitching madman,
From her eye where the storm begins,
The softness which fascinates, the pleasure which kills.)

In Benjamin's reading of Baudelaire's poem, the big city or the modern city forms the precondition for this encounter: 'What this sonnet communicates is simply this: far from experiencing the crowd as an opposed, antagonistic element, this very crowd brings to the city dweller the figure that fascinates' (*Illuminations* 169). Cécile/Lola does not appear, however, on a crowded boulevard, a passer-by among many. On the contrary, the setting for her exchange with George is markedly desolate: a mass of parked cars surrounds them, stationary in contrast to the moving crowd which carried along the protagonist of Baudelaire's poem. Along with the two protagonists, the only human presence is the car-park attendant. In this respect it is possible to categorise *Model Shop* as a postmodern reworking of Baudelaire's poem, the car park emblematic of Los Angeles as a postmodern city, sprawling without any recognisable centre. It is a city in which the pedestrian *flâneur* has been replaced by the vehicular *flâneur*. What is retained from the Baudelaire poem in *Model Shop*, however, is the fleeting nature of the initial encounter between Cécile/Lola and George. It is significant that the exchange takes place in a car park, a transitory or non-space through which people simply pass without lingering.

Of Baudelaire's poem, Benjamin writes: 'In a widow's veil, mysteriously and mutely borne along by the crowd, an unknown woman comes into the poet's field of vision' (*Illuminations* 169). Cécile/Lola also first appears in a veil, and although not a widow, she was abandoned by her husband, the same man for whom she patiently waited in *Lola* and with whom she was reunited at the film's close. This loss accounts for Cécile/Lola's melancholic character in *Model Shop*, which can only be fully appreciated with reference to Demy's earlier film. The veil too suggests loss. It is this melancholy, a source of fascination for George, which also links Cécile/Lola to the quintessential Baudelairean Parisienne. Here she recalls the protagonist of another Baudelaire poem from *Spleen et Idéal*:

> Je t'adore à l'égal de la voûte nocturne,
> O vase de tristesse, ô grande taciturne,
> Et t'aime d'autant plus, belle, que tu me fuis ... (57)
>
> (I adore you as much as the vault of night,
> O vase of sadness, great and taciturn,
> And I love you all the more, beautiful, because you flee from me ...)

Like the 'belle' of Baudelaire's poem, Cécile/Lola's initial reluctance to engage with George heightens his fascination for her: the more she flees from him the more he desires her.

George stands in for the poet in *Model Shop*. A dandy and a vehicular *flâneur*, he spends his time cruising the streets of Los Angeles in a vintage MG convertible he cannot afford to pay off. He refuses to work for money, and sees himself as an artist who wants to create 'something meaningful', quitting his job with an architecture firm because he does not want to spend his life building shopping malls and car parks. Moreover, George's dialogue is often lyrical and reflective and he is able to see beauty in urban degradation – itself a Baudelairean sentiment. More importantly, like the poet describing his encounter with the *passante*, George is our way into the film; we see everything filtered through him, most importantly Cécile/Lola. Indeed, the first shot we get of Cécile/Lola, starting on her feet and panning upwards, is bookended by reverse shots of George looking at her.

During his first encounters with Cécile/Lola, George experiences 'the kind of sexual shock which can beset a lonely man' (Benjamin, *Illuminations* 169). For Benjamin, Baudelaire's line 'crispé comme un extravagant' describes the poet's body contracting 'in a tremor' (*Illuminations* 169). While George and Cécile/Lola do consummate their relationship, it remains nonetheless nothing more than a passing event. During their first encounter, Cécile/Lola breezes in and out of the car park as effortlessly as she breezes in and out of George's life. Like the love between the poet and the *passante* of Baudelaire's poem, their love is 'spared, rather than denied, fulfilment' (Benjamin,

Illuminations 170). George's de facto relationship with would-be actress Gloria, when juxtaposed with his fascination with Cécile/Lola, stands in for the poverty of fulfilled love, a fact that further underscores George's loneliness and lack of a sense of meaning and place. Transience or placelessness pervades Demy's film. Cécile/Lola and George are both transitory figures, George waiting to be drafted for Vietnam and Cécile/Lola in Los Angeles only until she has enough money to return to Paris.

Baudelaire's poetry is not, however, the only literary prefiguration of Cécile/Lola. George's first encounter with Cécile/Lola also recalls Armand Duval's first encounter with Parisienne Marguerite Gautier in Alexandre Dumas *fils*'s *La Dame aux camélias*:

> La première fois que je l'avais vue, c'était place de la Bourse, à la porte de Susse. Une calèche découverte y stationnait, et une femme vêtue de blanc en était descendue .... Le souvenir de cette vision, car c'en était une véritable, ne me sortit pas de l'esprit comme bien des visions que j'avais eues déjà, et je cherchais partout cette femme blanche si royalement belle. (80–1)

> The first time I had seen her she was on the Place de la Bourse, at the doorstep of Susse's. An open carriage had parked, and a woman dressed in white stepped out .... The memory of this vision – because it truly was a vision – did not leave my mind, unlike many other visions I'd had before, and I searched everywhere for this woman in white who was so regally beautiful. (Schillinger 45)

This idea of the Parisienne first appearing as a vision, capturing the imagination of the male protagonist, is also taken up in another film featuring a cosmopolitan Parisienne, Billy Wilder's *Sabrina* (1954).

Sabrina: a transatlantic Parisienne

Sabrina tells the story of a chauffeur's daughter (Audrey Hepburn) living on a Long Island estate who is sent to study cookery in Paris. Under the influence of the French capital, and with the aid of a wealthy baron, Sabrina returns to Long Island transformed from humble servant girl to chic Parisienne. Hitherto unnoticed on the Larrabee

Estate, Sabrina now attracts the attention first of David and then Linus Larrabee (William Holden and Humphrey Bogart, respectively), with both men at different times declaring their love for her. It is above all this sojourn in Paris which is responsible for the marked change in Sabrina. As Uzanne remarks:

> Paris crée moins la Parisienne qu'il ne la perfectionne; son air ambiant est éminemment modeleur de jolies formes intellectuelles et physiques; il dégrossit, épure, affine, polit, dégage, élance, embellit, amenuise, subtilise tout ce qu'il enveloppe de son charme à la fois caressant et corrosif. (18)

> Paris may be said to complete rather than to create *la Parisienne*; the air of the capital develops all beautiful forms whether of the mind or of the body. It refines, polishes, beautifies, and spiritualises everything that undergoes the influence of its charm, which is at once a sting and a caress. (*The Modern Parisienne* 1)

Sabrina confirms this remark when she says: 'Oh, but Paris isn't for changing planes, it's for changing your outlook! For throwing open the windows and letting in ... letting in *la vie en rose*.'

Wilder's film is often read as a rags-to-riches or Cinderella story, and this is certainly the case in both Dina M. Smith's recent 'Global Cinderella: Sabrina (1954), Hollywood, and Postwar Internationalism,' and Rachel Moseley's 'Dress, Class and Audrey Hepburn: The Significance of the Cinderella Story'. However, Sabrina is much closer to the figure of *la Parisienne* than Cinderella, and aligning her thus calls into question such notions as innocence, passivity and domination. Indeed, *la Parisienne* is often associated with more active and complicit notions. In addition to cosmopolitanism and social mobility, Sabrina is associated with four key motifs of the Parisienne type: fashion, most notably through her costuming by Parisian couturier Hubert de Givenchy; prostitution, initially as the courtesan of the elderly Baron St Fontanel in Paris and later as an object of exchange, traded between the Larrabee brothers; consumption, as both subject (she returns to Long Island with an armful of packages) and object (she is immediately fixed within David Larrabee's gaze); and danger, since she presents a threat to the Larrabee Industries' plastics merger and by extension a threat to American economic interests as such.

In what follows, however, the cosmopolitan Parisienne will be considered primarily as a transnational figure. The term transnational is a recent concept in film studies, reflected in a journal, *Transnational Cinemas*, launched in 2010, entirely devoted to the subject. Transnationalism is, however, by no means self-evident, and scholars disagree over its meaning and use. One thing generally agreed upon is that the transnational occupies a transitional space between nation-states and their cultures on the one hand, and the fully globalised world on the other. What these debates around the notion of transnationalism demonstrate is not only the problematic nature of the concept transnationalism – and by extension the concept of cosmopolitanism – but more importantly the need to deconstruct the dichotomy between Hollywood cinema and the rest of the world, to include Hollywood as part of the world system and not simply as the dominant force. Indeed, Elizabeth Ezra and Terry Rowden remark that despite Hollywood's key role in US cultural imperialism, it is 'important to recognise the impossibility of maintaining a strict [binary opposition] between Hollywood cinema and its "others". Cinema has from its inception been transnational, circulating more or less freely across borders and utilising international personnel' (2).

The idea of the transnational can be traced back, at least in part, to the transatlantic cultural exchange between the film industries of America and France in the postwar period. I want to focus on one strand of this development: the Franco-American collaboration embodied in what Schwartz calls the 'cycle' of Hollywood 'Frenchness' films produced in the 1950s and 1960s, to which Wilder's *Sabrina* belongs. The Franco-American exchange embodied in these Hollywood Frenchness films of the 1950s and 1960s would stand, then, as part of an originary moment of this world system and of the cinema which emerged out of it. For Schwartz, this postwar cycle of films demonstrates cooperation and cultural exchange between the film industries of France and America in a period which is often characterised as one of Americanisation on the one hand, and French protectionism on the other. Schwartz demonstrates how the marketing of Frenchness, by both France and America, promoted a film culture based on internationalism and cultural exchange. 'Frenchness' both embedded in film images and as 'an organizing category of film production', promoted the appearance of cosmopolitanism on screen and its development off screen as a production practice in the postwar era (Schwartz, *It's So French!* 8). One way to interpret these Frenchness films is as reflections of the political and ideological climate: 'A weak and backward postwar France then encounters dashing America and, eventually seduced, "modernizes" and submits to the confident and forward-looking American way of life' (Schwartz, *It's So French!* 20). Thus the films appear to operate as ideological vehicles of Americanisation in post-war Europe, and this is most evident, for example, in the 'orphan' roles of Leslie Caron in Vincente Minnelli's *An American in Paris* (1951) and Jean Negulesco's *Daddy Long Legs* (1955) (Schwartz, *It's So French!* 20). Such interpretations tend to focus on the symbolic function of character and plot whilst ignoring the Frenchness aesthetic of the films. The aesthetic, however, tells its own story: the visual history of cinema and of mass art, the origins of which can be found in nineteenth-century Paris.

Regardless of the time and place in which they are set, these Frenchness films generally evoke fin-de-siècle Paris. In Minnelli's *Gigi* (1958), John Huston's *Moulin Rouge* (1952) and Walter Lang's *Can-Can* (1960), for example, the Belle Époque is directly evoked via a historical setting which demands the period's re-creation through sets and costumes. In contrast, *An American in Paris*, Wilder's *Irma la Douce* (1963) and George Cukor's *Les Girls* (1957), films set in a time contemporaneous with their production, re-create the Belle Époque indirectly through their aesthetic. This is generally achieved in three main ways: by incorporating symbols such as the Moulin Rouge, the cancan and the Eiffel Tower; through direct visual citation of Impressionist, post-Impressionist and nineteenth-century poster art; and through the use of an Impressionist and post-Impressionist palette.

According to the script summary for the ballet sequence occurring at the end of *An American in Paris*, the 'goal of the ballet was to accomplish choreographically, dramatically, and scenically, what the great Impressionist painters accomplished in their medium through the use of colour and light and forms' (qtd in Schwartz, *It's So French!* 38). The ballet evokes, and at times explicitly references, works by Raoul Dufy, Pierre-Auguste Renoir, Maurice Utrillo, Henri Rousseau,

Vincent Van Gogh and Henri de Toulouse-Lautrec. In order to account for this use of fin-de-siècle imagery, especially the work of Toulouse-Lautrec, Schwartz argues that rather than simply considering the films' immediate postwar context, these Frenchness films 'need to be recontexualized as part of a longer history of visual culture in which Paris served as a beacon' (*It's So French!* 21).

Schwartz offers four possible explanations for the use of this particular aesthetic. First, fin-de-siècle Paris 'coincided with the initial rise of mass culture, and thus became the single most repeated image of France' (13–14), synonymous with Frenchness in the international and American imagination. Secondly, because he also painted, Toulouse-Lautrec's commercial work (illustrations, lithographs and posters) was understood as art more so than the commercial work of his contemporaries. Hollywood directors, according to Schwartz, seized on 'the notion that commercial art was art nevertheless' (34). Thirdly, the use of nineteenth-century French art gave these productions an air of quality (29). This took place at a time when television posed a serious threat to cinema, and filmmakers sought to both reassert the magic of cinema and to connect it to an artistic tradition (21). Finally, these Frenchness films connect filmmaking with Belle Époque Paris in order to pay homage to the birthplace of cinema (21). To these can be added two, perhaps more ideological, reasons for the use of this aesthetic. First, representing France as fin-de-siècle Paris consigns her power to the past, reinforcing her status as an orphan in need of a father. Secondly, it creates nostalgia for the glory days of the Belle Époque and thus effaces the embarrassment of the Vichy years. For Schwartz, however, these explanations are reductive as they situate cultural expression as 'an outlet for the political' (20). Schwartz emphasises rather the way a new cosmopolitanism 'emerged in film during the late 1950s and early 1960s [which] depended upon a strong investment in "Frenchness" in both France and America' (7).

A figure who frequently occurs across this cycle of Frenchness films and who may be considered allegorical for the transatlantic exchange is *la Parisienne*. Just like the aesthetic of the Hollywood Frenchness films, *la Parisienne* is a figure borrowed from the plastic arts of nineteenth-century Paris. *La Parisienne* as she appears in this cycle of films is, however, as much an American invention as she is a French one.

This is due partly to the cosmopolitanism of the Parisienne type. As Justine De Young remarks: 'The *Parisienne*'s identity was not necessarily linked to her nationality, as being a *Française* or *Anglaise* was; the *Parisienne* embodied a set of qualities independent of country of origin that could be attained as long as one lived in Paris' ('Women in Black' 249). If *la Parisienne* is a myth, a social phenomenon which, according to Roland Barthes, can be 'adapted to a certain type of consumption' (118), from the end of the Second World War onwards this consumption became progressively globalised, and *la Parisienne* increasingly an object of global consumption. In the cycle of Frenchness films this global consumption is facilitated by obvious or stereotyped signifiers of Frenchness.

In Wilder's film, there is a scene in which Sabrina pens her final letter from Paris to her father in anticipation of her return to Long Island. She is seated at her desk, the Sacré Coeur visible from the window, and on the street an accordion plays 'La Vie en rose'. What is notable about this scene, aside from the use of obvious signifiers of Frenchness, is Sabrina's description of herself as a citizen of the world, as both '*in* the world and *of* the world'. Her letter, read in voice-over, includes the following passage:

> I want to thank you now for the two most wonderful years of my life. I shall always love you for sending me here. It is late at night and someone across the way is playing 'La Vie en Rose' – it is the French way of saying 'I am looking at the world through rose-coloured glasses' and it says everything I feel. I have learned so many things, Father. Not just how to make vichyssoise or calf's head with sauce vinaigrette, but a much more important recipe. I have learned how to live ... How to be in the world and of the world ... and not just to stand aside and watch. And I will never, never again run away from life ... or from love, either.

Even though her reflections are intended more philosophically, they can also be read as the expression of an emerging global identity, without nation or class. Indeed, Sabrina's father remarks to Linus that she is 'just a displaced person: she doesn't belong in a mansion, but then she doesn't belong above a garage either'.

The encounter between David Larrabee and Sabrina at Glen Cove station upon her return to Long Island demonstrates the way in which Paris has powerfully transformed the chauffeur's daughter. David, who had largely ignored Sabrina before her sojourn in Paris, is now captivated by the chic woman at the station who he misrecognises as someone of his own class. The scene opens with a shot of a toy poodle with a jewelled collar, standing beside two suitcases, and then the camera pans up to reveal Sabrina elegantly dressed in a Givenchy grey wool two-piece tailored suit with cinched waist and calf-length skirt. Her outfit is accessorised with a cream, turban-style hat, gold hoop earrings and black kid gloves. A sweeping orchestral version of 'La Vie en rose' plays as the camera follows Sabrina pacing the station platform. There is a cut to a mid-shot of David speeding down a road in his convertible whistling his signature tune, 'Isn't It Romantic?'. We see him look off-camera and there is a cut to a point-of-view shot of Sabrina. Cut to a close-up of David: we hear the screeching of brakes, see him reverse towards the station and bring the car to a sudden halt in front of Sabrina. 'Taxi, miss?', he says, raising his hat; 'Cheapest rates in Glen Cove'. Cut to a close-up of a surprised and bemused Sabrina, and the following dialogue ensues:

SABRINA: Well hello! How *are* you?
DAVID: Well I'm fine, how are you? And I might add, *who* are you?
SABRINA: Who am I?
DAVID: Am I supposed to know?
SABRINA: Come to think of it, no you're not supposed to know!

David offers to drive her home and on the way he tries to glean both her identity and her status. Sabrina keeps him guessing with ambiguous responses. Upon seeing his daughter on her return from Paris even Sabrina's father remarks that he would not have recognised her.

The above exchange, and David's sudden interest in Sabrina, is in stark contrast to the last time the two saw one another at a Larrabee soirée. In this scene Sabrina, having stolen away from the garage to look in on the lavish affair, is surprised by David. Wide-eyed, Sabrina gladly welcomes this chance meeting only to be casually dismissed:

DAVID: Oh, it's you Sabrina. I thought I heard somebody.
SABRINA: No, it's nobody.

Two years on, Sabrina finds herself invited, somewhat reluctantly, by David, to a Larrabee soirée. When she arrives dressed in a resplendent black on white embroidered evening gown featuring a fitted strapless bodice and a voluminous skirt, pearl-drop earrings and white elbow-length gloves, all heads turn to her. Sabrina has gone from invisibility to being highly visible, and it is this visibility which in turn aids her social mobility. Testifying to this, the butler bursts into the kitchen proclaiming to the other domestic staff: 'Oh, you should see her! You should see Sabrina! The prettiest girl, the prettiest dress, the best dancer, the belle of the ball! And such poise as though she belonged up there.' Later, at the party, Sabrina asks David's mother, Maude Larrabee: 'You didn't recognise me did you? Have I *changed*? Have I *really changed*?'; to which the older woman responds: 'You *certainly* have!'

Dina Smith remarks that *Sabrina* portrays postwar France as 'a glamorous ingénue waiting to be consumed, her cultural capital vital to postwar America's emerging cultural hegemony' (34). The film is not, however, simply about the French subjection to American economic and cultural domination represented by the hardnosed business-as-usual ethics of Linus Larrabee on the one hand, and the helpless orphan Sabrina on the other. Rather, Wilder's film, through its use of the Parisienne type, connects two forms of national art and popular culture in a way that may be considered transnational.

In terms of Sabrina's metonymic function, it is not for David Larrabee for whom she stands for Paris. Rather, it is for his brother Linus, whose notably un-Romantic life includes an experience of Paris limited to 'changing planes'. What Sabrina represents for Linus is another outlook, which might be defined as quintessentially or stereotypically French. Not only does she convince Linus to leave his umbrella behind when travelling to Paris, she also gives him the following piece of advice: 'Paris isn't for changing planes; it's for changing your outlook; for throwing open the window and letting in *la vie en rose*.' The end of the film is, however, ambiguous. While Linus does accompany Sabrina back to Paris, it is unclear whether the trip is a honeymoon or merely another attempt at neutralising this dangerous Parisienne who, through both her increasing visibility and mobility, poses a threat to the economic interests of the Larrabee family. The ambiguity of the ending, however, reflects the ambiguity of Sabrina, who may or may not be without schemes of her own.

The cosmopolitan Parisiennes discussed in this chapter can be defined according to four main concepts: visibility, mobility, transformation and metonymy. Visibility is demonstrated in the following ways: by their presence in the public sphere; by their fashionability; and by their mysterious demeanour. For these cosmopolitan Parisiennes, visibility holds the key to their mobility, both geographically and socially, and each cross borders of nation and class. In geographical terms, mobility is demonstrated in the setting of these films outside Paris (Algeria, Los Angeles and New York), while social mobility is achieved primarily through fashion, with chic appearance masking humble origins. Gaby, Cécile/Lola and Sabrina are, however, mobile in another way, in that each escapes or flees the film and, ostensibly, closure in both a narrative and an aesthetic sense. Each eludes the attempt of the male protagonist to pin her down or fix her in any one idealised image or representation. These three cosmopolitan Parisiennes also serve the metonymic function of standing in for Paris for the films' male protagonists, a Paris outside Paris. For Pépé, Gaby stands in for the lost Paris of working-class idyll; for Linus Larrabee, Sabrina symbolises the French way of life so different from the world of American big business; and Cécile/Lola stands in for three happy weeks George spent in Paris before returning home to Los Angeles and the reality of work, domestic life and the Vietnam War. Finally, central to the identity of the cosmopolitan Parisienne is the notion of transformation, which forms either part of the narrative proper to the films, as in *Sabrina*, or functions as a narrative subtext, as in *Pépé le Moko* and *Model Shop*. Sabrina is shown travelling to, residing in and returning from Paris, while Gaby's and Cécile/Lola's transformation is alluded to by other means: Gaby's transformation from working class to high class is alluded to in a conversation with Pépé which reveals their shared class origins, and Cécile/Lola's transformation from dancing girl in Nantes to chic Parisienne in Los Angeles emerges intertextually through Demy's prequel to *Model Shop*, *Lola*.

The ambiguity of these three cosmopolitan Parisiennes is the result of a constantly shifting identity which is facilitated by the interaction of these three functions: the visible, the mobile and the metonymic. Indeed, the only time they ever achieve stability is when they are momentarily fixed by the gaze of the male hero, and there are several points where this fixation is captured through the use of point-of-view shots. These fixations, however, invariably involve misrecognition on the part of the hero. Pépé misrecognises Gaby as a mirror image of himself; George misrecognises Cécile/Lola first as a respectable, wealthy woman from Beverly Hills, and then as a cheap 'slut' working in the euphemistic model shop; and David Larrabee misrecognises Sabrina as a member of the Long Island social set like himself. These fixations and misrecognitions are in part the expression of the male hero's desire, and each film shows the woman in question fulfilling a particular wish for the hero. From these misrecognitions, however, the figure of *la Parisienne* takes flight, moving with striking independence from the male hero. In spite of the latter's attempts to pin her down, she is never reducible to the fantasies she evokes.

An interesting exception to the use of point-of-view shot in these films occurs in *Sabrina*. As Moseley has noted, the first shot we have of Sabrina standing at a Long Island bus station having just arrived back from Paris occurs prior to the arrival of David Larrabee, and thus independently of any male gaze: 'A space is allowed before this focalisation, for an admiring gaze which is not specifically gendered male' ('Dress' 113). Moseley goes on to argue that in fact Hepburn's display is predominantly 'for a feminine audience, one which is competent in reading sartorial codes' ('Dress' 113). Hepburn as Parisienne here functions as a cosmopolitan or global image of French femininity and represents the exportability of French chic and luxury goods. In her article 'Parisienne femininity and the politics of embodiment', Humphrey identifies this link between the cosmopolitanism of *la Parisienne*, as put forward by such advertising campaigns as Yves Saint Laurent's perfume 'Parisienne', and the creation of a global market for the product:

> In keeping with its focus on a global market the Yves Saint Laurent promotional blog opens up the possibility that any

woman can represent the values of the city … . The identity of la Parisienne presented here is exclusive yet malleable enough to be potentially embodied by a global base of consumers with enough purchasing power. The idea that la Parisienne identity is transient and can therefore be assumed and adopted is an important dynamic in the marketing of consumer brands, both in their long-term general appeal and in their short-term fashions. (257)

The next chapter explores how the Parisienne type is established as an icon of fashion and style through cinema. While this present chapter examined costume and fashion in intra-filmic terms – that is, in terms of its function within both the film's narrative and diegesis – the following chapter looks more closely at extra-filmic considerations such as costuming the Parisienne type in cinema, and the role this plays in the creation of certain 'looks' associated with particular Parisiennes.

3
Icon of fashion

This chapter explores the relationship between *la Parisienne*, fashion and film within three contexts: the historical, which forms the groundwork for considering this relationship in general; the industrial, which considers the possibilities for costuming *la Parisienne* in a given film; and the textual, which considers the intersection of the first two contexts in specific films. The textual context demonstrates how cinema continues to maintain the association of *la Parisienne* with fashion and style but also how costume displays a range of meanings and references beyond simply denoting an elegantly dressed woman. Jo/Audrey Hepburn in a black turtleneck, black cigarette pants and black penny loafers performs an avant-garde dance in an 'Existentialist' cavern in Paris. Séverine/Cathérine Deneuve in a double-breasted military-style grey wool coat with wide collar and epaulettes, accessorised with a black pillbox hat, gloves, tote and Roger Vivier Pilgrim court shoes, steps into a Parisian brothel. Patricia/Jean Seberg with a pixie haircut, in cropped pants and a T-shirt bearing the *New York Herald Tribune* logo strolls down the Champs-Elysées.[1] These iconic images illustrate the connection between *la Parisienne*, fashion and film. They have been reproduced many times in both print and online style guides, and the clothing and hairstyles – or more generally, the 'look' – of the women has been much imitated. What makes these images so iconic, alongside the actresses and the films themselves, is the costuming of the Parisienne type in each scene.[2] Each look was styled by a costume designer, a couturier, and the actress herself, respectively.

La Parisienne and fashion in the nineteenth century

The development of Paris as a modern city in the second half of the nineteenth century took place alongside the development of both prêt-à-porter and haute couture. In marketing both high and ready-to-wear fashion, the image of *la Parisienne* was often used. Fashion plates, like those used in *La Mode Illustrée* and *La Gazette des Dames*, were central to the development of *la Parisienne* as a type. *La Parisienne* functioned as an ambassador for Paris generally, and for French fashion industries specifically. Iskin writes that by the 'second half of the nineteenth century, the chic Parisienne embodied French taste and fashionability as national traits' (185).

If *la Parisienne* is the embodiment of French fashionability, she is also distinct from the French woman as such. Although Uzanne argues that 'écrire sur la Parisienne, c'est également parler de la femme en général, c'est analyser le caractère, l'esprit, le gout de la Française qu'elle synthétise' (2), 'a description of the Parisian woman is a description of every Frenchwoman' (*The Modern Parisienne* 1), she has, however, also been described as not French at all (Bernstein 73). During the nineteenth century, the superiority of *la Parisienne* in matters of taste, fashion and dress was commonly established through her comparison with the French provincial woman: 'Les provinciales se vêtissent,' writes Delord, 'la Parisienne s'habille' (1) (provincial women put on clothes, *la Parisienne* dresses). According to Delord, literature imagined the provincial woman thus: a stout woman of 50, although treated condescendingly as a young girl, with a blotchy complexion, decked out in eccentric dresses and garish scarves, she excels in making apricot jam, has a predilection for colourful language and an imperceptible guttural pronunciation which will suffice to render even her most beautiful and innocent actions ridiculous (5–6). In spite of this unflattering portrayal of the provincial woman, however, Delord dedicates his physiology to the women of the provinces and remarks that *la Parisienne* – admired so much by the *provinciales* – is, in fact, a provincial herself:

> Frappez hardiment à toutes les portes, interrogez les passeports, les actes de naissance ... et vous verrez que toutes ces femmes charmantes ... sont nées en province, et qu'elles ont vécu en province, et vous ne les trouverez pas plus maussades pour cela. (9)

(Knock on any door, scrutinise passports, birth certificates ... and you will see that all of these charming women ... were born in the provinces, have lived in the provinces, and you will not find them any worse for it.)

Delord makes the distinction between women from the provinces who leave their home towns for Paris and those who remain in the provinces, and claims that a provincial woman can have Parisienne grace and spirit provided she does not live in the provinces (13). The opposition of *la Parisienne* and *la provinciale* is maintained geographically as well as conceptually. Agnès Rocamora comments on the prevalence of this opposition in nineteenth-century French cultural life: in Balzac's novels, for example, 'the distinction Paris/*province* is articulated along the lines of a discourse on fashion whereby Paris is synonymous with fashionability and *la province* with an unredeemable lack of fashion sense' (38). In a similar vein, Arsène Houssaye in *Les Parisiennes* also establishes the superiority of *la Parisienne* in matters of fashion by way of comparison with the provincial woman:

> La Parisienne n'est pas à la mode, elle est la mode .... Quand une provinciale passe sur le boulevard, on reconnait que sa robe est neuve. La robe de la Parisienne a beau sortir, à l'instant même, de chez la meilleure couturière, il semble qu'elle ait été portée depuis la veille: la provinciale est habillée par sa robe, la Parisienne habille sa robe. (268)

> (The *Parisienne* is not in fashion, she is fashion .... When a *provinciale* passes on the boulevard, one recognises that her dress is new. The Parisienne's dress even straight out of the best couturier, this very minute, appears as though it has been worn since the day before: the provincial is worn by her dress, the Parisienne wears her dress.)

Thus what *la Parisienne* really possessed, for Houssaye, was above all else a mastery of fashion.

With the increasing availability of fashionable clothing, the garments themselves became less important than how they were put together and worn:

> Le grand art du vêtement pour les femmes, l'art suprême – il ne faut pas l'oublier – consiste à ne jamais confondre le moyen avec le but, c'est-à-dire à s'arranger de manière que l'attention du spectateur, en se portant sur leur toilette, s'arrête à leur personne, et qu'ainsi la parure ne serve qu'à faire admirer la femme parée. (Uzanne 78)
>
> (The great art of dress for women, the supreme art – let us not forget it – consists of never confusing the means with the end, that is to say, to manage it in such a way so that the attention of the spectator, in falling on their toilette, fixes on their person, and that thus the finery serves only to attract the admiration of the adorned woman.)

Similarly, Justine De Young argues that 'following fashion came to mean perfecting one's taste, not merely paying for luxury goods, and the *Parisienne* represented the apotheosis of taste. The essential chicness of the *Parisienne* was tied to her mastery of fashion, not her submission to it' ('Women in Black' 249–50). Uzanne goes even further than this when he remarks:

> Une jeune femme sans fortune, à condition qu'elle soit svelte, bien proportionnée, et qu'elle ait le sens inné de la toilette, sera, 'avec un rien', pourvue de toutes les séductions qui seront refusées à la grosse dame sanglée dans les plus somptueux complets de tailleur. (77–8)
>
> A woman who is well-proportioned and slender, and has an instinctive taste for dress, even though she is poor, will look a thousand times more attractive than a stout woman in the most sumptuous clothes. (*The Modern Parisienne* 32)

Thus to an innate feeling for fashion was added a certain physical type, the waif or gamine.

The clever or resourceful Parisienne will always appear to have spent more than she has on her dress. According to Uzanne, there is a multitude of such women in Paris, as well as many women who, with a modest budget for dressmaking and toilette, are obliged to follow more rigorous frugality, aided by 'un certain génie spécial dont nos Parisiennes ne sont pas avares' (76), 'a sort of genius peculiar to Parisiennes' (*The Modern Parisienne* 31).

There is a contradiction at the heart of *la Parisienne*. On the one hand, she seems to possess a peculiar genius: the ability to be elegant without necessarily spending a lot of money. On the other hand, however, the French economy relies, in part, on the marketability of *la Parisienne* and women are encouraged to consume French luxury goods in order to attain Parisian chic: 'France's fashion industry and all of its ancillary enterprises depended on ... the "Parisienne" as a living monument to modern femininity' (Garb, 'Painting' 98). During the nineteenth century, Parisienne actresses in particular helped promote France's fashion industry. Indeed, links between Paris, *la Parisienne*, fashion and actresses were well established before the advent of cinema and film stars. Patrice Higonnet suggests that 'the identification of Paris with fashion might be expanded into a series of equations: Paris = La Parisienne = fashion = actress' (117). Actresses functioned as 'spokeswomen for fashion, or rather fashions, since each actress had her own favourite couturier: for Réjane it was Jacques Doucet' (Higonnet 117). Actresses from the theatre of the Third Republic often publicised couturiers: Sarah Bernhardt, for example, was dressed by Worth. Uzanne claims that in return for advertising the fashions of various designers, women who held privileged positions in the artistic world such as popular actresses and music-hall singers benefited from a reduction of more than 60 per cent on their purchases (*The Modern Parisienne* 39). The relationship between actress and designer continued with the advent of cinema, in which the actress promoting French couture had an ever-widening reach, as images of display could now be presented not just to a localised audience, as in the theatre, but disseminated throughout the world. It is not, however, only designers of haute couture who provide costumes for *la Parisienne* in cinema.

Costuming *la Parisienne* in cinema

There are three possibilities for costuming *la Parisienne*. First, a costume designer creates the costumes. Second, a couturier designs costumes or provides clothing from his or her collection (a couturier may design for a star with whom they are strongly affiliated both on and off screen, or may design for an actress with whom they have little or no affiliation prior or subsequent to the film in question). Third, the actress wears her own clothing and brings her own personal style to the role.

Generally speaking, the costume designer's approach is to remain in the background, allowing costume to serve, aid and/or demonstrate the development of character and plot. Commenting on the distinction between the approach of the costume designer and the couturier to fashion in film, Stella Bruzzi writes: 'The creation of clothes as spectacle is the prerogative of the couturier; the overriding ethos of the costume designer is conversely to fabricate clothes which serve the purposes of the narrative' (3). A further key difference between the costume designer and the couturier is that while the couturier tends to be a very public figure with a distinct brand or style, the costume designer does not generally have a high public profile.

During the 1920s, many couturiers worked in cinema, designing new costumes or lending gowns from their collections. These included Paul Poiret for Marcel l'Herbier, Jeanne Lanvin for Abel Gance's *Napoléon* (1927) and Jean Patou for Louise Brooks in G.W. Pabst's *Pandora's Box* (1929). Depending on the film, the couturier may design costumes for the entire film or work in conjunction with a costume designer, and it is common that in Parisienne films the couturier dress the Parisienne while the costume designer creates costumes for the rest of the cast. In Billy Wilder's *Sabrina*, for example, French couturier Hubert de Givenchy provides the wardrobe for Sabrina following her transformation into a Parisienne, while costume designer Edith Head designs Sabrina's pre-Paris costumes as well as those of the rest of the cast. Commenting on the distinction between the couturier and the costume designer in *Sabrina* and *Funny Face*, Bruzzi remarks:

> Both films centre on the transformation of Audrey Hepburn from gauche girl to sophisticated gamine, and in both the roles filled by Head and Givenchy are clearly demarcated: whilst Head is given the pre-transformation clothes, it is Givenchy who designs all the show-stopping Parisian fantasies. (6)

Following their first collaboration on *Sabrina*, Givenchy became Audrey Hepburn's regular designer, both on and off screen. Most notably, he dressed her in Blake Edward's *Breakfast at Tiffany's* (1961) and in her Parisian films including Richard Quine's *Paris When It Sizzles* (1963), Stanley Donen's *Charade* (1963) and *Funny Face* (1956), and William Wyler's *How to Steal a Million* (1966). Similarly, Cathérine Deneuve had a long professional and personal association with Yves Saint Laurent and was his model, muse and close friend for decades. The French designer provided costumes for her notable roles in Luis Buñuel's *Belle de jour* (1967), Alain Cavalier's *La Chamade* (1968), and François Truffaut's *La Sirène du Mississippi* (1969). Indeed, Bruzzi has noted that in Buñuel's film Deneuve 'in effect models a Saint Laurent "capsule wardrobe"' (21). French designer Pierre Cardin provided costumes for Jeanne Moreau in Jacques Demy's *La Baie des anges* (1963), François Truffaut's *La Mariée était en noir* (1968), Louis Malle's *Viva Maria!* (1965), Anthony Asquith's *The Yellow Rolls Royce* (1964) and Joseph Losey's *Eva* (1962), as well as designing outfits for her off screen. Hepburn, Deneuve and Moreau all assumed ambassadorial roles in the global export of French high fashion.

A couturier, however, may also design for an actress with whom they have no particular affiliation or with whom the affiliation is not strong or exclusive enough to constitute an artist/muse collaboration. For example, Maison Dior provides costumes for Ingrid Bergman in Anatole Litvak's *Goodbye Again* (1961) and also dresses Marlene Dietrich for her cameo in *Paris When It Sizzles*; Coco Chanel dressed Michèle Morgan in Marcel Carné's *Le Quai des brumes* (1938) and Carole Bouquet in Bertrand Blier's *Trop belle pour toi* (1989). While a costume designer creates a generic image of Parisian chic which may help to perpetuate the myth of the superiority of the French fashion industry and Paris as the fashion capital of the world, with the introduction of couturiers in cinema the Parisienne shifts from selling a universal ideal towards being the ambassador of a specific brand. Arguably, the marketing of Parisian chic realises its full potential with the intersection of star and couturier which extends beyond the screen.

In addition to a costume designer and/or a couturier, a further possibility for costuming the Parisienne in cinema involves the actress providing her own wardrobe, ostensibly wearing her own clothes, or at least espousing a look synonymous with her off-screen style. This was particularly the case with Nouvelle Vague actresses. As Ginette Vincendeau remarks:

> New Wave stars sported a natural look – little visible make-up, hair usually darkish in a low-key coiffure (Moreau), a bob (Karina) or tousled in a 'just out of bed' look (Lafont). When they did not wear discreet couture clothes (Moreau, Seyrig), actresses tended to downplay their figures with girlish outfits which were often their own – blouses with lace, twin-sets, skirts and petticoats – or sometimes boyish jeans, T-shirts and flat shoes, showcasing the new, younger and more casual fashion. ('The Star Reborn' 20)

Henry Chapier claims that with the 'triumph' of the Nouvelle Vague 'costume design is no longer the same aesthetic sanctuary' and that 'fashion henceforth seeks its inspiration in the street' (8). The New Wave, with its budgetary constraints and desire to break with the tradition of quality in French cinema and develop a more personal style, dispensed with the role of the costume designer and moved away from cinema's relationship with haute couture. This shift allowed for the self-fashioning aspect of *la Parisienne* to come to the fore, with stars like Brigitte Bardot, Jean Seberg and Anna Karina bringing their own style to New Wave films and later becoming style icons in their own right.

Films about fashion: *Reunion in France* and *Funny Face*

Reunion in France and *Funny Face* are both explicitly about the production, consumption and marketing of fashion. The plot of Dassin's film takes place in and around a fictional haute couture fashion house in Paris during the Occupation. The action centres on Michèle de la Becque (Joan Crawford), a high-society Parisienne whose easy life is turned around when she suspects her fiancé Robert Cortet (Philip Dorn), a wealthy industrialist, of collaborating with the occupying Nazi forces. Rather than maintain her status as a kept woman in compromising circumstances, Michèle subsequently eschews Cortet's money. In order to make a living, she takes a job as a sales assistant at Montanot, the fashion house where she had once been a wealthy client. Crawford's Michèle is the chic Parisienne of the film, dressed in lavish gowns by costume designer Irène. The role is a reprisal of an earlier film, Edmund Goulding's *Paris* (1926), in which Crawford plays a demimondaine Parisienne. Randy Roberts describes the plot of Dassin's film as 'the trials and clothes of Michele de la Becque' and goes on to point out that the film was poorly received, and failed the war effort on several fronts, least of all in the way France 'falls with great elegance. Everyone we see is beautifully gowned, comfortably housed, and apparently well fed' (159–60). What is interesting from the point of view of *la Parisienne* and fashion is the way in which Dassin establishes her identity relationally, through the deliberate juxtaposition of Michèle's elegance with the crude tastelessness of the German provincial women. In this way, the film demonstrates the claim, made by nineteenth-century physiologists and authors of twenty-first-century style guides alike, that simply purchasing expensive haute couture will not guarantee one's transformation into a chic Parisienne. *Reunion in France* was never considered a serious film about war and occupation; even MGM remarked that the real war depicted in the film 'was between fat German and thin French women, with fashion hanging neatly pressed in the balance' (R.W. Roberts 160). Indeed, a key scene in the film depicts the wives of the German forces rummaging through a table of garments at Montanot; a high-angle shot gives the women the unmistakable appearance of pigs at a trough.

The stereotyping of German women as both crude and overweight further undermines their attempts to attain Parisian chic. A more slender Michèle, still elegant in spite of her new workaday clothing, looks on, while designer Montanot remarks: 'I have been designing for very different tastes and figures.' When Michèle asks former clothes model Juliette: 'When did you become a saleswoman?', Juliette casts an ironic glance in the direction of the German women and replies: 'Mannequins are running to larger sizes now.' In a review of the film, the Office of War Information Bureau of Intelligence remarked that 'the most striking feature of France shown in the picture is a genius for designing and wearing women's clothes … . The preservation of this genius from the bad taste of the Germans is the big issue' (qtd in R.W. Roberts 160).

Stanley Donen's Hollywood musical *Funny Face* (1956), shot both on location in Paris and in the Paramount studios, is also explicitly about fashion, and the film plays on tropes associated with the fashion world, fashion journalism and fashion photography. Givenchy provides the couture clothes worn by Parisienne Jo Stockton (Audrey Hepburn), while costume designer Edith Head provides the other costumes for the film. Donen's film depicts the image of the fashionable Parisienne through two essential looks associated with Paris: the *rive gauche* or Left Bank look, and the *rive droite* or haute couture look. In *Fashion and Film*, Adrienne Munich argues that the term look 'implicitly draws together the act of deliberate seeing in both fashion and film, but is perhaps most recognizable as a fashion term describing a fashion ensemble' (2). Munich distinguishes the term look from the term the gaze, put into circulation in film studies in 1975 by Laura Mulvey. In contrast to the gaze, the look 'as a fashion concept, is about character and fashion information' (Munich 3). *Funny Face* establishes the look as the conjunction of figure, fashion and film through the juxtaposition of movement and still, film and photography, and between the fleeting moods of fashion and the eternal image that creates a style.

The narrative of Donen's film centres on the transformation of Jo from a bookish intellectual from Greenwich Village into a Parisian couture model. After discovering Jo while on a fashion shoot, photographer Richard 'Dick' Avery (Fred Astaire) convinces editor Maggie Prescott (Kay Thompson) that Jo should be the new face of *Quality* fashion magazine. Opposed to any involvement in the fashion world on principle, Jo accepts Dick's offer to be a model in Paris when she sees an opportunity to attend the lectures of 'empathicalist' philosopher Flostre, a parody of Jean-Paul Sartre. Jo calls the trip a 'means to end', to which Dick replies 'or a means to a beginning, according to how it works out'.

As the face of *Quality*, Jo has an entire collection designed for her by Parisian couturier Paul Duval, based on Givenchy. She is photographed by Dick, a fictionalised version of fashion photographer Richard Avedon, who served as the film's visual consultant. *Funny Face*, at times, indeed resembles a fashion magazine; most notably during the opening credit sequence and the Paris 'fashion shoot' sequence. Avedon's technique of 'high shutter speed and shallow-focus images, to catch his subjects as if in flight' contributes to the film's fashion-magazine aesthetic (Sheridan 87–8). Similarly, Bruzzi describes the film as a 'prolonged catwalk show' in which the clothes 'intrude on, dominate the scenes they are couched in' (13).

Jo is an interesting incarnation of *la Parisienne* because she embodies two contrasting yet quintessentially Parisienne personae or looks: Left Bank existentialist and Right Bank glamour. Alongside these two looks, Donen gives us two contrasting and stereotypically American images of Paris: the dimly-lit cafés, jazz clubs and existential caverns of the Left Bank, and the sumptuous couture quarter of the Right Bank. Uzanne describes this fashion quarter in the late nineteenth century as

[u]ne ville dans la ville, une sorte de ruche brillante où convergent les mille activités industrieuses de l'élégance, où les formes multiples du costume et de la parure s'élaborent pour l'embellissement des plus riches et des plus jolies femmes qui soient. (81–2)

[a] town within a town, a brilliant hive humming with the thousand industrial activities devoted to the elaboration of costumes for the adornment of the richest and prettiest women in the world. (*The Modern Parisienne* 135)

These contrasting spaces are established from the moment the characters arrive in Paris in the ebullient 'Bonjour Paris' song-and-dance sequence, shot on location. While Maggie anticipates Paris as a capital of fashion ('I want to wander through the Saint-Honoré / Do some window shopping in the Rue de la Paix'), Jo sees Paris as an intellectual city ('I want to see the den of thinking men like Jean-Paul Sartre / I must philosophise with all the guys around Montmartre and Montparnasse'). As an artist working for a fashion magazine, Dick bridges the gap between these two worlds for Jo, and facilitates her transformation. In a way too, it might be argued that Dick deconstructs or demystifies the whole Left Bank 'scene' for Jo, revealing it to be precisely that, a scene with its cultural signifiers and in-crowd politics. Flostre himself turns out to be little more than a charlatan, using highfalutin jargon to seduce young women like Jo.

However, while Jo is Dick's muse, she is also an artist in her own right. During a fashion shoot at the Louvre with Dick, Jo seizes control of her own image when she emerges from behind the marble sculpture of the Winged Victory of Samothrace, descends the Daru staircase and directs the shoot herself. She chooses her own pose and tells Dick when to take the picture. The use of freeze frame in this sequence creates the effect of a photograph and demonstrates the way photography establishes an iconic image by lifting it out of history or the stream of time. Immortality or timelessness is, according to Georg Simmel, a defining feature of fashion itself: 'Each individual fashion to a certain extent makes its appearance as though it wished to live forever' (qtd in Carter 77).

In *Funny Face*, the spatial reinforces the sartorial: Jo's wardrobe alternates between the intellectual of the *rive gauche* and chic Parisienne of the *rive droite*. While these two styles are diametrically opposed in the film, they are both the embodiment of different types of Parisian chic. While haute couture has always been associated with fashion and notions of chic, the *rive gauche*, 'beat' or 'existential' look was initially intended as an anti-fashion statement. However, due in part to Hepburn's adoption of this look off screen, it soon became fashionable in its own right. Mairi Mackenzie outlines the component features of this look as follows: 'Oversized fisherman-sweaters, drainpipe trousers or jeans, turtleneck jumpers, undressed hair and duffle coats' (92). In terms of style, it is Jo's existential or beatnik look which is the more iconic of the two looks she embodies in the film. Moseley argues that this is due largely to the 'achievability' of the look ('Dress' 118). Testament too to the iconic status of what Moseley describes as the 'student' or 'Bohemian Chic' Hepburn look ('Dress' 118) is the use of her beatnik dance sequence in a 2006 advertising campaign for clothing company Gap (Sheridan 85). This campaign underscores the commercial potential of the Parisienne type, established, during the nineteenth century, contemporaneously with her status as the image of both French and global femininity.

The spectacle of modern life in *Gigi*

Vincente Minnelli's Hollywood musical *Gigi* (1958), shot both on locations in Paris and in the studio for MGM, demonstrates the association of Paris and *la Parisienne* with fashion through its use of setting and period costumes designed by Cecil Beaton, who also served as production designer. The film, based loosely on Colette's novella, tells the story of a young girl (Leslie Caron) who is being groomed as a courtesan. In its vivid re-creation of Belle Époque Paris, Minnelli's film perpetuates the myth of Paris both as a city of spectacle and as the home of the elegant Parisienne who parades the boulevards and public parks and gardens, displaying her superiority in matters of dress, taste and style. Minnelli's film is particularly significant in terms of *la Parisienne* and fashion because of the detailed attention the director pays to the art of the spectacle; that is, to the art of observing and being observed, which was an important aspect of life dating back to Second Empire Paris.

Commenting on the Haussmanisation of Paris in his *Arcades Project*, Walter Benjamin points to the interrelationship between the boulevards and fashionable women (133). Before Paris was reconstructed by Haussmann, both visibility and mobility were virtually impossible. Under Napoleon III, some forty to fifty parks, squares and gardens were also created and installed. By the 1890s, the reconstructed gardens of the Bois de Boulogne had become a popular venue for leisure, where all of Paris went to see and be seen, and where high society met the demimonde.

In the opening scene of *Gigi* boulevardier Honoré Lachaille (Maurice Chevalier) observes the meticulously dressed women as they promenade through the Bois or ride in handsome landaus in an informal parade of the latest fashions. The film opens with a shot of an elegant lady reclining in the back of a landau, dressed in a splendid canary-yellow gown with a matching bonnet tilted coquettishly and cream-coloured gloves. She rests one hand languidly on the side of the landau and in the other holds a parasol. We then cut to an establishing shot of a crowd enjoying a leisurely afternoon in the Bois. Seated on chairs so angled as to take in the passing parade of carriages, the fashionable women are both subjects and objects of this spectacle of modern life, there to observe and to be observed. The scene is awash with the fabrics, colours and silhouettes of the Belle Époque. The popular fabrics of the era were silk chiffon, crêpe de Chine, mousseline de soie and tulle, while soft, dreamlike, pastel tones dominated the palette of such fabrics. The favoured silhouette was that of an S-bend created using corsetry while a profusion of trimmings of lace, ruffles, feathers and embroidery was used to achieve a frilly or frou-frou look.

That all of the women in this opening sequence carry parasols is significant. During the Belle Époque, a parasol was an important accessory for *la Parisienne* and played a part in the game of concealing and revealing: 'Women knew how to filter their charm through the dappled light cast by the sunshade' (Simon 197). Late nineteenth-century artworks and fashion plates often depict Parisiennes with parasols, including Édouard Manet's *Jeanne* (1882) and Henri Gervex's *Madame Valtesse de la Bigne* (1879). The opulent and romantic costumes designed for *Gigi* capture the splendour and importance of display in Paris circa 1900. David Harvey argues that during the Second Empire the transformation of the Bois de Boulogne into a place of sociality and leisure 'helped to emphasize an extrovert form of urbanization that emphasized public show of private opulence' (212). In its vivid re-creation of the Belle Époque, *Gigi* perpetuates the myth of Paris as a city of spectacle and foregrounds the Parisienne type as the epitome of taste and style.

Transformation in *Frantic* (1988) and *8 femmes* (2001)

Fashion in film can also serve a symbolic or mythical function, and can signify narrative tropes such as metamorphosis or transformation. Jill Nelmes includes costume as an integral part of the *mise en scène*, a 'variant of the prop but ... , of course, tightly connected to the character' (67). Costume often operates as a code and a change in costume can signify a 'change of status, attitude and even the passing of time' (67). Transformation is one of the key concepts or motifs associated with *la Parisienne*, and points to a deeper ontological mystery about her identity or essence. As Houssaye remarks: 'Aujourd'hui, ce n'est plus la même femme; demain, nouvelle métamorphose. Elle surprend par l'imprévu' (273) (Today, she is no longer the same woman; tomorrow, new metamorphosis. She surprises with the unexpected). In films featuring *la Parisienne*, costume is perhaps the main way of signifying transformation or change. In *Frantic* and *8 femmes* this change takes place in different ways. In *Frantic*, Michelle (Emmanuelle Seigner) is transformed from fashionable 1980s Eurotrash into *femme serpent*, one of the mythical incarnations of *la Parisienne* derived from the nineteenth century. In *8 femmes*, transformation is depicted as more formative for *la Parisienne*; from *provinciale* to chic Parisienne in the figure of Augustine (Isabelle Huppert), and from maid to *maîtresse* in the figure of Louise (Emmanuelle Béart).

Polanski's *Frantic* follows the plight of happily married American doctor, Richard Walker (Harrison Ford), whose wife mysteriously vanishes during a business trip to Paris. His quest to find her leads Walker into an underworld of seedy nightclubs, drug dealers and political espionage. While there, Walker meets Michelle, a young, streetwise Parisienne, who perhaps knows more than she lets on about the disappearance of his wife. Michelle is reluctantly enlisted in the search and, like the spiritual guides of classical mythology, leads Walker through Hell and back. Davide Caputo claims that Michelle plays a complex role in the film: 'She acts as perpetual guide to Walker, helping navigate both the landscape and French language, but she is also a demonic agent in her own right' (207).

In one particular scene during their foray into the Paris underworld, Walker and Michelle attend the Touch of Class nightclub, where Michelle performs her *danse serpentine*. The scene opens with an exterior shot of the nightclub over the door of which the name is somewhat ironically emblazoned in neon. Walker and Michelle enter the shot from below right of the frame and are shot from behind. Immediately notable is the sudden change in Michelle's costume, which differs radically from the her usual street-style look of high-waisted jeans or leather miniskirt, midriff tops, black leather biker jacket and boots, cheap, oversized jewellery, and fingerless gloves. She now appears dressed in a short, slinky, figure-hugging red dress with a lace-up back, the diamonds of skin formed on her back by crisscrossing laces giving the appearance of snakeskin. Inside the club, Michelle and Walker dance to Grace Jones's 'I've Seen that Face Before'. Michelle's writhing movements create the effect of the *danse serpentine*, which was often performed in music halls in fin-de-siècle Paris and which was the signature dance of Loïe Fuller. Both Fuller and fellow demimondaine Jane Avril wore costumes featuring serpent motifs for their performances of the *danse serpentine*. Elizabeth K. Menon describes 'an anonymous 1893 poster [which] transforms Loïe into a serpent-woman, her head and chest are melded to a serpent', and remarks that both on and off stage, Fuller cultivated her serpentine image, underlining the 'attractive but dangerous aspect to snake imagery' ('Images' 66). Jane Avril also embraced this motif and is depicted alternatively as both snake-charmer and *femme serpent*, most famously in a poster by Toulouse-Lautrec, entitled *Jane Avril* (1899). Indeed, the motif of the Parisienne and the serpent was popular in the visual culture of nineteenth-century Paris and this symbolism even found its expression in everyday accessories, from snakelike feather boas to serpent brooches. The sinuous lines of art nouveau reinforced this imagery (Menon, *Evil* 243). In 'modern French society, depictions of snakes with contemporary women conjured up the fille d'Eve. Fashionable Parisiennes came to be depicted as part-snake' (Menon, *Evil* 227). Baudelaire's poetry also helped to establish the mythology of the woman–snake, particularly the poems 'Le serpent qui danse' and 'Avec ses vêtements ondoyants et nacrés' of *Les Fleurs du Mal*.

Michelle's transformation is linked to a depiction of Paris as a demi-monde, underworld, or Hell, a popular trope in nineteenth-century visual art and literature. Ewa Mazierska remarks that in *Frantic* Paris 'reveals itself as a nocturnal space, even an inferno' (76). Polanski himself remarks that he wanted to 'get rid of everything that was too obviously quaintly Parisian and tried to show the city of today – the way I see it and not as Americans might imagine it to be' (qtd in Cronin 129). Indeed, the opening sequence of *Frantic* in which the Walkers arrive in Paris in a dirty taxi on a nondescript motorway is the direct antithesis of the jubilant 'Bonjour Paris' sequence of *Funny Face* which heralds the arrival of American 'tourists' Dick, Jo and Maggie and which depicts a clean, Technicolored Paris of famous monuments and tourist attractions. Polanski presents a de-romanticised vision of Paris because he 'wanted to show Paris to those Americans whose idea of the city is still based on *Irma la Douce* and *Moulin Rouge*' (qtd in Cronin 126). Paris may be deromanticised in *Frantic* but it is nonetheless heavily mythologised: 'the "Orphean" Walker survives his journey to Hell and brings his "Eurydice" back from the dead, sacrificing his guide in her stead' (Caputo 218). Walker manages to remain faithful to his wife, having resisted the temptation of Parisienne *femme-serpent* Michelle, 'transformed, briefly, from guide to temptress' (Caputo 208).

In François Ozon's *8 femmes*, clothing plays a symbolic role in two key transformations: from maid to *maîtresse* and from *provinciale* to Parisienne. A cursory glance at Ozon's film reveals the significance of costume. Each of the eponymous eight women wears, more or less, the same distinct outfit and coiffure throughout the film and is assigned a dominant colour palette in her wardrobe, just as each is assigned a particular flower in the opening credit sequence. The costumes, by costume designer Pascaline Chavanne, are used effectively to underline the different temperaments and social/familial positions of each of the women. In terms of the Parisienne type, I am most interested in the costuming of Augustine and Louise, primarily because they are the two characters who undergo significant transformation in the film. Louise's costuming is significant not only in the way that her archetypal *femme de chambre* uniform strongly references her Parisienne prefigurations, but also in the way that she subtly refashions her uniform to subvert her subservient and servile position within the household. Augustine's dramatic change in costume midway through the film signals her transformation from uptight, rigid spinster to glamorous Parisienne reminiscent of Jo Stockton's transformation from bookish geek to haute-couture model in *Funny Face*. Both Augustine and Louise demonstrate a kind of mastery over clothing and harness its potential to transform themselves and take control of their own image.

Set in an isolated, snowed-in mansion in the French countryside in the 1950s, *8 femmes* is a murder-mystery musical in which the eight women try to discover who among them is guilty of the murder of their patriarch, Marcel. The film was the result of Ozon's desire to remake George Cukor's *The Women* (1939). Having discovered that the rights to Cukor's film were unavailable, Ozon decided to adapt Robert Thomas's play *8 femmes*, first performed in Paris in 1961. Ozon's debt to Cukor is nevertheless evident in his all-female cast, acerbic dialogue and the cattiness of the women. The costumes also 'pay homage to stars of classic Hollywood' (Schilt 67). The film is, however, also firmly rooted in French culture and cinema. The presence of iconic French actresses Cathérine Deneuve, Fanny Ardant, Isabelle Huppert, Emmanuelle Béart and Danielle Darrieux especially makes for layered references to earlier French films. The women also sing popular French *chansons*, including Françoise Hardy's 'Message personnel', and George Brassens's 'Il n'y a pas d'amour heureux', from a poem by Louis Aragon. The plot rehearses popular narrative tropes and motifs of Parisian femininity: the *ménage à trois*, transformation, Sapphism, striptease, the *garçonne*, the 'belle et riche' sophisticate, the gamine, the scarlet woman, the mistress, the prostitute. Darren Waldron argues that 'by overexaggerating conventional caricatures, [Ozon] alerts his viewers to the artificiality and nonsensicality of society's limited and mythical constructions of "womanhood"' (73).

Louise is an archetypal chambermaid straight out of Octave Mirbeau. In her uniform, consisting of a black dress featuring starched white collar and cuffs with a frilly white cap and ruffled-edged white apron, Louise references the generic figure of the *femme de chambre* in cinema: her blonde hair swept back in a French twist calls to mind Paulette Goddard's Celestine in Jean Renoir's *Diary of a Chambermaid* (1946), while her black lace-up *bottines* and fetishistic relationship with the master of the house links her to Jeanne Moreau's Celestine in Luis Buñuel's *Le Journal d'une femme de chambre* (1964), which was adapted from Mirbeau's play. Louise's uniform also denotes her social position within the house. However, if the act of putting on clothing can denote social standing, its removal can also create meaning. Louise removes the collar of her dress and her maid's cap and lets down her hair in an act of defiance towards her *maîtresse* Gaby (Cathérine Deneuve), her first step towards liberation and usurpation. Having removed these outward symbols of her domestic status, Louise further relaxes into her new role when she puts on Gaby's luxurious fur-trimmed coat – an item of clothing that she had hitherto dutifully collected for Gaby. The coat is used as both costume and prop as a signifier of social standing, and Gaby is both surprised and unimpressed at seeing Louise in it. As Louise alters her clothing she also alters her behaviour; with her change in appearance she begins to disobey orders, answer back her *maîtresse* and take liberties such as sitting down and taking tea, as though she were part of the family, rather than simply serving it. Despite occupying an inferior position to the other women, Louise displays her superiority over them in matters of feminine charm, particularly in the song and dance number she performs for an inquisitive and captivated Augustine, who backwardly asks Louise how one might seduce a man.

Taking inspiration from Louise, Augustine too sets about refashioning herself. From a prudish, uptight, neurotic spinster dressed in heavy and rigid woollen and tweed fabrics in austere and conservative brown, green and auburn tones, Augustine emerges elegantly dressed in more fluid and luxurious fabrics in softer feminine tones. She abandons her provincial schoolmarm glasses and severe chignon, allowing her flowing auburn hair to fall loosely on her shoulders. Augustine wears an elegant luminous blue satin dress with a luxurious fur stole draped loosely around her shoulders, both borrowed from her sister Gaby who had previously declared herself 'belle et riche' and labelled Augustine 'laide et pauvre'. Augustine's act of borrowing is tied up with the mythology of *la Parisienne* as a resourceful woman who takes inspiration or borrows from various sources (both visually and materially) to piece together her look. Augustine has borrowed Gaby's clothes but she has created a new look all of her own which does not resemble Gaby at all.

Augustine's transformation rehearses an established narrative trope of the Parisienne type. Remarking on the transformation of women into Parisiennes, Houssaye remarks: 'Il y a deux naissances pour la femme: celle du berceau et celle de la robe' (273) (There are two births for woman: that of the cradle and that of the dress). Augustine's transformation is revealed cinematically through a typical transformation–revelation trope: the heroine descends a staircase and her transformation is revealed in stages. First, there is a shot of Augustine's satin-slippered feet, and then her hips and legs draped in material enter the frame before the camera pans up to reveal a mid-shot of her body from the neck down to just below the knees. With each shot we anticipate a glimpse of her face, and the camera then finally unveils Augustine's new coiffure and make-up in a mid-shot. Upon seeing her newly transformed sister, Gaby exclaims: 'Mais Augustine, qu'est-ce qu'il t'arrive?' (But Augustine, what has got into you?), to which Augustine, in her newly adopted cool and detached manner, replies: 'Rien de special. J'avais juste envie d'être belle' (Nothing special. I just felt like looking beautiful). Gaby expresses her surprise thus: 'C'est incroyable, ce changement est tellement surprenant' (It's unbelievable, such a surprising transformation), to which Augustine just coolly sighs as she bathes in the other women's surprise and admiration.

Both Louise and Augustine demonstrate their mastery over clothing and harness its potential to transform themselves and take control of their own image. Ozon's film, in this way, provides yet another cinematic figuration of *la Parisienne* and strengthens her association with fashion and style. Yet, as Waldron has pointed out, the exaggerated nature of the performances also points to a challenging of the dominant stereotype of the chic Parisienne through its reduction to caricature (73).

Self-fashioning in *À bout de souffle*

In a reversal of the fashion/film relationship explored in the other films in this chapter, *À bout de souffle* was not linked to fashion in the sense of a prevailing standard set by couture or design. While the aforementioned films all used costume designers and/or couturiers, in *À bout de souffle* the actress herself, Jean Seberg, provides her own wardrobe. This was in keeping with both the aesthetic and industrial demands of the Nouvelle Vague, the films of which were not only limited by budgetary considerations, but also by the promotion of a certain quotidian realism or everydayness (Marie 81). One of the features of the naturalness of New Wave films was that the outfits – it no longer makes sense to refer to them as 'costumes' – were often the actors' own. The quest for this naturalness also resulted in a simplicity of dress not found in the cinema of the preceding decades. This relative simplicity of dress was described by Uzanne as a keystone of the grace of *la Parisienne* in the early twentieth century:

> Aujourd'hui, plus l'habillement est riche, c'est à-dire surchargé de broderies, d'ornements, envahi par les passementeries, moins il est seyant. Les femmes parées comme des châsses sont le plus souvent pesantes, massives et sans l'adorable ondulation de la ligne. — L'ostentation tue la grâce. (77)

> [T]he more expensive the gown, the more loaded with embroidery, trimmings and ornaments, the less becoming it is. Women decorated like shrines are apt to be heavy, massive, and without any beauty of line – grace is killed by ostentation. (*The Modern Parisienne* 32)

It is Patricia's simplicity in dress which marks her out as a Parisienne. The result too was that an actress's personal style, what she wore every day, was through the medium of cinema promoted as fashionable in its own right. The scene in which Patricia, with her cropped hair, cigarette pants, T-shirt and penny loafers, strolls up and down the Champs-Elysées with Michel is described by Pamela Church-Gibson as 'an iconic moment – not only in cinema, but within fashion imagery' (99). What makes the figure of Patricia/Jean Seberg in *À bout de souffle* Parisienne is precisely this self-fashioning or *sui generis* aspect of her character.

À bout de souffle has 'become a fashionista's favourite' (Church-Gibson 99). The October 1990 edition of *Vogue* magazine features a fashion spread in which models Christy Turlington and Stephane Ferrara are carefully dressed and posed to resemble Patricia and Michel. More recently the March 2014 edition of *Marie Claire Australia* featured a 12-page fashion spread entitled 'Breathless', photographed by David Gubert and styled by Valeryi Yong. The spread featured model Liv Driscoll, hair cropped, in the role of Patricia/Jean Seberg. The magazine writes: 'Looking for a little inspiration? Let '60s film star and style icon Jean Seberg be your muse and opt for stripy T-shirts, cropped pants, pencil skirts and simple knits' (118).

Patricia/Seberg's much imitated style typified the *garçonne* look and was part of a more general backlash against the excessively feminine women of the 1940s and 1950s. When Patricia remarks to Michel, 'Je trouve que les robes des parisiennes sont trop courtes et que ça fait poule' (I find that Parisiennes' dresses are too short and that it makes them look cheap), she sets herself against the prevailing standards of French femininity at the time. Patricia's outlook is undoubtedly modern, expressed not only in her remarks but in her style. The *garçonne* style was the culmination of a movement which began some time after the First World War when 'writers and social observers produced a new image of female identity: *La femme moderne*, they called this new creature, or sometimes *la garçonne*' (M.L. Roberts 19). In 1924, Jacques Boulenger, the editor of the weekly *L'Opinion*, described this phenomenon as follows: the *femme moderne* is above all a creation of the war … . Nestled in the arms of her partner, she dances without a corset; she swims in a maillot … . Above all, she has a taste or desire for independence (qtd in M.L. Roberts 19). Patricia expresses on more than one occasion her desire to live independently of men. During the long hotel bedroom scene she says to Michel: 'Tu sais que je suis très indépendante' (You know that I am very independent). Later, when Michel enquires as to why she writes articles, Patricia responds: 'Pour être indépendante des hommes' (to be independent from men). This newfound desire for independence also found expression in the short, cropped hair which 'exemplified the dramatic, provocative changes sweeping the world of French Fashion' (M.L. Roberts 66).

Fashion is ubiquitous in the depiction of *la Parisienne* and demonstrates the variations within the type. The films set for this chapter demonstrate these variations through the eclectic array of film genres in which the fashionable Parisienne appears. This is why Alloway insisted iconography not follow usual paths of criticism such as auteurist or genre approaches, but rather develop different ways of grouping films.

The association of *la Parisienne* with fashion can be traced back to the nineteenth-century democratisation of fashion, when the image of the chic Parisienne was first exported, both throughout France and abroad. It was further strengthened through depictions of the Parisienne in art, literature and mass culture, and culminated in her role as the ambassador for French luxury goods and style. Parisian chic is one of the myths of the twentieth and twenty-first centuries, and this chapter in part demonstrates how this mythology developed historically, culturally and industrially. Cinema took up this mythology, and its treatment of the Parisienne type depicts on one level at least the conjunction of two industries: the film industry and the fashion industry. The relationship between *la Parisienne* and fashion is perpetuated in cinema primarily through the way the type is costumed (couturier, costume designer or self-fashioning), but also includes extra-cinematic considerations such as the actress/couturier relationship and the way a certain look, designed or self-styled, was achieved and subsequently marketed, whether directly or indirectly. Here the importance of the star comes into play; this is something that is significant to the type and will be taken up later in Chapter 6.

Cinematic treatments of the fashionable Parisienne both draw on and develop the pre-existing iconography of the type, and demonstrate the way costume displays a range of meanings beyond simply denoting an elegantly dressed woman. These treatments included films explicitly about fashion (*Reunion in France*, *Funny Face*); films which, in other words, take fashion as their overt subject matter, drawing the fashion industry into the textual fabric of the film. In Minnelli's *Gigi*, on the other hand, fashion is not the subject matter as such but rather forms an essential part of the *mise en scène* in the film's construction of Belle Époque Paris, foregrounding the importance of clothing and appearance for that era. *Gigi* begins with the idea that fashion is a spectacle, and that as a spectacle it is related to the development of the public sphere in nineteenth-century Paris primarily as the site of leisure and display. In *Funny Face*, this relationship between the public sphere, leisure and fashion is emphasised through the transformation of the public spaces of Paris into 'locales' for the fashion shoot: the Louvre, the Opéra Garnier, the banks of the Seine, the Gare de l'Est, the Place de la Concorde. Fashion is also employed in cinema as a narrative device, primarily for depicting transformation, a motif integral to the Parisienne type. In *Funny Face*, Jo Stockton is transformed from an 'austere and bluestocking New York bookseller' (Viviani 171) into a chic Parisienne who embodies two looks, that of the Left Bank existentialist and Right Bank glamour, bringing the sartorial into relationship with the geographical or spatial. Transformation also plays a part in both *Frantic* and *8 femmes*; however, in the latter film it is somewhat emptied of its meaning and narrative function, reduced to transformation for its own sake, a pure aesthetic phenomenon.

In terms of the three contexts within which these films have been considered – the historical, the industrial and the textual – the following two main conclusions can be drawn:

(1) cinema is part of the fashion industry, but can also take the fashion industry as the subject of films; the figure of the Parisienne is in part an ongoing construction of the conjunction of the fashion and film industries, yet she also maintains a relative autonomy from these industries;

(2) costume forms part of the cinematic *mise en scène*, functions by aiding in periodising a film and establishing its epoch, possesses meaning beyond its denotation, and draws on a pre-existing iconography.

In terms of the first of these conclusions, *Funny Face* may be a showcase for Givenchy's elaborate gowns and tailored suits; however, the enduring fashion legacy of the film, the one which entered the popular consciousness, belongs to Hepburn's own personal style, the outfit worn during the dance sequence in the cavern, which has come to be associated with beatnik or Existential Left Bank culture. Indeed, in the popular fashion press, the Hepburn look in this scene takes its place among the most influential fashion statements of the twentieth century. While both Hepburn's couture and existential looks appear in Paula Reed's *Fifty Fashion Looks that Changed the 1950s*, it is the uniform-like nature of the latter outfit which facilitated its easy adoption into ready-to-wear fashion. Alongside Hepburn, we can also cite Deneuve's Yves Saint Laurent capsule wardrobe of *Belle de jour* and Jean Seberg's T-shirt and cigarette pants of *À bout de souffle* as examples of iconic simplicity. Indeed, these looks all exemplify Uzanne's remark that the Parisienne is opposed to ostentation, instead embracing a quiet elegance. In the relationship between the Parisienne and fashion, in an iconographical sense at least, the former dominates the latter: fashion is depicted following the Parisienne rather than the Parisienne following fashion. The second of the above conclusions, that costume possesses a range of meanings beyond mere denotation or periodisation – for example, danger depicted through ambiguity of dress – will be taken up further in the following chapter on the Parisienne as femme fatale, indicating the extent to which, for the Parisienne type, costume conceals as much as it reveals, and plays a narrative function greater than mere decoration.

Notes

1. I use both the name of the character and actress, as these images are just as much about the actress and her image as the character in the film.
2. The films are Stanley Donen's *Funny Face* (1956), Luis Buñuel's *Belle de jour* (1967) and Jean-Luc Godard's *À bout de souffle* (1960), respectively.

4
Femme fatale

The association of woman with Paris was a popular trope of nineteenth-century French culture. To this association of woman with Paris was joined a third image, that of death. This is most apparent in Charles Baudelaire's poetry, where the representation of women is divided between the abominable and the holy. As Walter Benjamin remarks: 'It is the unique provision of Baudelaire's poetry that the image of woman and the image of death intermingle in a third: that of Paris' (*The Writer of Modern Life* 41). As a prostitute or courtesan, *la Parisienne* posed another threat, that of venereal disease, something which led to the association of these women with death. Patrick Bade notes how, as there was no cure for syphilis in the nineteenth century, 'women often were quite literally the carriers of hideous disease and death' (9). This nineteenth-century cultural tradition finds its expression in cinematic representations of the Parisienne type as femme fatale.

This chapter considers manifestations of *la Parisienne* as femme fatale in Jules Dassin's *Du Rififi chez les hommes* (1955), Marcel Carné's *Le Jour se lève* (1939) and *Le Quai des brumes* (1938) and Jean-Luc Godard's *À bout de souffle* (1960). These films, each in its own way, are examples of French film noir and their female protagonists read as femme fatales. However, the femme fatale of French film noir is different from the femme fatale of American film noir; she comes from a different cultural tradition and is informed by a different cultural figure. The femme fatale moves easily between American noir and French noir, and while her narrative function remains the same – to bring closure through the hero's death or demise – this is brought about in different ways. French and American noir, I would argue, offer two differing manifestations of the femme fatale, which can be called the 'unintentional' and the 'intentional', respectively. The term 'unintentional' is used by Susan Weiner to describe Nelly (Michèle Morgan) in *Le Quai des brumes*; however, I want to extend the use of this term both to include other femme fatales in French film noir and to connect them to the type *la Parisienne*. In contrast to the intentional femme fatale of American film noir, the actions of the unintentional femme fatale only indirectly or incidentally lead to the hero's demise. Indeed, the unintentional femme fatale does not need to act in order to bring about the hero's downfall: her mere presence on screen is enough. This is because she is the embodiment of the nineteenth-century French tradition which associates women and the city with death, an association continued in the primarily urban settings of film noir.

In the nineteenth century, *la Parisienne* was often associated with danger:

> Inevitably, not far beneath the surface of la Parisienne as the personification of pleasure lurked the primitive, the invert, and the modern degenerate. Even though theater pressmen meant to celebrate the charms of actresses by describing them as very Parisian, the label carried implications of danger. *L'Illustration* made beauty the key feature of la Parisienne but noted that 'it is the beauty of the devil!' (Berlanstein 117–18)

In 'Femme fatale: fashion and visual culture in fin-de-siècle Paris', Steele argues that 'Behind the image of the femme fatale, the irresistibly attractive woman who leads men to destruction, lurked the specter of the fashionable Parisienne' (316). Through her representation in nineteenth-century literature, art and popular culture, *la Parisienne* became one manifestation of the *fille d'Eve* or daughter of Eve. In *Evil by Design: The Creation and Marketing of the Femme Fatale*, Menon looks at 'the manifestation of fatality within the supposedly real (but in fact stereotypical) contemporary woman known as the Parisienne and termed a *fille d'Eve* by nineteenth century writers' (4). Popular-culture stereotypes of the Parisienne as femme fatale informed Salon painting, which in turn solidified this image of her as the embodiment of evil. For Menon, this had implications for the development of French feminism; however I am less interested in this aspect of Menon's work than in the way she accounts for the origins of the fatal Parisienne in terms of cultural stereotypes of French femininity: 'The femme fatale's origins are intimately related to the Biblical Eve and the narrative of the Fall in the book of Genesis. Eve is arguably the first femme fatale; her daughters the filles d'Eve – defined broadly as all women who came after her – are also femmes fatales by implication' (4).

Helen Hanson and Catherine O'Rawe also claim the femme fatale can be traced back to Eve and that during the late nineteenth century she emerged as a clear and identifiable type in Western art and literature (3). However, they point out that Eve is not the only biblical precursor to the femme fatale, citing also Adam's first wife, Lilith, 'turned demon and succubus' (3). In fin-de-siècle European literature and art there is an 'extraordinary proliferation of femmes fatales' and this 'preoccupation with evil and destructive women is one of the most striking features of late nineteenth-century culture' (Bade 6). Bade argues that artists working in the nineteenth century formed their femmes fatales from a diverse range of literary and historical sources and reworked and transformed many traditional themes (7). In addition to these biblical precursors, the ancient world provided endless inspiration: 'From Greek mythology came Helen of Troy, Circe, Medusa, Medea, and the Sirens, and from Babylonian mythology Astarte, who was the bringer of death and decay as well as fertility, and who in the manner of certain insects destroyed her lovers' (Bade 7). In France in the nineteenth century the figure of the fatal woman appeared alongside her opposite, the saint or 'good' woman. What Virginia M. Allen in *The Femme Fatale: Erotic Icon* calls the 'the French Contribution' to the figure of the fatal woman can be found most notably in the writings of Baudelaire and Théophile Gautier, especially the latter's novel *Mademoiselle de Maupin*:

> Neither Gautier nor Baudelaire gave the label of 'femme fatale' to their women. Rather they …gave radical emphasis to particular feelings about the opposite poles of the Eternal Feminine. The work of both provided new images of oriental exoticism, androgyny, and sinful sterility for the oncoming generations. (81–2)

In popular representations, these two aspects of the eternal feminine[1] were given representation in two separate characters: the archetypal bad woman, and her opposite, the good woman. One of the most recognisable nineteenth-century examples of this opposition is found in Bizet's opera *Carmen* (1875), based on Prosper Mérimée's 1845 novella, in which Carmen is juxtaposed with 'good' woman Micaela. This popular trope is taken up in cinema and we often see this juxtaposition between the 'good' and the 'bad' woman in both French and American noir.

The term femme fatale has been used since the beginning of the twentieth century, while many of the images (both literary and visual) to which writers apply the term pre-date its use. According to Allen, the term 'is now being applied retroactively to nearly any image of a seductive woman, even those who are not noticeably evil' (viii). Allen speculates that the term may have been coined in popular journalism and theatrical reviews around 1912:

> The fact that the term is French does not necessarily mean that the French invented the phrase. It illustrates more than anything else the profound Anglo-Saxon conviction that sexy – erotically dangerous – women are usually French, and as a corollary, most French women are sexy. (viii)

These remarks about the connection between the femme fatale and the French woman further strengthen the link between the femme fatale and the figure of *la Parisienne*. Crisp identifies the development of the femme fatale in 1930s French cinema as follows:

> Two female stereotypes developed in the later thirties which contrasted …with each other: the flighty elegant and the sensual seductive. Earlier, female stars had tended to be described in somewhat varied terms, as delightful, gay, vivacious, or capricious, but by 1937 the adjectives had become more distinctive, and the interest, tastes, and appearance of the stars described in ritualized terms. On the one hand, are 'feminine' stars, flighty, frivolous, and somewhat superficial whose main interest is their self-presentation to the world; on the other hand are sensual,

mysterious, somber, and potentially dangerous women, who had initially been termed 'vamps,' but who are soon refashioned as 'femmes fatales'. (262)

The term femme fatale, at the beginning of the decade, was initially applied only to foreign actresses, especially blonde Nordic vamps. It was in the late 1930s that 'sultry French brunettes [were] incorporated into the sisterhood of the vamp' (Crisp 263).

It is useful to reinforce the relationship between *la Parisienne*, the femme fatale and French cinema because in film studies the femme fatale is most often considered within the context of American film noir, and thus in relation to American characters. For example, the archetypal femme fatale of cinema is invariably Phyllis Dietrichson (Barbara Stanwyck) in Billy Wilder's *Double Indemnity* (1944), Brigid O'Shaughnessy (Mary Astor) in John Huston's *The Maltese Falcon* (1941), Cora Smith (Lana Turner) in Tay Garnett's *The Postman Always Rings Twice* (1946) or Kathie Moffat (Jane Greer) in Jacques Tourneur's *Out of the Past* (1947). As a general rule, any study of women in film noir centres on the concept of the femme fatale, the main narrative hinge on which the fate of the hero turns. Hanson and O'Rawe, however, express the need to transcend the established connections between film noir, Hollywood and the femme fatale, and emphasise the importance of

> tracing the roots of the *femme fatale* figure across cultures and periods, and on restoring much-needed context by exploring the transnational and historical origins and intertexts out of which this complex feminine archetype has arisen. Each manifestation of the *femme fatale* has to be studied in relation to its local context and history, as well as in relation to the ways it may have absorbed other traditions of representation. (3)

With this in mind, then, it is possible to move beyond the narrow generic limits of film noir by opening up the concept of femme fatale to broader cultural histories and contexts. In the context of French film noir, it is possible to consider these characters not only as femmes fatales, but also as incarnations of the nineteenth-century figure of *la Parisienne*.

The chanteuse and the courtesan in *Du Rififi chez les hommes*

Du Rififi chez les hommes belongs to a particular strain of French film noir, the mid-1950s French gangster film. The mid-1950s saw the emergence of a group of influential gangster films in France which showed greater similarities with American cinema, including, along with Dassin's film, Jacques Becker's *Touchez pas au grisbi* (1954) and Jean-Pierre Melville's *Bob le flambeur* (1955). These films were, usually negatively, characterised as film noir by critics at the time of their release (Vincendeau 'French Film Noir' 24); however, there are discernible generic differences, including the role of women in these films. Ginette Vincendeau claims these French gangster films eliminate the femme fatale. Women in these films, she writes, are 'too marginal to be of consequence: when they betray it is by mistake rather than by design' ('French Film Noir' 38). This is true of both Mado (Marie Sabouret) and Viviane (Magali Noël) in *Du Rififi chez les hommes*. Neither are femmes fatales in any classic sense typical in American film noir; they are not lead characters, nor are they afforded as much screen time as the male protagonists. However, while they are secondary characters, they are by no means inconsequential to the development of the plot. Thus the gangster film does not strictly eliminate the femme fatale, as Vincendeau claims. Mado and Viviane qualify as fatal women because of their destructive effect on the male protagonists; however, recognising these women as femmes fatales perhaps relies on a different set of signifiers from a different cultural tradition than those associated with the femmes fatales of American noir, such as screen time or narrative consequentiality.

Du Rififi chez les hommes pioneered a new sub-genre of crime film, the heist film. Ageing gangster Tony le Stéphanois (Jean Servais), upon his release from prison, initially refuses to take part in another jewel heist. However, after discovering his former girlfriend Mado has taken up with enemy Pierre Grutter, he changes his mind. The heist goes smoothly but its aftermath proves disastrous, and it is both Mado and Viviane who unintentionally cause the deaths of Tony and fellow gang member Cesare. During Viviane's song-and-dance performance, Cesare (Jules Dassin) is bewitched by the seductive chanteuse. It is Cesare's infatuation with Viviane which prompts him to steal a ring during the heist, a decision which will set off a chain of events that ends in his death. Unbeknownst to herself, Viviane betrays Cesare by offhandedly telling one of Grutter's men that 'a crazy little Italian' gave her the ring, which Grutter's men know to be part of the loot. Viviane proves fatal for Cesare; however, she is neither scheming nor calculating, nor does she even ask Cesare for the ring. In fact, far from deliberately scheming against Cesare, Viviane is sentimental, and when the ring is confiscated asks for it back, even though she believes it to be a fake. In a similar way, Mado is unintentionally fatal for Tony. As a kept woman and gangster's moll, with Tony in prison and no longer able to support her, Mado had little choice but to consort with other men, including Grutter. It is only after Tony discovers Mado's infidelity that he decides not only to take part in the heist but to mastermind a more elaborate and potentially lucrative plan than initially proposed by the gang.

This unintentional fatality is related, I would further argue, to Viviane and Mado's status as Parisiennes. Both are glamorous and fashionable demimondaines. Mado is linked to the figure of *la Parisienne* primarily through her status as a kept woman and is prefigured by the Parisienne courtesans of the Second Empire. She consorts with criminals and receives money, expensive clothes and jewellery in return for sexual favours: when Mado tells Tony that she 'earned them', he replies: 'Tu as toujours su te défendre'; the verb *défendre* meaning both 'to look after' and 'to prostitute' oneself. Mado is cut from the same cloth as Émile Zola's nineteenth-century prostitute Nana. Like Nana, who switches between various lovers and suitors, Mado has no particular allegiance to any one man. Her loyalty is literally bought and sold as any other commodity in the marketplace. As soon as Tony is in prison, Mado goes to the Riviera where she liaises with another man and ultimately meets Tony's successor Grutter in Morocco.

Viviane, too, can be characterised as Parisienne primarily through her occupation as a nightclub singer or chanteuse. She is a descendant of the music-hall and café-concert tradition characterised by Parisiennes such as Jane Avril, Fréhel, Yvette Guilbert and Josephine Baker. Like the courtesan, the chanteuse is a member of the demimonde and relies on her sexuality but in a more indirect way. The song Viviane performs at Grutter's nightclub, *L'Âge d'Or*, would at first seem to continue the predilection of American film noir for including a musical number, usually staged in a nightclub setting, examples of which include Lauren Bacall singing 'And Her Tears Flowed Like Wine' at Eddie Mars's casino in Howard Hawks's *The Big Sleep* (1946), Claudia Drake singing 'I Can't Believe You're In Love With Me' in Edgar Ulmer's *Detour* (1945), and Rita Hayworth singing 'Put the Blame on Mame' in Charles Vidor's *Gilda* (1946). However, the inclusion of a musical number in film noir also has its antecedents in French film noir of the 1930s. For example, Maurice Chevalier performs both 'Il pleurait comme une madeleine' and 'Mon amour' in Robert Siodmak's *Pièges* (1939); Jean Gabin performs a song in Julien Duvivier's *Pépé le Moko* (1937), which perhaps seems out of place in a gangster film; and Jean Renoir's *La Bête humaine* (1938) features the music-hall number 'Pauvre petit cœur de Ninon'.

The identification of both Mado and Viviane as femmes fatales is reinforced in *Rififi* by the deliberate juxtaposition of these two Parisiennes with the film's two other female protagonists, Mario's wife Ida (Claude Sylvain) and Jo's wife Louise (Janine Darcey). In contradistinction to Mado and Viviane, who are the bearers of death, these women represent a different kind of femininity and are the bearers of traditional values of hearth and home.

A film which also treats this dichotomy of the Eternal Feminine (Good Woman/Bad Woman) in an interesting way is Marcel Carné's *Le Jour se lève*. Here Carné undermines this strict dichotomy by rendering his female protagonists more ambiguous: while both Françoise (Jacqueline Laurent) and Clara (Arletty) play a part in the demise of François (Jean Gabin), their deceptive appearances prove more fatal to the hero than their actions. This ambiguity or deception is what links the women of Poetic Realism to the nineteenth-century figure *la Parisienne*. Like Viviane and Mado, the women of Poetic Realism can also be read in terms of the unintentional femme fatale and *la Parisienne*.

'Not what they seem': Clara and Françoise in *Le Jour se lève*

According to Vincendeau, Carné's *Le Jour se lève* and *Le Quai des brumes* are often cited, along with other films of Poetic Realism, as precursors to American film noir ('French Film Noir' 23–8). Poetic

Realist films are generally pessimistic and nostalgic urban dramas of the working-class, artisan or criminal milieus. The films are usually set in Paris, although there are also colonial examples, such as *Pépé le Moko* and Duvivier's *La Bandera* (1935). A common feature of Poetic Realism, which it shares with film noir, is the darkness in atmosphere, narrative trajectory and *mise en scène*. They deal particularly with the tragic destiny of a popular hero, usually played by Jean Gabin. The films have a distinctive lyrical style characterised by chiaroscuro lighting, constructed sets, evocative visual imagery and witty and often poetic dialogue, usually scripted by poet Jacques Prévert. Marcel Carné is generally considered to be the foremost filmmaker of Poetic Realism. The main reason for this, according to Dudley Andrew, is that Carné 'genuinely offers to the spectator a feeling for the populism of the age in conjunction with …images of fatalism figured through his pessimistic love stories' (*Mists* 260).

While German Expressionism is frequently considered a source of American film noir, for a long time the influence of Poetic Realism was overlooked. This was mainly due to the fact that influential French critics Raymond Borde and Emile Chaumeton, in their 1955 book *A Panorama of Film Noir*, dismiss Poetic Realism as a possible forerunner to noir. They write: 'Did *Pépé le Moko*, *Quai des brumes* and *La Bête Humaine* announce American film noir? We think not' (23). In this way Borde and Chaumeton were typical of French commentators in conceiving film noir as a solely American phenomenon, a tendency continued in Anglo-American criticism. More recently, however, the influence of Poetic Realism on film noir has been more widely acknowledged (Spicer 6). Aside from the obvious visual and narrative aspects that Poetic Realism and film noir share, there are other connections between the two. First, a number of émigrés from the German studios worked in France before working in Hollywood, including directors Siodmak, Fritz Lang, Billy Wilder and Max Ophüls, as well as cinematographer Eugene Schufftan and set designer Alexandre Trauner. The increasing transnationalism of the film industry meant that personnel moved between Berlin and Paris working on co-productions. Secondly, there was a transatlantic dimension to film noir, too, derived in part from a reaction to the pressures of wartime conflict in Europe and America. Many of noir's most noted directors, including Siodmak, Lang, Wilder and Edgar G. Ulmer, were émigrés from Germany and central Europe. Thirdly, several poetic realist films were remade in Hollywood by noted film noir directors: Jean Renoir's *La Bête humaine* was remade by Fritz Lang in 1958 as *Human Desire*; Duvivier's *Pépé le Moko* was remade by John Cromwell as *Algiers* in 1938; and Carné's *Le Jour se lève* was remade by Anatole Litvak as *The Long Night* in 1947, with Henry Fonda in the Gabin role. Conventional noir history claims that these émigré directors simply imported something loosely termed German Expressionism to Hollywood. Recent scholarship, however, argues that the question of European influence is more dynamic, unstable and multifaceted (Hillier and Phillips; Spicer). What these directors brought with them, along with various technical and stylistic knowledge, was a double perspective on American society: a benign interest in popular American culture, particularly detective fiction, was combined with the wariness of its many excesses.

If Poetic Realism is to be considered a forerunner to American film noir, then the women of Poetic Realism may be seen as prefigurations of the femme fatales of American noir. Helmut Gruber notes that Gabin 'consorts with a woman or women who act as foils, define his aims and desires, create or add to his sense of entrapment, and ultimately turn an uncertain destiny into a doomed fate' (24). In *Le Jour se lève*, Gabin consorts with two such women, each of whom in their own way prove fatal for him: café-concert performer Clara and the young florist's assistant Françoise. Carné's film proceeds as a series of episodic flashbacks detailing the events which lead to François killing Valentin (Jules Berry) and then committing suicide. Both Clara and Françoise feature prominently in these events.

Clara is the quintessential Parisienne; a demimondaine and artiste, she is more openly seductive than Françoise and obviously kept by her manager, dog-trainer and performer Valentin. Françoise, on the other hand, is the perfect image of the good woman, innocent and sexually reserved. This is, at least, the way François sees them. Carné's treatment of the two women, however, disrupts our expectations of their narrative function. It would seem at first that Clara is to be the femme fatale to Françoise's innocent just as François plays the hero to Valentin's villain. However, as Maureen Turim remarks:

If the hero and villain follow the generic pattern of melodrama, the two women are harder to categorize. Françoise 'should' be the ideal innocent heroine and Clara, the other, fallen, woman, but here is where the film performs some of its most interesting play with character. The first flashback introduces both women, placing them in parallel roles in the working-class and marginal *café-concert* milieu of the film. (69)

We might assume that the film will impose a strict opposition, with Clara as the bad woman and Françoise as the good. However, this strict delineation of roles does not take place. To begin with, as Turim points out, 'the opposition between the heroine and the other woman is modified by Françoise being far more worldly and far less innocent (in her attraction to Valentin) than she initially appears to François' (69). Moreover, Clara and François find themselves allied through their mutual dislike of Valentin, and their shared sense of working-class communality which rejects the bourgeois world of appearances and faux elegance of Valentin and the social-climbing Françoise.

Arletty/Clara is Parisienne in four main ways: through her identity as *parigote*, through her androgynous appearance (*la garçonne*), through her chicness, and through her association with the café-concert. To use Edgar Morin's term, Arletty's star persona 'infects' the character of Clara. Clara's working-class status is reinforced through the star persona of Arletty who embodies the *parigote* – the Parisian working-class woman. Hussey describes Arletty as both the 'supreme working-class *parigote*' (346) and the 'archetypal *parigote*' (385). Susan Hayward writes: 'Arletty, predominantly characterised as a *parigote*, attracts in a way that is different and ambiguous' (2005: 176). Arletty's complex star persona – simultaneously woman and 'one of the men' (Hayward *French* 175) – is also expressed through her androgynous appearance. Ellen Pullar remarks that 'on-screen Arletty was frequently associated with an androgynous sexuality that some audiences may have found shocking, in roles that granted her a "masculine" assertiveness or allowed her to appear dressed in masculinized costumes' (11). Arletty's androgyny links her to the femme fatale in the French conception, at least, particularly as articulated in Gautier's androgyne Madeleine/Théodore in *Mademoiselle de Maupin*

(1835). In this novel, the beautiful young woman Madeleine assumes the dress and identity of a man, calling herself Théodore. The novel's protagonist D'Albert, a leisured young man unaware of the true sex of Théodore, meditates on the compelling beauty of the androgyne. In recent popular discourse, too, the influence of both male and female dress on the style of *la Parisienne* has been noted. French actress Carole Bouquet, in a short piece on the subject of elegance for the book *Parisiennes: A Celebration of French Women*, remarks: 'The Parisienne strikes a perfect balance between what she shows of herself, and what she is – whether that balance is true or false, calculated or learned, whether her femininity is communicated or acquired through the looks of others, be they men or women' (175). Similarly, a recent style guide, *Paris Street Style*, advises readers to borrow clothing from their boyfriend's wardrobe in order to attain Parisian chic (154).

In the 1930s, Arletty cultivated the *garçonne* look, and frequently appeared in men's attire both in her role as a fashion model and in her publicity photographs (Pullar 13). It was a look closely associated with art deco, and the prevailing liberalism and the emancipation of women played a decisive role in its development (Lussier 8). Through her anti-domesticity, eccentricity and intellectualism, Arletty was distinct from the prevailing ideal of French femininity embodied by Simone Simon or Annabella. However, she 'represented an alternative form of stardom that was equally French' (Pullar 8). In her analysis of how Arletty's star persona was articulated in French movie fan magazines of the 1930s, Pullar notes that her 'eccentricity and her intellectual nature were rendered as specifically Parisian qualities' (17). If Arletty represents the working-class Parisian as *parigote,* she equally represents the chic Parisienne, not only through her association with fashion (Arletty was a fashion model during the 1920s for designers such as Paul Poiret, Georges Fouquet and Chez Tiburce), but also with the café-concert, where she began her career. Arletty's peculiar ambiguity was the result of a union of opposites: she possessed, according to one journalist, 'a faubourg accent and the chic of the Champs-Élysées' (qtd in Pullar 14).

Clara and François carry on a liaison of sorts, even while François continues to pursue Françoise. It is François's involvement with the two women which leads to his death. While Clara and Françoise certainly do not set out to calculatedly plot François' demise, they do play a part in his downfall. The turning point in the narrative, in which François's doomed fate is sealed, occurs in the scene in which François goes to Clara's apartment to end their liaison by telling her he is going to marry Françoise. Clara offers François her brooch as a parting gift, a souvenir to remember her by. François instantly recognises the brooch as the same in kind as that owned by Françoise. When he questions Clara about it she explains the brooch was given to her by Valentin, and that he gives one to all his sexual conquests. Realising the extent of Françoise's involvement with Valentin and shattering his illusions of her as an innocent and naïve simple-hearted florist's assistant, François now knows that all of his hopes of working-class domestic happiness will never materialise. The brooch which, through Clara, links Françoise with Valentin, becomes the narrative catalyst which leads François to first kill Valentin and then himself.

Both Clara and Françoise are the embodiment of the ambiguity of *la Parisienne*. Iskin writes of *la Parisienne*'s 'inexplicable mystique', which 'emerged as another facet of the discourse on the figure in books and popular journals in the nineteenth century' (197). In *Le Jour se lève*, this ambiguity is expressed primarily through dress or costume. Françoise, dressed alternately in a utilitarian work dress of coarse fabric of the *midinette* or *grisette* and a prim and demure simple long-sleeved floral dress which falls below the knee, with Peter Pan collar which sits high up around her neck, symbolises working class-values of fidelity and simplicity. The collar and style of her dress, which keep her well covered, suggest innocence and purity. The only time her arms are exposed is when she has rolled up her sleeves, a sign of her status as a working woman. Françoise appears meek and mild, diminutive, almost backward, and her dress and demeanour reinforce this.

In contrast, the first time we see Clara, she appears in a far more revealing stage costume. Clara is tall and statuesque; she wears a tutu with a very short, ruffled skirt comprising layers of see-through organza material which sits low on her hips and falls about the top of her thighs, her long legs in sheer black stockings highly visible. The tight-fitting shiny black bodice of her tutu features a plunging deep V-neckline, and her shoulders, back, arms and décolletage are all exposed. In contrast to Françoise, Clara's hands and forearms are among the few parts of her body covered up: she wears long black shiny gloves which recall those of music hall star Yvette Guilbert and also prefigure the famous black gloves of a femme fatale of American film noir, Gilda (Rita Hayworth). In contrast to the demure Françoise, Clara's appearance is bold, brash, forward and far more overtly sexually; the fabrics she wears are ostentatious and flashy compared to those of Françoise's garb. Valerie Steele notes that ambiguity of dress was a feature of the Parisienne type in the literature of nineteenth-century France, and gives the example of Valérie Marneffe from Balzac's *Illusions perdues*, a woman with many lovers but who 'dresses like a respectable married woman, in simple tasteful fashions' (*Paris Fashion* 67). Steele goes on to cite Balzac from the novel: 'These Machiavellis in petticoats are the most dangerous women – far more to be feared than honest *demimondaines*' (*Paris Fashion* 67). In *Le Jour se lève*, neither Clara nor Françoise is what they appear to be. François misrecognises Françoise as the innocent flower seller, the bearer of traditional working-class values, and mistakes Clara for the easy-going *parigote* with whom it is possible to have a good time without any serious implications. He is wrong on both counts.

'Mac Orlan's ghost': Nelly in *Le Quai des brumes*

The Parisiennes of *Le Jour se lève*, Clara and Françoise, function as unintentional femmes fatales by inadvertently causing the demise of the hero played by Jean Gabin. The ambiguity of these women, expressed through their respective modes of dress, is the catalyst in the film's narrative resolution, in which Gabin's double misrecognition leads to his death. In *Le Quai des brumes*, *la Parisienne* also appears as an unintentional femme fatale in the character of Nelly (Michèle Morgan). This is determined and overdetermined in Carné's film in three ways: first, by Nelly's cinematic innocent being haunted by the literary prostitute of the film's source novel; secondly by Michèle Morgan's star persona and the mysterious sexuality it imparts to the character of Nelly; and thirdly by Nelly's androgynous mode of dress. Thus two textualities are at work in constructing the figure of the fatal Parisienne: the intra-textual, that is her narrative function and costume; and the extra-textual, namely Mac Orlan's novel and the importation of aspects of Morgan's persona into the role.

Following their initial meeting at Panama's Hut, a quayside shack which serves as a half-way house for transients, artists and outsiders, army deserter Jean (Jean Gabin) develops a fascination with the mysterious Nelly. They embark on a romance which is complicated by both Nelly's jealous suitor Lucien Legardier (Pierre Brasseur) and her covetous and resentful guardian Zabel (Michel Simon). Jean's attraction to Nelly embroils him in a sordid world and leads to his brutal murder of Zabel and in turn to his own death at the hands of Lucien. Susan Weiner remarks that Nelly is 'a femme fatale: unintentionally but nonetheless. While she herself does not seem to act, men scheme, die and kill for her. At the end of Carné's film, Nelly is the only one left standing, a survivor of the narrative web she has inadvertently spun' (130).

A key difference between Mac Orlan's novel and Carné's film is the transposition of the setting from Montmartre in 1903 to Le Havre in 1938. Even though the action is set in Le Havre, and it is implied that Nelly has ostensibly spent her life in the port town, she is unmistakably Parisienne. Primarily, this is because the Parisienne of Mac Orlan's novel is imported to, or overlaid onto, the Nelly of the film. Weiner offers a dual reading of the novel and Carné's film to demonstrate how the former informs the latter, particularly in relation to the transformation of Nelly from a prostitute to an orphan and from a 19-year-old self-reliant woman to a 17-year-old minor legally requiring a guardian. Weiner writes: 'On the level of the signifier alone, Nelly's transformation from novel to film, from prostitute to orphan, conjures a chain of associations that allows an initial reflection on the implications of such a rewriting: woman to girl, sexuality to innocence, street to hearth, badness to good. A sullied femininity is recast as pure' (130). Weiner goes on to claim that the 'fearsomeness' of Nelly's survival at the end of the film only really surfaces when the novel is read alongside the film, where there is a continuity which transcends the narrative: 'One incarnation of Nelly haunts the other: the prostitute's powers are never far from the vulnerability of the orphan, and female innocence is more monstrous than it would seem' (130). Nelly has been transformed, first and foremost, to fulfil certain generic or narrative requirements of Poetic Realism, and this transformation is necessary for the male hero to be able to identify with the women in these films. In Jean's world-view, a prostitute is not a victim or outcast but someone who, unlike himself, possesses a métier or plies her trade. It is only after Jean learns of Nelly's plight that his attitude towards her softens into narcissistic love. Like all such love in Poetic Realism, it is doomed from the outset, and this is depicted in the film in a shot of Jean and Nelly framed in a window, the jamb of which passes between the two, signifying the impossibility of their union. The mystery of Nelly's sexuality, the 'obscure guilt' which seems reflected in every look she directs towards Jean, can be explained in part by the fact that on the occasion of their first meeting Jean assumes she is a prostitute ('faire le turf?'). He later discovers she is an orphan, taking refuge in Panama's hut after fleeing her guardian Zabel. However, just when we assume her to be an innocent victim, it is revealed that she has had a lover, has a sexual relationship with Zabel, and frequents seedy bars such as *Au Petit Tabarin*, where she met her first doomed lover Maurice. That Maurice's fate mirrors that of Jean's only underscores the danger Nelly poses to the men she loves.

The peculiar conjunction of guilt and innocence in the figure of the prostitute-orphan is only partly responsible for the power Nelly has over the men she encounters. Another overdetermining factor in her mysterious sexuality is Michèle Morgan's star persona. According to Crisp, Morgan brings to Nelly 'incompatible or even contradictory elements', making her simultaneously 'familiar and inaccessible, dazzling and reserved, pure yet bearing some obscure guilt, dependent on a man to whom she is committed, yet apart, mysterious' (277). Morgan's mysterious sexuality constitutes what Crisp calls a 'gentler mystery', which renders the character Nelly 'no less fascinating, and ultimately no less deadly, but lacking the calculation, self-interest, and ruthlessness' usually associated with more intentional femme fatales (117).

Morgan's gamine or boyish appearance is accentuated in the film by her androgynous mode of dress. This allows for further narcissistic investment in the heroine on the part of the hero. Edmund Turk remarks that 'androgyny is an essential component of the Carné œuvre ... . In their first encounter, Jean jokes about Nelly's slender, boyish frame' (123). When Nelly comments on the 'jolie tête' of the puppy which incessantly follows Jean, Jean replies: 'Toi aussi t'as une belle tête, tiens t'es belle et tu me plais, sans blague t'es pas épaisse mais tu me plais' (You too you got a pretty head; look, you're pretty and you're easy on the eye, no joke you're not well built but you're all right). The framing of their initial meeting and the exchange of looks between Jean and Nelly is reminiscent of the archetypal first encounter between the American film noir hero and the femme fatale, particularly between Cora (Lana Turner) and Frank (John Garfield) in *The Postman Always Rings Twice* and Walter (Fred McMurray) and Phyllis (Barbara Stanwyck) in *Double Indemnity*. Nelly is, however, unlike her American counterparts, not overtly sexual in appearance. In contrast to Cora's midriff blouse and high-waisted short shorts and Phyllis's towel, Nelly wears a raincoat over a modest dress and a black beret and a scarf tied high up around her neck. As Turk remarks: 'Nelly's trench coat, her beret, and her habit of walking with head bent and hands in her pockets are indeed tomboyish variants of Gabin's own uniform and gait' (123). The choice of Morgan's costume, designed by Coco Chanel, was, however, purely accidental. Exasperated at not being able to meet the needs of a female character so unpretentious as Nelly, Chanel remarked unkindly: 'Why not just give her a raincoat and a beret!' (qtd in Turk 123). In spite of the haphazard way in which Nelly's outfit was conceived it does take on a signification of its own within the context of the film. That Chanel designed it adds a dimension of Parisian chic which might otherwise have been absent in the clothing of an orphan from Le Havre; while on the other hand, the sartorial layering of the transparent raincoat reflects a narrative layering in which the protective yet ultimately see-through outer layer or persona reveals that which it conceals.

Both Nelly's appearance and her presence at Panama's Hut evoke for Jean the image of a typical streetwalker. He addresses her candidly in language he considers suitable for an exchange between a soldier and a whore, language which in fact suggests the prelude to a possible liaison. His use of the colloquial phrase 'faire le turf' (do the rounds) indicates the matter-of-factness with which he approaches the subject. Nelly's mystification at this turn of phrase ('le turf, qu'est-ce que ça veut dire?') establishes, at least in Jean's mind, that Nelly is no prostitute in this narrow sense. However it must be remembered that the story she tells of her tragic life is in fact a first-person account viewed through the eyes of a male protagonist who has an investment in the story she tells, right down to the fact that they are both orphans. Nelly may not be a prostitute in the narrow sense with which Jean is acquainted, and indeed her reaction to his language suggests she is largely unfamiliar with the world Jean inhabits. However, like her nineteenth-century Parisienne precursors, Nelly is a kept woman; she is dependent on men for her livelihood, and this involves, whether willingly or not on her part, an exchange of sex.

The rewriting of the character of Nelly in Le Quai des brumes involves two things: the transposition of the setting from Paris to the provincial port town of Le Havre, and Nelly from 19-year-old prostitute to 17-year-old orphan. The Nelly of the novel does not, however, disappear but is repressed in the Nelly of the film. What makes Nelly Parisienne is this repressed returning to haunt Carné's film. This manifests itself in Nelly's mysterious sexuality, which is in turn reinforced by Michèle Morgan's star persona. This rewriting, facilitated by the generic requirements of Poetic Realism, in fact obscures an essential aspect of Nelly's character, creating an ambiguity without which the narrative could not function. It is this ambiguity, rather than any single one of her actions, that proves fatal for Jean. The repression of Mac Orlan's prostitute creates a textual unconscious in which prostitution functions as an underlying subtext to innocence.

From 'La belle dame sans merci' to 'La belle Américaine': Patricia in À bout de souffle

Jean-Luc Godard's À bout de souffle has been described as a parody, homage and pastiche of film noir, and is filled with direct and obvious references to the genre. The plot is relatively simple, and appears to follow a standard B-grade formula. Michel Poiccard (Jean-Paul Belmondo) steals a car and during the ensuing chase shoots and kills a policeman. He returns to Paris and tries to persuade his American girlfriend Patricia (Jean Seberg) to run away with him to Rome. The police establish his identity, and after a series of misadventures and betrayals, Michel is finally cornered and killed. Patricia is among those who betray him, and Vincendeau describes her as a 'playful little girl who is also a dangerous *femme fatale*' (*Stars* 120).

Patricia's role in *À bout de souffle* is profoundly ambiguous. Steve Smith remarks:

> On the one hand, Michel constructs her as the typical noir mistress as a kind of challenge to his male power, in which she is indissolubly desirable and dangerous. On the other hand, just as the spectator is insistently invited to construct Michel as different from his 'own' self image, so Patricia's role in the film may similarly be read in two conflicting ways. At one obvious level, Patricia's role is consistent with that of the classical noir *femme fatale*. Indeed, Godard himself has acknowledged his debt to Otto Preminger's *Laura* (1946) and *Fallen Angel* (1947) [*sic*], in which, presumably he was referring to the female leads in these films. (69)

Patricia fills the noir model of the femme fatale on other interrelated levels. Like Laura (Gene Tierney) in Preminger's film of the same name, she narcissistically hangs an image of herself on the wall of her room. Likewise, Patricia's betrayal of Michel directly implicates her in his downfall, but unlike the intentional femme fatale of American noir she does not, initially at least, set out to destroy Michel. Ultimately, Patricia is ill-suited to the stereotypical role of femme fatale and a clue to this is provided by her economic status. In film noir, women are typically barred from the male world of money and power and the femme fatale sees in the male an opportunity to use her attractions to gain access to this world. By contrast, Patricia sees in Michel nothing more than an opportunity for diversion 'from a modern, youthful bourgeois lifestyle which promises her ... a secure career, financially at least independent of men, within these patriarchal structures' (S. Smith 71). This is partially true. Patricia stands to gain very little economically or socially from her association with Michel, but there is an inference in the film that Patricia does use her sexuality to get ahead in the world. When Michel suggests Patricia should have stayed with him instead of spending the night with journalist Van Doude, Patricia replies she had to see the journalist because he promised her articles to write.

Like *la Parisienne*, the femme fatale is an ambiguous figure; that is, in the successive modes of her appearance there is doubt as to the truth of her appearance. It is possible to read Patricia's betrayal of Michel in more than one way. First, as a simple act of self-interest: Patricia is not prepared to accept the risks of criminality, which, she realises, will compromise her privileged position within the social order. When questioned by the French police regarding her association with Michel she is warned of the trouble she could face by not cooperating with them. Her relationship to Michel, which for her was only a casual holiday romance, now threatens her stay in Paris. Secondly, denouncing Michel is an easy way to get rid of him; he is as disposable for Patricia as the American commodities flooding the postwar European marketplace. After she has what she wants from him, she literally throws him away. The final shot of the film, in which Patricia stares unashamedly at the camera, defying judgement, invites such a reading. Thirdly, Patricia's betrayal can be seen as the fulfilment of Michel's desire, the culmination of his cinema-fuelled fantasy to live out the narrative of a noir-gangster hero. He has the gestures, the cigarette, the hat and several flashy American cars; all he needs is a femme fatale, and he casts Patricia in this role. His persistence with her, despite his continual assessments of her lack of character, is testimony to this desire. Finally, following on from this last point, Patricia's denunciation can be read allegorically as the clash of two different world-views. Michel's simple, naïve and Romantic worldview, in which 'grassers grass, burglars burgle, murderers murder, and lovers love' is juxtaposed with the more complicated world of Patricia, in which 'lovers also grass'.

While Patricia is an incarnation of the femme fatale of film noir, she is also prefigured by *la Parisienne* in two main ways: she is cosmopolitan, an American temporarily residing in Paris; and she is both fashionable and self-fashioning. Like Michèle Morgan and Arletty, Jean Seberg brought her own style to the role of Patricia. Paula Reed remarks that it was Seberg's 'American preppy style passed through the filter of French chic, that ended up creating the stereotype of the French gamine ... . It was also in Paris that she got the famous pixie haircut for which she is most remembered' (1960s 10). As a fashionable Parisienne, Patricia's look symbolises her modernity and everything that is forward-looking and progressive. Her *garçonne* look marks her out as modern and connects her to the *garçonne* of post-First World War art, most notably the work of American expatriate painter Romaine Brooks. A portrait of the painter Gluck (Hannah Gluckstein) by Brooks depicts the subject in male attire. The title itself, *Peter, a Young English Girl*, draws attention to the gender ambiguity of the portrait (Elliott 20). Gluck's short, cropped Eton bob and predilection for men's clothing were frequently commented upon in the press of her day, and Gluck saw her project of dressing in men's attire as synonymous with that of the so-called Modern Girls (Doan 117–19). Following the release of Victor Marguerite's novel *La Garçonne* in 1922, young Frenchwomen were inspired to cut their hair short and dress *à l'allure garçonnière*. This new style was particularly 'associated with the young, sexy, independent *garçonne* or *femme moderne*' (M.L. Roberts 66). Commenting on Frenchwomen's penchant for short hair between the two world wars, Roberts remarks: 'Short hair exemplified the dramatic, provocative changes sweeping the world of French fashion. Notions of female beauty had undergone a profound transformation since the beginning of the century' (66). Similarly, Whitney Chadwick writes:

> The social upheaval caused by the war led to fundamental changes in gender roles in European society. Belle-époque conceptions of femininity and female sexuality gave way to the emerging figure of the modern woman. An ambiguous symbol of postwar modernity and the new social freedom women obtained, the modern woman had distinctly different sartorial strategies and bodily forms than her symbolist counterparts. Along with her masculine-tailored clothes and close-cropped hair, the modern woman often had a job and remained single. Brooks' artistic practice registered these changes. (85)

Real-life Parisiennes Brooks and Gluck are the direct ancestors not only of the Arletty of the late 1930s, but also Patricia's *garçonne* of the late 1950s and early 1960s.

Patricia is a modern woman: she has close-cropped hair, a job at the *New York Herald Tribune* and refuses to commit to Michel. In addition to her cropped hair, Patricia's adoption of the *marinière* or Breton stripes in the film contributes to her *garçonne* look and links her to Chanel's penchant for men's clothing. Before being appropriated by Chanel in 1917, the *marinière* was, according to Lynn Phillips, 'the French deckhand's badge of proletarian masculinity' (56). Patricia's hairstyle is especially distinct from the voluminous hairstyles of the femme fatale, both in American film noir and in the representations of the nineteenth-century *fille d'Eve*. Indeed, hair is one of the key motifs which established *la Parisienne* as femme fatale in the nineteenth century. Typically it is long and thick, and shown falling mane-like around the woman's face and shoulders. During the nineteenth century the 'femme fatale's hair was her most effective and lethal weapon' (Bade 13). Commenting on Dante Gabriel Rossetti's fatal women, Bade notes the 'abundance of their hair' (13). This is particularly the case in Rossetti's oil painting *Lady Lilith*. Rossetti painted a replica in watercolour of this work, to which he attached a quatrain from Goethe's *Faust*, translated by Shelley:

> Beware of her fair hair, for she excels
> All women in the magic of her locks,
> And when she twines them round a young man's neck
> She will not ever set him free again. (qtd in Allen 292)

Baudelaire, too, makes frequent reference to the abundant head of hair of the heroines of his poems. In 'La chevelure', the poet is intoxicated by the perfumed tresses which transport him to exotic locales.

Recently, Alain Bergala has drawn attention to the importance of women's hair in cinema and includes Godard among the 'great immortalisers of women's hair'. In 2010, Bergala curated an exhibition for the Cinémathèque française, 'Brune/Blonde', on women's hair in cinema. He writes:

> It was cinema that compiled and broadcast the central models with regard to women's hair. Film stars were the leading icons of the time in this respect. Under the control of the major studios, they imposed styles of femininity that often guided the fashion of entire generations: the short bob of the 1920s (Louise Brooks); the

platinum blonde of the 1930s (Jean Harlow); long wavy locks in the 1940s (Veronica Lake); the flowing tresses of Brigitte Bardot in the 1950s, the androgynous cut of Jean Seberg in the1960s. (*Brune, Blonde* n.p.)

Patricia offers a new image of *la Parisienne* and an updated or modern version of the femme fatale which can be linked to a tradition other than the American femme fatale, to the modern, chic Parisienne and to the unintentional femmes fatales of French cinema, specifically those of Poetic Realism. Patricia's modernity, announced through her clothing and style, is contrasted with Michel's more traditional values or world-view, particularly emphasised through his insistence on the romantic conflation of sex with love, something Patricia does not share. Even though Michel models himself on Bogart and tries to align himself with the typically American hardboiled hero, he is actually much closer to the sentimental and romantic doomed hero of Poetic Realism embodied by Jean Gabin. Michel Marie likens Michel to Gabin in both *Le Quai des brumes* and *Le Jour se lève* (106). Andrew remarks that Gabin is 'the model Bogart would bring to life in America during the war passing down his reticence to Dana Andrews, Fred MacMurray, and the catatonic Richard Widmark. This is the tradition that comes back to France in *Breathless*' (*Mists* 15–16). Indeed the closing scenes of *À bout de souffle* are strikingly reminiscent of the ending of *Le Jour se lève*: both men spend their final hours chain-smoking and playing with their girlfriends' teddy bears. Likewise, Michel's ultimate fate mirrors that of Gabin's Jean in *Le Quai des brumes*: both are shot in the back in a crowded street. What Michel shares with the Gabin heroes of Poetic Realism is a very old-fashioned or anti-modern idea of love and a fundamental misrecognition of these women who are modern women and cut from a different cloth. This is in contrast to the hardboiled noir hero, typically played by Humphrey Bogart, who will come to dominate American noir and who, by reasoning his way out of sentimental notions such as love and fidelity, ups the ante on the femme fatale. In the final scene of *The Maltese Falcon*, for example, Bogart's Sam Spade coldly explains to Mary Astor's Brigid O'Shaughnessy: 'I won't play the sap for you; this time you're taking the fall.'

In Poetic Realism and in *À bout de souffle*, however, it is the Parisienne and not the hero who walks away unscathed. Carné's films form a subtext for *À bout de soufflé*, which also links Patricia to a different cultural tradition than American noir. Like the femme fatales of Poetic Realism, Patricia's dress and androgynous appearance symbolise a narcissistic attraction for the hero: she is both a love object for Michel as much as she is a mirror image of himself. This is depicted literally when the two exchange items of clothing: Patricia wears Michel's shirt and hat, Michel wears Patricia's bathrobe. It is Michel's overinvestment in Patricia – exacerbated by the ambiguity and mystery reflected in the modernity of her outlook and dress – and not any real action on her part that leads to Michel's death. Even her eventual denunciation of Michel to the police is less out of any attempt to dispose of Michel than to force him to leave Paris. Michel's fate is less the result of Patricia's actions than that of a destiny lived out through cinema, and the self-referential treatment of noir narratives in Godard's film.

The femme fatale is associated, somewhat narrowly, with Hollywood noir of the 1940s and 1950s. By drawing the figure of *la Parisienne* into the context of French film noir, different readings of the femme fatale become possible. The focus of this chapter has been on the Parisienne type as femme fatale in French film noir, tracing its development from the popular nineteenth-century trope of the association of woman with the city and death through the development of a particular type of femme fatale in Poetic Realism and the French heist film, to a self-reflexive treatment of the type, including her 'Americanisation', in New Wave cinema. Each of the films discussed in this chapter demonstrate both an aesthetic and narrative overdetermination of the femme fatale by the figure of *la Parisienne*, particularly through iconographical motifs associated with the type, like fashion, ambiguity, sexuality and danger. Unlike the femmes fatales of classic or American film noir, however, the danger *la Parisienne* poses is unintentional and only indirectly leads to the hero's demise.

One of the features of the Parisienne femmes fatales in the films discussed here is danger communicated primarily through ambiguity of dress and appearance. This underscores the importance of clothing and hairstyles in the symbolic economy of cinema. Secondly, these fatal Parisiennes all share another common motif: they are, in one way or another, kept women or courtesans. Nelly in *Le Quai des brumes* is kept by Zabel, Françoise in *Le Jour se lève* is kept by Valentin, and Mado in *Du Rififi chez les hommes* is the property first of Tony and then Grutter. This is less obvious perhaps in the character of Patricia in *À bout de souffle*, although her much-prized independence is ambiguously maintained through a suggestive sexual association with Van Doude. These two motifs – dress/appearance and prostitution – will be taken up further in the next chapter in relation to another Parisienne type, the courtesan. Parisienne courtesans, like the femmes fatales of French film noir, are often unintentionally fatal to the men with whom they associate, however this fatality – not always literal – is usually worked out within a *ménage à trois* narrative structure in which the courtesan is forced to choose between love and luxury.

Note

1 The notion of the eternal feminine was used by de Beauvoir to demonstrate the way patriarchy reduces woman to her sex, regardless of the apparent multiple representations. As Deborah B. Bergoffen has pointed out: 'Whether she is figured as the erotic, birthing, or nurturing body, woman is imaged as the sex and wrapped in a mythical body. Embodied as the eternal feminine, woman is barred from the domain of the subject' (144). While *la Parisienne* has certainly been defined as a myth, part of her mythology is precisely the resistance to the patriarchal objectification intended by de Beauvoir's use of the term 'eternal feminine'.

5
Courtesan

Paris at night. Marie arrives at a chic restaurant on the arm of a rich suitor, an ornament of, and testament to, his wealth. At an elegant soirée, Lucile's expensive earrings attract the compliments of other guests; explaining they are a gift from her older benefactor, she incites the jealousy of her young lover. On the terrace adjoining her dressing room, Satine, the Sparkling Diamond, explains through song to a lovestruck penniless poet: 'the only way of loving me, baby, is to pay a lovely fee'.

Parisiennes Marie, Lucile and Satine are all cinematic incarnations of the courtesan. In Charles Chaplin's *A Woman of Paris* (1923), Marie St Clair (Edna Purviance) leaves her unnamed provincial town to reinvent herself in Paris and becomes the kept woman of wealthy man-about-town Pierre Revel (Adolphe Menjou). He sets her up in a plush apartment with domestic staff, provides her with expensive clothing and jewellery, and gives her access to the glamorous world of Parisian high society. In Alain Cavalier's *La Chamade* (1968), based on Françoise Sagan's novel of the same name, Lucile (Cathérine Deneuve), a hedonistic young woman, is kept by the generosity of the older affluent bachelor, Charles (Michel Piccoli). She falls for a poor, young editor Antoine (Roger Van Hool), and finds herself torn between two worlds, luxury and leisure with Charles, or waged labour and relative poverty with Antoine. Baz Luhrmann's *Moulin Rouge!* (2001) recounts the love affair between Belle Époque courtesan Satine (Nicole Kidman) and bohemian writer Christian (Ewan McGregor). Satine's ambition threatens her happiness with Christian when she solicits the attentions of a wealthy duke (Richard Roxburgh) in order to finance the production that will 'make her a star'. Each of the aforementioned films draws on the iconography of *la Parisienne* as courtesan, highlighting the association of the Parisienne type with prostitution and consumption.

La Parisienne is frequently associated with prostitution, whether in the narrow, literal sense of the purveyor of sex, or in the more general sense of the 'seller and sold in one' (Benjamin, *Arcades* 10), both the object and subject of consumption. Taking together Benjamin's idea of ambiguity and Georg Simmel's idea of the 'purely momentary' nature of a monetary exchange of prostitution, Hollis Clayson argues that the nineteenth-century prostitute 'is the living embodiment of the cold cash nexus but is ambiguous, evanescent and transient as well' (8). Russell Campbell notes that cinema adds another layer of ambiguity to the prostitute: 'If in life it is sometimes difficult to define just what constitutes a "prostitute", it is even more so in the cinema, which often thrives on a tantalizing ambiguity' (6). In order to limit the scope of his study, however, Campbell focuses only on characters who implicitly engage in 'cash transactions for sexual services with multiple clients' (7), a definition which does not include the courtesan. However courtesanship is a form of prostitution most usually associated with the Parisiennes of the nineteenth century, and the courtesan too possesses an ambiguity revealed not only through the material or monetary nature of the exchange she makes with men, but also because this exchange is, unlike that of prostitution, veiled by appearances. There are examples of the Parisienne type as prostitute in cinema, such as the streetwalker (for example, Billy Wilder's 1963 *Irma la Douce* and Jean-Luc Godard's 1962 *Vivre sa vie*), the gigolette (for example, Jacques Becker's 1952 *Casque d'or*, Laure Charpentier's 2010 *Gigola* and Marcel Carné's 1938 *Hôtel du nord*), or the inhabitant of a brothel or *maison close* (for example, Luis Buñuel's 1967 *Belle de jour* and Max Ophüls's 1952 *Le Plaisir*). However in this chapter the focus will be on the courtesan as the form of prostitution most usually associated with the figure of *la Parisienne*.

Both Paris and *la Parisienne* carry connotations of desire, pleasure and prostitution. Abigail Solomon-Godeau suggests that *la Parisienne* can be seen as a symbol for Paris in the nineteenth century, a city 'constructed through capitalism as the capital of desire' (142). The association of Paris with a 'sexually available woman' can be found in the female figures that characterise the city, the prostitute and the courtesan, which 'draw attention to the representation of Parisian women as sexually promiscuous' (Rocamora 114). Rocamora acknowledges the influence of cinema on contemporary print culture, and by extension, on the representation of Paris in the modern day fashion press: 'Buñuel's famous Parisian *Belle de Jour*, in which Deneuve plays a prostitute, certainly contributed to the production of the Parisian woman as a figure of sexual consumption' (115). In her study of present-day representations of *la Parisienne* in *Vogue Paris*, Rocamora argues that Paris is depicted as a feminine city and a city of pleasure, and cites the August 2006 issue dedicated to *la Parisienne* which makes particular reference to the Parisian prostitute in a fashion spread entitled 'Nocturne Parisien' (116). Here the Parisian prostitute is linked to pleasure, desire and nocturnal Paris. Commenting on Zola's *Nana*, Rita Felski argues that not only does the eponymous courtesan blossom in the consumer society of Belle Époque Paris but she is 'at the heart of the cash nexus, her social and sexual identity shaped by fashion, image, and advertising, her perverse erotic desires linked to modern urban decadence' (75).

The prostitute was a ubiquitous figure in the art, literature and mass culture of nineteenth-century Paris and often functioned as a symbol of the French capital. Art and literature during the Second Empire (1851–70) featured the prostitute and the adulteress as the main subjects of modern life. In particular, the Second Empire was associated with the 'glittering courtesan' who imitated the fashions and comportment of the haute bourgeoisie and the imperial court (Clayson 2). The representation of the prostitute during this period focused on the courtesan for two main reasons: the greatly visible presence of 'real' courtesans and the Haussmanisation of Paris which 'produced social fears explicitly tied to a discomfort with the blurring of social boundaries in Paris – a state of affairs that artists and moralists alike often found embodied by the courtesan' (Clayson 2).

The exceedingly well-paid courtesan, belonging to the demimonde, constituted the 'pinnacle of a continuum of women who traded their bodies and their company for financial reward in mid-nineteenth century France' (Rounding 9). The hierarchy of prostitution was decided not only by the price a woman commanded, but also by the level of choice she exercised with regard to her clients. Prostitutes at the lowest end of the scale 'had to take whatever was on offer', whereas those at the other end of the scale, 'the élite of the *demi-monde*, the renowned courtesan, had an almost infinite number of aspirants to pick from' (Rounding 17–18). The luxury to choose is one defining feature distinguishing the courtesan from other lower forms of prostitution. This raises the question of how a courtesan or demi-mondaine can be defined. Joanna Richardson provides the following definition of the archetypical courtesan:

> A courtesan is less than a mistress, and more than a prostitute. She is less than a mistress because she sells her love for material benefits; she is more than a prostitute because she chooses her lovers .... She may have been a respectable woman, cast by some unhappy affair into the demi-monde; she may be a woman of humble birth, whose only hope of fortune seemed to be her physical attraction. She may be an actress who willingly abandoned her inadequate hopes in the theatre; she may simply be a careerist, set on a life of adventure. (1)

Richardson also highlights the role of choice, and offers possible reasons as to how a woman becomes a courtesan. In *A Woman of Paris*, Marie St Clair is a woman of humble origins who comes to Paris following the breakdown of the relationship with her fiancé, Jean. A fallen woman, Marie finds her place in the demimonde and is depicted enjoying the material benefits such a life affords. *La Chamade* does not explain how Lucile became a kept woman, and Sagan's novel only reveals that she lived a meagre existence 'à vingt ans et elle n'amait pas l'idée de ne pouvoir recommencer à trente' (190), 'at twenty, and she did not care for the idea of beginning again at thirty' (Murray 120). Cavalier's film does, however, provide two incidental references to Lucile's background: in the first, Lucile expresses a wish to book the same hotel room her mother booked when she came to Paris, a reference to Lucile's potentially provincial origins; and in the second, Lucile thanks Charles for continuing to send her mother money, hinting at her humble or working-class upbringing. Like Marie, Lucile also takes pleasure in material wealth and the idleness the courtesan's lifestyle provides. In Lurhmann's film, Satine finds herself in the demimonde after deciding to become an actress. Rather than abandon her ambition, however, she uses her position as a courtesan to finance a theatre venture which promises to make her a star, like her idol Sarah Bernhardt. Unlike Lucile and Marie, for whom courtesanship and its material benefits is an end in itself, Satine sees it purely as a means to achieving her ambition. This does not, however, mean Satine would willingly embrace a penniless bohemian existence: after telling Christian she 'can't fall in love with anyone', the stupefied poet responds: 'Can't fall in love but a life without love, that's terrible.' To this Satine retorts: 'No, being on the street, that's terrible.'

Central to the notion of the courtesan is the idea of selling one's body for material benefits, which implies not the prostituting of oneself for mere survival or subsistence, but rather the active choice to prostitute oneself in order to gain access to the world of luxury and material goods. The Second Empire was the golden age of the courtesan:

> There have, of course, been *grandes cocottes* since 1870, but the fall of the Second Empire ended the empire of the courtesan. She was a brilliant, exotic bird that flourished in the days of a permissive Imperial Court, of widespread social license and political irresponsibility. There could be no such careless *joie de vivre* after 1870. The courtesan could not thrive so well in the new Republican world. (3)

Richardson's book follows the lives and careers of twelve of the Second Empire's most famous courtesans, a group often known as *la Garde*. Richardson remarks how not all of these courtesans were 'French by birth, but all were French in spirit, and all of them were, at some time, established in Paris' (3).

Rounding traces the origin of the terms 'demimonde' and 'demimondaine' and the latter's initial distinction from the term courtesan. Rounding's study covers a smaller but more detailed field than Richardson's book; however, while she limits herself to the 'lives and legends' of only four of *la Garde* – Marie Duplessis, Cora Pearl, La Païva (Thérèse Lachmann) and La Présidente (Apollonie Sabatier) – *Grandes Horizontales* focuses not only on the real lives of these women but also on the very process of 'myth-making' itself (5). Rounding remarks that the four courtesans chosen for her study 'were subject more than most to the image-making of others, and of themselves' (5). Not only were these women represented and imagined in the writings and art of others, but they themselves took an active part in creating their own persona, image or myth. Thus they demonstrated the penchant for self-fashioning which forms part of the iconography of the Parisienne type.

Rounding defines the demimonde in nineteenth-century Paris as a half-world which exists between the upper echelons of respectable society and the common life of the lowly prostitute. The term demimonde is, according to Rounding, 'suggestive of twilight, of a world of shifting appearances and shadow, where nothing is quite what it seems, a world between worlds' (1). The term demimondaine initially gained widespread currency with the first performance of Alexandre Dumas *fils*'s play, *La demi-mondaine*, in March 1855. The term, however, soon found wider usage as a synonym for courtesan, in spite of Dumas *fils*'s insistence that the demimondaine 'does not accept money for her favours ...and she is thus distinguished from the courtesan, for whom love is a financial transaction' (Rounding 2). One of the features of the demimondaine identified by Rounding is her ambiguous appearance; that is, it is often difficult to distinguish a woman belonging to the *haute monde* from a demimondaine. Here Rounding cites a remark of Maxime du Camp, who declared that 'one does not know today whether honest women are dressing like prostitutes, or prostitutes are dressed like honest women' (2). This remark recalls an episode from Dumas *fils*'s *La Dame aux camélias* in which Armand Duval recounts the following tale:

> Il y a dans un livre d'Alphonse Karr, intitulé: *Am Rauchen*, un homme qui suit, le soir, une femme très élégante, et dont, à la première vue, il est devenu amoureux, tant elle est belle. Pour baiser la main de cette femme, il se sent la force de tout entreprendre, la volonté de tout conquérir, le courage de tout faire. À peine s'il ose regarder le bas de jambe coquet qu'elle dévoile pour ne pas souiller sa robe au contact de la terre. Pendant qu'il rêve à tout ce qu'il ferait pour posséder cette femme, elle l'arrête au coin d'une rue et lui demande s'il veut monter chez elle. (82)

In a book by Alphonse Karr called *Smoking*, a man follows an elegant woman one night and falls in love with her at first sight because she is so beautiful. Overcome by his desire to kiss the woman's hand, he feels in himself the strength to undertake everything, the will to conquer all, the courage to do anything. He hardly dares look at the coquettish glimpse of leg she reveals as she raises her skirt to keep the earth from besmirching her dress. As he dreams of everything he will do to win this woman, she stops on a street corner and asks him if he wants to come up to her place. (Schillinger 45)

Films featuring *la Parisienne* as courtesan often employ the narrative trope of the *ménage à trois*, consisting of the Parisienne, the wealthy suitor and the poor, romantic lover/artist. The sensitive and sincere artist generally possesses true feelings for the Parisienne but owing to his poverty cannot hope to compete for her affections with the wealthy bachelor. Indeed, as Dumas *fils* writes in *La Dame aux camélias*, 'être réellement aimé d'une courtisane, c'est une victoire bien autrement difficile' (141), 'to be truly loved by a courtesan, that is a much harder-won victory' (Schillinger 88). In *A Woman of Paris*, Marie is caught between the poor painter Jean Millet and rich bachelor Pierre Revel. In *La Chamade*, Lucile must choose between Antoine, an editor at a small publishing house and the rich, older businessman Charles. In *Moulin Rouge!* Satine finds herself the object of desire for both the wealthy Duke of Monroth and the penniless poet Christian. In each of these cases the presence of a poor lover introduces a complication for the courtesan – and, by extension, the narrative – into the otherwise clear-cut notion of love as a financial transaction.

Adorned and ornamented: Marie in *A Woman of Paris*

Dressed in a sleek, floor-length black evening gown, with a deep V-neck and dropped waistline, and embellished with a circular pearl motif, Marie enters an exclusive Parisian restaurant alongside her wealthy suitor, Pierre Revel. While her fashionable 1920s silhouette evokes the film's contemporary setting, the composition of the shot and the symbolism of Marie as ornament to Pierre Revel's wealth recall nineteenth-century Paris and the figure of the glittering Parisienne courtesan. Indeed, Chaplin's silent film draws on the iconography of the Parisienne courtesan in its construction of Marie, in particular the notions of transformation and fashionability or style.

Iconographic typology is an important part of the economy of silent cinema because it does away with the need for complex explanations or reiteration. Jacqueline Nacache remarks that in *A Woman of Paris*:

> La principale contrainte, d'ordre stylistique, venait de Chaplin lui-même, qui s'était donné pour but d'obtenir un ton nouveau, fondé sur un style de jeu à la fois expressif et sobre, une grande économie de moyens, au moins au sens figuré du terme. (197)
>
> (The principal stylistic constraint came from Chaplin himself, who set himself the task of achieving a new tone, founded on a style of acting both expressive and sober, a great economy of means, at least in the figurative sense of the term.)

Nacache gives the example of the use of light passing over the face and body of Marie standing in for an absent train as the canonical example of a rhetoric of economy in silent cinema (197). A further, and perhaps more central, example of economy in Chaplin's film is the use of the Parisienne, who, according to Tamar Garb, is 'so suggestive a spur to narrative and so much the product of narrative structures that her figure alone could function as a distilled story' (*Bodies* 83). Garb goes on to argue that 'one only had to say the word "Parisienne" to invoke a series of well-rehearsed narrative associations, expectations and assumptions' (*Bodies* 83). In the silent medium there can be no such utterance, and indeed the word Parisienne appears nowhere in the titles of *A Woman of Paris*. We rely, rather, entirely on visual and narrative iconography to realise the story distilled in Chaplin's film.

The key moment in Chaplin's film in which the economy of the type comes into play is during a transition between two scenes. In the first scene, we see Marie, a humbly and somewhat drably dressed woman, standing alone on the platform of a provincial train station. In the shot immediately following we are given a title which reads: 'A year later in the magic city of Paris, where fortune is fickle and a woman gambles with life –'. In the sequence following this title, Marie appears, or rather is presented, at a chic upmarket restaurant in Paris, on the arm of Pierre Revel, who is described as 'a gentleman of leisure whose whims have made and ruined many a woman's career'. What occurs here is the cinematic equivalent of an ellipsis in which a whole history of processes and assumptions are subsumed, processes and assumptions that can only be realised by way of the iconography of *la Parisienne*. One of these processes is transformation, an established narrative trope of the Parisienne type. Primarily, this transformation takes place in Paris. Uzanne remarks: 'Paris crée moins la Parisienne qu'il ne la perfectionne' (18) (Paris perfects rather than creates *la Parisienne*). In films featuring *la Parisienne*, costume is one of the main ways of signifying transformation or change.

Costume also works in Chaplin's film to emphasise the connection between Marie and the nineteenth-century courtesan who was renowned for her style and fashionability. Valerie Steele writes that during the Second Empire 'the famous *grandes horizontales* were as notorious for their sartorial splendour as for their amatory abilities' (*Paris Fashion* 159). In his confessions, *Man about Paris*, Arsène Houssaye juxtaposes the ladies of society and the demimondaines as they appeared at the races and charity balls: 'At first glance they were the same women dressed by the same dressmakers, with the only distinction that the *demi-mondaines* seemed a little more *chic*' (qtd in Steele, *Paris Fashion* 170). Emmanuelle Rétaillaud-Bajac remarks that 'la courtisane joue un rôle décisif dans la propagation des modes, vouée qu'elle est, par sa fonction, à faire valoir l'argent de ses riches protecteurs et à magnifier le vêtement par sa plastique et son "chien"' (17) (the courtesan plays a decisive role in the propagation of fashions, devoted as she is, by her function, to highlighting the wealth of her rich protectors and to magnify the clothing by her physique and her 'sexiness'). Clayson argues that the interconnected relationship between prostitution and fashionability 'lay at the heart of the history and myth of the later nineteenth-century courtesan, because once having secured a means of support, her life was consecrated to the display of her fashionable possessions and idleness' (60–1).

In contrast to the simple, drab and utilitarian ensemble she wore in the provinces, once in Paris Marie wears elegant evening dresses in luxurious fabrics, adorned with beads and pearls, and evening coats trimmed with fur. These outfits are accessorised with strings of pearls and elaborate headpieces featuring a froth of feathers. Her gowns and dresses hang loosely and do not follow the contours of the body, conforming to the typical 1920s silhouette. Marie also wears her hair in the fashionable 1920s-style shingled bob. At home in her apartment, Marie lounges in a fashionable peignoir and wears a satin bandeau headdress when receiving guests. In Second Empire Paris, the peignoir was a wardrobe staple for the chic Parisienne. Simon remarks: 'In the first hours of her day, a woman put on a luxurious peignoir – or housecoat – embellished with bows, lace and crimped flounces. This indoor robe grew more and more sumptuous until it became a truly elegant form of attire in which to receive visits from intimate friends' (22). To depict Marie in her peignoir also conforms to the iconography of *la Parisienne* in late nineteenth-century art and including 'peignoir-clad figures became de rigueur in modern-life scenes' (De Young, 'Fashion'120). Many painters, including Stevens, Renoir and Manet, depicted women in their peignoirs. In modern depictions of women, in both painting and literature, the peignoir signified not only leisure but sexual availability: 'Contemporary French literature is filled with references to peignoirs, inevitably in the context of undressing, a recent bath, preparing for the day, rising from bed or going to bed, and, above all, availability for sex' (Tinterow 30).

Marie's sartorial style and interest in fashion is further depicted in a scene which shows her contemplating the various outfits she might wear for the portrait she commissions Jean Millet to paint. Marie is concerned with projecting a chic appearance and wants to control and fashion her own image. She is disappointed when she realises Jean has painted her in the plain and understated suit of her provincial days rather than in the glamorous, floor-length gown accessorised with a spectacular headdress of white feathers she had chosen. Indeed, Chaplin's film highlights Marie's conspicuous consumption of luxury goods, particularly fashionable clothing and fine dining. At the same time this consumption becomes itself something consumed, not only by the gaze of other characters but also by that of the audience. *La Parisienne* participates in the spectacle of modern life both as a consumer and as an object for consumption and is 'characteristically represented either adorning herself for public appreciation, posing for public acclamation of her physical charms, or selling something, the slippage between the merchandise on sale and the woman herself being easy to make' (Garb, *Bodies* 84).

The composition of the shot in which Marie arrives at the restaurant is suggestive of a performance and the very entrance to the restaurant resembles an empty stage ready to receive the arriving guests. The fashionable and expensive restaurants of Paris, along with the theatre, the racetrack, and the Bois de Boulogne, functioned as a setting for both a fashion parade and subsequent ostentatious display of wealth. Here, one came not only to dine, but more importantly to see and be seen. The composition of this shot also recalls a shot from Vincente Minnelli's *Gigi* (1958) in which Gigi (Leslie Caron) makes her debut at Maxim's on the arm of the wealthy sugar magnate and playboy Gaston Lachaille (Louis Jourdan). Gaston, like Pierre Revel, is dressed in a simple and formal egalitarian black tuxedo, using Gigi, in her opulent, floor-length, white satin gown embellished with two vibrant exotic turquoise birds and long white satin opera gloves, as the primary indicator of his wealth. In an earlier scene at Maxim's, Honoré Lachaille (Maurice Chevalier) ironically remarks: 'What a marvellous place Maxim's is! Not only gay and beautiful, but in one thing unique: in Maxim's everybody minds his own business. No one is the slightest bit interested in whom one is with.'

Marie's entrance at the restaurant also calls to mind James Tissot's painting *L'Ambitieuse* which belongs to a series of paintings known as *La Femme à Paris*. Comprising 15 large canvases, Tissot's *La Femme à Paris* was first exhibited in Paris in 1885 and then in London the following year under the title *Pictures of Parisian Life*. *L'Ambitieuse* is set during a grand soirée and the young Parisienne occupies the central space of the canvas. The excessive frills and flounces of her rose-coloured dress, along with her matching ostrich-feather fan, dominate the space. She is framed on the right by her escort for the evening, a diplomat dressed in black whose face is obscured by her large chignon and feathered headpiece. On the left she is framed by a sea of people, many of whom turn to gaze at her. In contrast with the austerity of her escort's attire, the young kept woman 'represents the glamour and superficial excesses that money and modernity could buy' (Garb, 'Painting' 95). Uzanne remarks that men of the world keep a woman 'comme ils entretiennent un yacht, une écurie ou un domaine de chasse, tout ce qui peut concourir au bon renom de leur fortune' (441), 'as they keep a yacht, a stud, or a sporting estate, everything that can augment the reputation of their fortune' (214). They therefore do not require love or even sensual pleasure from the courtesan but rather simply 'la consécration de leur renom de viveurs' (Uzanne 442), 'the consecration of their celebrity as *viveurs*' (214). While a courtesan could choose her suitor(s), the choice was often based on disposable income rather than personal attributes. However, the more money she received the more her expenses would increase, in addition to which she was expected to spend and not save her money (Rounding 18). Once a woman had embraced the lifestyle of a demimondaine and become accustomed to a high income, it was generally difficult to abandon, not unlike the common streetwalker who found herself ensnared in a life of poverty and prostitution. Moreover, hardly any courtesans managed to arrange sufficient provision for middle age, let alone old age (Rounding 18).

The scene at the restaurant in Chaplin's film introduces the figure of the courtesan and her wealthy protector, but it also contains a reference to another type which clusters around representations of the Parisienne as courtesan: the demimondaine past her prime. In *A Woman of Paris* this type is described as 'one of the richest old maids in Paris'. Seated at a table with a young gigolo, the aged courtesan is a parody of her former self, with her wrinkled face elaborately made-up and her flabby, corpulent body squeezed into a revealing sequined gown. The aging demimondaine is found in French literature and best described by Colette in her novel *Chéri*:

> Peut-être soixante-dix ans, un embonpoint d'eunuque corseté, – on avait coutume de dire de la vieille Lili qu' 'elle passait les bornes' sans préciser de quelles bornes il s'agissait. Une éternelle gaîté enfantine éclairait son visage, rond, rose, fardé, où les gros yeux et la très petite bouche, fine et rentrée, coquetaient sans honte. La vieille Lili suivait la mode, scandaleusement. Une jupe à raies, bleu révolution et blanc, contenait le bas de son corps, un petit spencer bleu béait sur un poitrail nu, à peau gaufrée de dindon coriace; un renard argenté ne cachait pas le cou nu, en pot de fleurs, un cou large comme un ventre et qui avait aspiré le menton. (89)

Perhaps seventy years of age, with the corpulence of a eunuch held in by stays, old Lili was usually referred to as 'passing all bounds', without these 'bounds' being defined. Her round pink painted face was enlivened by a ceaseless girlish gaiety, and her large eyes and small mouth, thin-lipped and shrunken, flirted shamelessly. Old Lili followed the fashion to an outrageous degree. A striking blue-and-white striped skirt held in the lower part of her body, and a little blue jersey gaped over her skinny bosom crinkled like the wattles of a turkey-cock; a silver fox failed to conceal the neck, which was the shape of a flower-pot and the size of a belly. It had engulfed the chin. (Senhouse 42)

The demimondaine past her prime is also found in Zola's *Nana* in the character of Gaga, 'une grosse femme, sanglée dans son corset, une ancienne blonde devenue blanche et teinte en jaune, dont la figure ronde, rougie par le fard, se boursouflait sous une pluie de petits frissons enfantins' (11), 'a stout, tight-laced woman whose once fair hair had turned white and been dyed yellow, and whose round face, heavily rouged, looked puffy under a rain of little childish curls' (Holden 28). In Chaplin's film the aging demimondaine represents what Dumas *fils* called the 'première mort' (24) of the courtesan, old age, and serves as a cautionary tale for Marie. The film does not conclude with Marie's fate left thus in the balance. Rather, she is redeemed, 'transformed by the purifying love of an honest man' (Richardson 196), a popular theme in literature and theatre dealing with the subject of courtesans. Like Marguerite Gautier in Dumas *fils*'s novel, Marie too is a courtesan capable of love. Realising her part in the suicide of the young painter, Jean, Marie seeks redemption by forsaking her life as a courtesan and returning to the provinces to open an orphanage with Jean's mother. The scene of the orphanage opens with the title: 'Time heals, and experience teaches that the secret of happiness is in service to others', a notion juxtaposed with the self-serving life of the Parisienne courtesan.

The conclusion of Chaplin's film, along with the cautionary figure of the demimondaine past her prime, paint *A Woman of Paris* as a moral tale. The narrative loops around to return Marie to the provinces a chastened, but now ultimately happy, woman. This is in stark contrast both to the character of Lucile and the narrative trajectory in *La Chamade*. While both films depict the life of luxury and material wealth enjoyed by the courtesan, in *La Chamade* this enjoyment in not complicated by any moral position or ideology. Further, the narrative of *La Chamade* proceeds in the opposite direction to that of *A Woman of Paris*: Lucile is depicted moving from luxury to poverty before finally choosing luxury again.

The pleasure of living: Lucile in *La Chamade*

A quiet Paris boulevard in the grey dawn light; grand Haussmann buildings line one side of the street and a row of lamp-posts the other. Cut to a shot of a wide boulevard leading to the Place de la Concorde, the Madeleine and Obelisk prominent in the centre of the screen. The buildings which line the street on the right hand of the screen take on the golden hue of the morning sun. The sky lightens and Paris begins to wake. Cut to a tree-lined residential street, the sky now pale blue; the camera pans slowly to the right to reveal a sandstone mansion with large curtained windows framed by gently moving leaves. Cut again to an interior shot, a close-up of a gossamer curtain lightly billowing in the breeze, before the camera pans slowly right to settle on a close-up of Lucile, her head resting on a soft white pillow, her face the picture of serenity. Cut to a long shot of Lucile, alone in a large bed in a high-ceilinged, tastefully decorated room. She slowly rises, walks languidly over to the open window and inhales with almost sensual pleasure the first hint of spring air. The slow pace of her elegant movements, accompanied by the dreamy score, suggests she is a lady of leisure. Dressed in a flowing white negligee, she gracefully walks into the adjoining bathroom. In the mirror, she contemplates her reflection before applying a light mist of floral water to her face and perfectly coiffed blonde hair.

The opening credit sequence of *La Chamade* establishes a languorous pace and emphasises the pleasure of simply existing, a pleasure that is afforded to a kept woman who has ample time to enjoy life. The grandeur of the *mise en scène* suggests opulence, luxury, pleasure and wealth. The sequence mirrors the opening passage of Sagan's novel on which the film is based:

> Elle ouvrit les yeux. Un vent brusque, décidé s'était introduit dans la chambre. Il transformait le rideau en voile, faisait se pencher les fleurs dans leur grand vase, à terre, et s'attaquait à présent à son sommeil. C'était un vent de printemps, le premier: il sentait les bois, les forêts, la terre, il avait traversé impunément les faubourgs de Paris, les rues gavées d'essence et il arrivait léger, fanfaron, à l'aube, dans sa chambre pour lui signaler, avant même qu'elle ne reprît conscience, le plaisir de vivre. (13)

> She opened her eyes. A bluff, determined wind had entered the room, billowing the curtain into a sail, bending the flowers in a large vase on the floor, and now attacking her sleep. It was a spring wind, the first: it smelt of earth, woods, forests, and having swept unscathed over the suburbs of Paris and the streets reeking of gas fumes it arrived, brisk and swaggering, in her room, at dawn, to point out, even before she was awake, the pleasure of living. (Murray 11)

The opening paragraph of Sagan's novel depicts the pleasure of living, of the utmost importance to Lucile and afforded her by Charles. Lucile tries, ultimately unsuccessfully, to maintain this pleasure of living when she abandons her life with Charles to embark on a relationship with the younger and significantly poorer Antoine. After deciding to live with Antoine and, at his instigation taking a job to occupy herself, Lucile finds herself at an overcrowded bus shelter in the rain. Her exasperation with her new situation is expressed thus in Sagan's novel:

> Lucile attendait l'autobus place de l'Alma et s'énervait. Le mois de novembre était spécialement froid, spécialement pluvieux et la petite guérite devant la station était bondée de gens frileux, maussades, presque agressifs … . Le seul charme réel de l'argent, pensait-elle, c'était qu'il vous permettait d'éviter cela: l'attente, l'énervement, les autres. (189)

> Lucile impatiently awaited the bus at the Place de l'Alma. It was a particularly cold and rainy November, and the little bus shelter was crowded with shivering, sullen, almost aggressive people …. The only real charm of money, she thought, was that it permitted one to avoid all this: the exasperation, the other people. (Murray 119)

Lucile returns to Charles, and her choice to be a kept woman is ultimately tied up with her idea of what constitutes the pleasure of living. What Charles's money affords Lucile above all is leisure time and solitude. Lucile's philosophy of life is given voice in Harry's monologue from William Faulkner's *Wild Palms* (1939), which she reads aloud in a bar after having walked out on her job. The lengthy monologue, which espouses the virtues of idleness, ends with the line: '[N]othing is better, nothing to match, nothing else in all this world but to live for the short time you are loaned breath, to be alive and know it' (113).

The opening credit sequence of *La Chamade* also highlights three important motifs: the city of Paris, pleasure, and Lucile/Deneuve's hair and face. The setting is significant as it places Lucile within the tradition of the Second Empire and Belle Époque courtesan living in Paris, the city of pleasure: 'One of the myths of the *belle époque* that was not wholly untrue was that Paris was now the world capital of pleasure' (Hussey 296). Lucile/Deneuve's hair plays a significant role in establishing her character, and in connecting it to the greater themes of affluence and idleness. Her well-groomed hair connotes a sophisticated elegance associated with *la Parisienne* but also identifies Lucile with the star image of Cathérine Deneuve. Ginette Vincendeau makes a direct comparison between Deneuve's hair and her physical gestures which are both 'graceful and controlled', while her blondeness connotes 'sophisticated affluence' and her hairstyle signifies 'the well-groomed woman' (*Stars* 200). Deneuve's hair both frames and illuminates her face, accentuating what Guy Austin describes as its mask-like quality (40). This quality contributes to the elusiveness and ambiguity of the characters Deneuve incarnates but also lends itself particularly to the roles of kept woman and prostitute.

As a modern-day version of the nineteenth-century courtesan, Lucile continues the association of the kept woman with fashionability, style and elegance through her hair and make-up, and her wardrobe by Yves Saint Laurent. Lucile wears chic ensembles in a classic neutral colour palette throughout the film: her everyday look consists of neat mid-length A-line skirts, turtleneck sweaters, paisley-print collared shirts, trench coats, double-breasted coat dresses, and low-heeled court shoes. For evening events, Lucile wears eye-catching, seductive couture dresses, including a long-sleeved, candy-pink, floor-length gown featuring sequinned details; a red, white and navy geometric-patterned, long-sleeved, knee-length dress featuring a pussy-bow tie neckline; and a high-neck, floor-skimming black gown worn with an elaborate black coat featuring a froth of feathers. Deneuve once remarked of Saint Laurent's designs:

> His clothes for daywear help a woman to enter a world full of strangers. They enable her to go wherever she wants without arousing unwelcome behaviour, thanks to their somehow masculine quality. However, for the evening, when she may choose her company, he makes her seductive. (qtd in Reed, *1960s* 62)

Lucile's costuming in *La Chamade* constitutes a fashionable, highly polished look in which she is mostly covered up, which adds to the clothing's restraint and elegance: there are no plunging necklines, short hemlines or excess exposure of skin; her arms and décolletage are seldom on display. Even when she is holidaying on the Riviera, Lucile eschews a bikini in favour of jeans or chino pants worn with crew-neck T-shirts or collared shirts with the sleeves casually rolled up. In particular, Lucile's tailored skirts and double-breasted coat dresses recall Saint Laurent's costuming of Deneuve in Buñuel's *Belle de jour*. Paula Reed characterises Deneuve's costuming in Buñuel's film as 'chaste eroticism and French chic' and remarks that in her 'tailored coats and dresses, she is the perfect Parisienne' (*1960s* 62).

Lucile's status as both a kept woman and a Parisienne is communicated through her fashionability and style; the result, on the one hand, of her costuming by Yves Saint Laurent, and on the other, of Deneuve's star persona. By the mid-1980s, Deneuve was already an 'institution' with an established image, that of elegance (Vincendeau, *Stars* 37). Deneuve has been described as possessing a 'provocative elegance' (Middleton 242), 'famous for her chic type of French beauty' (Williamson 26) and 'relentlessly typecast as the elegant and expressionless bourgeois woman' (Austin 40). Rocamora describes Deneuve as the 'ultimate *Parisienne*' (50), claiming that Deneuve's identity 'cannot be dissociated from the glamorous fictional images – the imagined Parisian women that have made her famous the world over' (94). Sabine Denuelle refers to Deneuve's 'elegance naturelle' (196), while

James Fox, writing for *Vanity Fair*, describes her as 'a living symbol of French style' (103).

As a kept woman, Lucile's most notable cinematic precursor is the eponymous heroine of Max Ophüls's film *Madame de* ... (1953), played by Danielle Darrieux. Alongside her clothing, hair and make-up, Lucile's jewellery also connotes her fashionability and represents the gifts that she receives as a kept woman. However, her jewellery does not only serve to highlight her elegance; it also functions as a prop that propels the narrative which links her to Ophüls's heroine. In *La Chamade*, Lucile's earrings serve the function both of indicating to Antoine Lucile's ongoing association with her rich benefactor Charles and of underscoring for Antoine the impossibility of keeping Lucile in the manner to which she has become accustomed. Similarly, the action of Ophüls's film turns around the circulation of a pair of gifted earrings which 'complete the circle to give the husband proof of his wife's infidelity' (Armes 155). In Ophüls's film, Madame de sells her earrings to pay off certain pressing debts. In *La Chamade* Lucile sells a necklace given to her by Charles in order to leave her job and still meet the expenses of her life with Antoine.

The title of Ophüls's film is deliberately elusive: it refuses to reveal to whom the eponymous Madame belongs. Instead, we are left with an intriguing ellipsis. This raises the question of ownership and of the woman as property or chattel. Madame de's very appearance on screen is preceded by all of her accoutrements. In the opening scene of the film, Ophüls's camera pans around her boudoir, focusing on the contents of her wardrobe and her jewellery box, before finally settling on her face. This creates an inextricable link between Madame de and her accessories. In a similar vein, Lucile is also connected to her material possessions. When Lucile decides to leave Charles, he insists she take everything with her. She refuses, and he consoles himself with the thought that he can at least look at her dresses in the wardrobe and see her car in the garage. Like Madame de, Lucile's belongings are, in Charles's mind at least, an extension of her being, a reminder of her; they stand in for her and are indissociable from her.

For Sabine Denuelle, Danielle Darrieux as Madame de is a quintessential Parisienne: 'La Parisienne est encore est toujours du côté du plaisir, de la beauté et de l'amour, et Max Ophüls lui donnera pour longtemps les traits de Danielle Darrieux dans *Madame de'* (145) (La Parisienne is still and always associated with pleasure, beauty and love, and Max Ophüls will long give her the traits of Danielle Darrieux in *Madame de*). Lucile, like Madame de, is also a Parisienne strongly associated with pleasure, beauty and love. The association of Lucile and Madame de also operates on an inter- and extra-cinematic level. Indeed, Lucile/Deneuve can be considered the spiritual daughter of Madame de/Darrieux, a fact highlighted by the fact that Deneuve also plays Darrieux's actual daughter in Jacques Demy's *Les Demoiselles de Rochefort* (1966) and again, more recently, in François Ozon's *8 femmes* (2001). Darrieux is considered in both her French and Hollywood films as incarnating the quintessential Parisienne type. Jean-Christophe Ferrari includes Darrieux (with Leslie Caron, Claudette Colbert and Audrey Hepburn) as among the main actresses who personified Hollywood's Parisienne: 'Darrieux had the elusiveness, piquancy and carefree manner of speech that Hollywood associated with the Parisienne' (74). In her Hollywood Parisienne films *The Rage of Paris* (1938) and *Rich, Young and Pretty* (1951) Darrieux was, according to Ferrari, 'easily able to assume the role of the Parisienne thanks to her inimitable style and elegance' (85). Deneuve's star persona shares the qualities of style, elegance and elusiveness with Darrieux, all of which are accentuated in *La Chamade*.

Deneuve's role as Lucile is preceded by several other famous roles which inform Deneuve's star persona and infect the character of Lucile. When Truffaut cast Deneuve in *La Sirène du Mississippi* (1969) she had just finished filming *Belle de jour* for Buñuel, in which she played bourgeois housewife-turned-prostitute Séverine Serizy. At the time, Truffaut wrote that what he liked about Deneuve was her mysterious quality: 'She is wonderfully suited to parts involving a secret, or a double life. Cathérine Deneuve adds ambiguity to any situation and any screenplay, for she seems to be concealing a great many secret thoughts, we sense there are things lurking behind the surface' (qtd in de Baecque and Toubiana 253). Lucile's elusiveness is informed by two of Deneuve's other roles: her portrayal of Séverine in Buñuel's film, and Marion in *La Sirène du Mississippi*. Marion is visually linked to Lucile by way of a long, black coat trimmed with ostrich feathers which she wears to a soirée with Charles. The coat, especially in the snow-covered context of Truffaut's film, creates another visual connection, this time to Jean Béraud's painting, *Parisienne, Place de la Concorde* (1890), in which a black feather boa encircles the neck of a chic Parisienne crossing the snow-covered Place de la Concorde. In this way, Lucile's costume not only connotes the elegance of the chic Parisienne but connects her to her nineteenth-century predecessors in art. The black feathered coat also points to the way in which Deneuve's other roles infiltrate the character of Lucile.

Deneuve's star persona, particularly the specificity of her face, plays a vital role in the treatment of Lucile as both kept woman and elusive Parisienne. The following description of Lucile is found in Sagan's novel: 'Lucile était insaisissable. Elle était gaie, polie, souvent drôle mais elle se refusait obstinément à parler d'elle, de Charles ou de ses projets' (27), 'Lucile was a most elusive person. She was gay, polite, often amusing, but stubbornly refused to talk about herself, or Charles, or of any plans for the future' (Murray 19). In Cavalier's film this elusiveness is communicated primarily through the use of Deneuve's face, which is often shot in close-up. Geoffrey Nowell-Smith remarks that Deneuve is an 'actress who always remains behind the screen, drawing the spectator towards her rather than projecting outwards, let alone inviting complicity' (36). For Austin, Deneuve is 'glacial' and incarnates 'the white woman, a figure of control, of unattainable beauty, refinement and rigidity, pallor and poise' (34). Austin argues that Jacques Demy's *Les Parapluies de Cherbourg* (1964) established Deneuve's star persona: 'Deneuve drives out of the film a star, the white woman incarnate, with her mask in place' (42). Linked to this concept of the mask or the screen is Deneuve's acting style, which Austin describes as 'typically minimalist and impassive' (41).

If the face of Lucile/Deneuve always remains metaphorically behind the screen (Nowell-Smith 38), then Cavalier at times literalises this notion by way of *mise en scène*. Lucile is often shot behind glass. In a scene at a café she is shot from the outside looking in. In the many scenes in which she is driving or riding in the passenger seat of a car, she is filmed through the front windscreen. In a key scene, in which Antoine meets Lucile at the airport, their initial reunion takes place with a glass partition between them. In this scene, it is always Lucile, and never Antoine, who is shot behind the glass. This treatment creates another barrier, in addition to the mask of her face, between Lucile and the outside world and those who look at her. Being placed behind glass also suggests the way in which Lucile, as a highly paid courtesan, is a luxury good or precious commodity, who can be courted but not owned by the poor lover and who can be bought but not courted by the wealthy suitor.

The sparkling diamond: Satine in *Moulin Rouge!*

'I can't fall in love with anyone', remarks music hall performer and courtesan Satine to the enamoured young writer Christian. However, following an extravagant song-and-dance number, a pastiche of love songs in which the pair sing and dance their way across the rooftops of Paris against a Méliès-inspired sky, Satine does fall for Christian. The courtesan, the woman accustomed to seeing men only in terms of their economic potential, becomes a *camélia*, the 'loving prostitute' (Rounding 19).

Baz Luhrmann's *Moulin Rouge!* draws both directly and indirectly on the diverse iconography of *la Parisienne* as courtesan, derived from nineteenth-century art, literature and mass culture, and on this iconography as it has been reworked in cinema. The film is a palimpsest and demonstrates, in its treatment of the Parisienne type, the mythological foundations of the type as the representation of a representation, a succession of images with no clear discernible beginning or end point. Indeed, the film has been described as a 'postmodern pillaging of imagery' (Fuller 15), which alerts us to the highly constructed nature of the images, narrative and characters. The aim of what follows is to trace the specific iconography of *la Parisienne* Luhrmann's film draws on in order to illuminate some of the representations that inform the representation of Satine as a Parisienne courtesan.

The character of Satine draws on the iconography of *la Parisienne* as courtesan established in nineteenth-century French literature. Indeed, Zola's *Nana* features a prostitute named Satine, the French word for 'satin', a popular nineteenth-century fabric which 'also carried erotic connotations' (Steele, 'Édouard Manet: *Nana*' 127). The main literary source of Luhrmann's film, however, is Alexandre Dumas *fils*'s *La Dame aux camélias*. The novel was published in 1848, adapted for the stage in 1852, and became the basis for Verdi's opera *La Traviata*, which opened in Venice in 1853. The novel opens with the narrator attending the auction of the deceased estate of consumptive courtesan Marguerite Gautier. He subsequently makes the acquaintance of Armand Duval, who recounts his doomed love affair with Marguerite. Like Marguerite Gautier in Dumas *fils*'s novel, Satine dies young, of consumption. The scenes which depict Satine dying slowly of the fashionable and romantic disease of consumption draw on an iconography established, in part, by Dumas *fils*'s portrayal of Marie Duplessis, which, in the Romantic imagination, connects the disease with the courtesan as redeemed woman. Even the word consumption in these circumstances is heavily aestheticised, invoking 'the image of someone languorously wasting away, while occasionally coughing a little blood' (Rounding 68–9), and this is how Satine's death is depicted in *Moulin Rouge!* In the words of the narrator of *La Dame aux camélias*, she is spared the 'châtiment ordinaire' (Dumas *fils* 24), 'the ordinary punishment' (Schillinger 3) of courtesans by being allowed to die 'dans son luxe et sa beauté, avant la vieillesse, cette première mort des courtisanes' (Dumas *fils* 24), 'in luxury and beauty, before old age set in, that first death of courtesans' (Schillinger 3). Through her death, and by having her story told by the bohemian writer Christian, Satine becomes a redeemed courtesan in the same way as Marguerite, who is redeemed, through narration, by Armand Duval. The narrator of *La Dame aux camélias* comments: 'Les penseurs et les poètes de tous les temps ont apporté à la courtisane l'offrande de leur miséricorde, et quelquefois un grand homme les a réhabilitées de son amour et même de son nom' (Dumas *fils* 42), 'The thinkers and poets of the ages have bestowed the gift of mercy upon the courtesan, and sometimes a great man has rehabilitated them by virtue of his love, and sometimes even with his name' (Schillinger 17). That Satine is the narrative construct not of her own story, but of Christian's, is the first indication of the ambiguity of the Parisienne courtesan in Luhrmann's film: Christian becomes the unreliable narrator who presents us with a version of the life of the courtesan suited not only to his, but ultimately to our own, tastes and ideals.

In *La Dame aux camélias*, Dumas *fils* himself draws on an older tradition of the Parisienne courtesan handed down from Victor Hugo,

Balzac and Alfred de Musset, in which the narrative begins 'with the end of the story [by] having the narrator learn its details from the lovesick hero' (Kavanagh x). *Moulin Rouge!* provides a variation on this theme: the lovesick hero and narrator of Dumas *fils* are combined in the character of Christian. In the opening scene of the film, Christian is shown seated alone at his Underwood typewriter in a rundown garret in Montmartre, composing the story of his love affair with Satine which begins at the end with the words: 'The woman I love is dead.' Luhrmann's film continues the narrative trope of the redeemed courtesan, which comes to him through Dumas *fils*'s novel.

Significantly, *La Dame aux camélias* passed through many reworkings and transformations on its way to Satine and *Moulin Rouge!* The story became standard in the nineteenth century and the character of Marguerite Gautier has been depicted not only by visual artists like Aubrey Beardsley and Cecil Beaton, but also 'portrayed on stage by Sarah Bernhardt, Eleanora Duse, and Isabelle Adjani, in ballets by Margot Fonteyn and Sylvie Guillem, and in films by Greta Garbo and Isabelle Huppert' (Kavanagh xiv). Not only is Luhrmann's work one among many (re)presentations of Marguerite Gautier; Satine subsumes not only the original Marguerite but many of the subsequent depictions of her.

The character of Marguerite Gautier was inspired by the real-life Parisienne courtesan Marie Duplessis and in *La Dame aux camélias* she is 'transformed into the "prostitute with a heart of gold", Marguerite Gautier' (Rounding 59). Thanks to Dumas *fils*'s novel, Duplessis 'became the prototype of the virtuous courtesan' (Rounding 5). Satine is also a descendant of real-life Second Empire courtesan, Duplessis. However, even this real-life courtesan was herself a self-fashioned aesthetic construct: the identification of Duplessis with the heroine of *La Dame aux camélias* 'affected all subsequent judgements and even physical descriptions of her, with the result that the "real" Marie (who was also in part a fabrication of her own making) slipped into the shadows' (Rounding 5). Moreover, due to Dumas *fils*'s use of recognisable elements of Duplessis's life alongside invented or modified elements in his construction of Gautier, and due to the rapid popularity of his novel and play, it quickly became 'impossible to disentangle the myth from the reality, to know whether various descriptions of her are based on genuine memories of Marie or whether they have become entirely overlaid with the image of Marguerite' (Rounding 62). Further, Dumas *fils*'s novel contributed to the 'mythologising of [Marie] into the type of the saintly courtesan, the acceptable face of the fallen woman' (Rounding 64), and it is this type of courtesan that is depicted in Luhrmann's film.

Alongside Marie Duplessis, Satine is also the spiritual descendant of another Second Empire courtesan, Blanche d'Antigny, although the reference to d'Antigny forms part of a more complex system of references in need of some unravelling. In a key scene in *Moulin Rouge!*, the 'Sparkling Diamond Medley', Satine sings 'Diamonds Are a Girl's Best Friend', a song-and-dance number originally performed by Marilyn Monroe in Howard Hawks's *Gentlemen Prefer Blondes* (1953). Luhrmann's version of this iconic number includes a brief transition to Madonna's 1984 pop song 'Material Girl'. This referencing makes sense on both a thematic and iconographic level, on the one hand because it expresses the materialist and hedonistic sentiments of the courtesan and on the other because Madonna's video clip also makes reference to the musical sequence in Hawks's film. Fuller argues that this sequence, among many others in *Moulin Rouge!*, recontextualises well-known popular culture moments. He writes that when Satine 'segues into "Material Girl", it's not simply Madonna who is inscribed, but Monroe again, since in her video for the song Madonna dressed as Monroe in her pink gown from the "Diamonds' number"' (15). Satine's rendition of 'Diamonds' and 'Material Girl' 'harnesses the erotic power of those earlier formidable sirens (Jane Russell, Marilyn Monroe, and the latter's simulacrum, Madonna)', thus situating Satine in 'a familiar paradigm of paramours' (Kinder 5). Satine's song, then, initially appears to be more a reference to American popular culture than to nineteenth-century France. Yet in *Gentlemen Prefer Blondes*, Lorelei Lee (Marilyn Monroe) performs 'Diamonds' on a Parisian music-hall stage. Monroe's character is a modern-day courtesan intent on marrying the wealthy Gus Esmond, Jr (Tommy Noonan). She makes no attempt to hide her intentions of marrying for money in the following scene:

ESMOND SR: Have you got the nerve to tell me you don't want to marry my son for his money?
LORELEI: It's true.
ESMOND SR: Then what do you want to marry him for?
LORELEI: I want to marry him for *your* money.

Lorelei is a direct descendant of Blanche d'Antigny, a lineage traced not only through her physical resemblance – the blonde hair and curvaceous figure – but also her much publicised penchant for diamonds. Indeed Richardson describes Blanche d'Antigny as a 'diamond-covered deity' (21). Following a stage performance by Blanche d'Antigny in 1868, Barbey d'Aurevilly, critic for *Le Nain Jaune*, remarked:

> One curious fact ... is the part played by this lady's diamonds. They certainly perform better than she does ... Diamonds are the women's decoration. They aren't always the Legion of Honour, it is true, but I can see quite well that women like to have them and display them. (qtd in Richardson 10).

Appearing in the opéra bouffe *Le Chateau à Toto* in 1868, d'Antigny performed a song which detailed her humble beginnings and her rise to fame. It is a common theme for the Parisienne courtesan, and one which is also reflected in the narrative of the 'Little Rock' number performed by Monroe and Jane Russell in *Gentlemen Prefer Blondes*. Both songs juxtapose the glamorous life of the courtesan with that of the simple country girl:

> J'ai maintenant quatre voitures
>   Au lieu de deux sabots.
> Autrefois je gardais vingt têtes
>   De bétail dans les champs,
> Je n'ai fait que changer des bêtes ... (qtd in Richardson 19)
>
> (I now have four cars
>   Instead of two clogs.
> I used to look after twenty head
>   Of cattle in the fields,
> All I have really done is change the stock ...)

Costume is perhaps the most important motif for establishing a Parisienne iconography. Satine's wardrobe references other Parisiennes, and has its precursors in both Hollywood and French cinema. The red dress she wears at the end of the 'Sparkling Diamond Medley' resembles Monroe's candy-pink dress from *Gentlemen Prefer Blondes*, designed by William Travilla. Both dresses are similar in style; floor length, satin gowns featuring an oversized bow. The notable exception is the vivid red of Satine's gown which is substituted for the pink of Lorelei's gown in the 'Diamonds' number. The red of Satine's gown, however, recalls the red dresses worn by Lorelei and Dorothy in the 'Little Rock' sequence in Hawks's film. These scarlet, sequinned gowns are themselves referenced in Jacques Demy's *Les Demoiselles de Rochefort*, which also tells the story of two provincial stage performers who leave their home town, seeking fame and fortune in Paris. Satine's red satin gown and black opera gloves, worn with her hair piled on her head, also recall a poster of Belle Époque music-hall performer Yvette Guilbert and another poster of Satine's idol Sarah Bernhardt. This dress and, more specifically, the black opera gloves, are also similar to the strapless black satin gown and gloves worn by Rita Hayworth during the famous 'Put the Blame on Mame' nightclub performance sequence in Charles Vidor's *Gilda* (1946). Monroe's pink gown in *Gentlemen* 'bears a striking similarity to Rita Hayworth's black *Gilda* gown, also strapless and worn with opera gloves' (Young 139). Just as Monroe's Lorelei Lee is prefigured by a nineteenth-century Parisienne Blanche d'Antigny, Hayworth's Gilda is also prefigured by a notable Parisienne. In designing Hayworth's gown for *Gilda*, Jean-Louis was 'inspired by the John Singer Sargent painting *Madame X*' (Young 107). The painting caused a scandal when first exhibited at the 1884 Salon because of its depiction of a woman with the strap of the dress 'brazenly falling from off her shoulder' (Young 107). *Madame X* is a portrait of Virginie Gautreau, an American expatriate living in Paris, famous in Parisian society in the late nineteenth century for both her beauty and her infidelities.

A further iconographic use of costume in *Moulin Rouge!* is found in Satine's bustier and top hat, which recall the character of Lola Lola (Marlene Dietrich) in Josef von Sternberg's *The Blue Angel* (1930). This reference, however, comes to Luhrmann's film through the intermediary of stage performer Lola (Anouk Aimée) from another of Demy's films, *Lola* (1961), who wears a similar top hat and bustier in her signature song and dance number.

In making the heroine of *Moulin Rouge!* both a stage performer and a courtesan, Luhrmann draws on the iconography of *la Parisienne* as venal female performer, a popular trope in the late nineteenth century. During this time female entertainers were, according to Michael Garval, 'privileged objects of desire' (49) who were either courtesans or at least regarded as such: 'With "virtuous" women relegated to the domestic sphere, performers were enticingly public figures – *femmes publiques* being, in an absolute sense, prostitutes' (49). Many courtesans in nineteenth-century Paris were also stage performers, including Blanche d'Antigny, Lina Cavalieri, Lise Fleuron, Caroline Otero, Liane de Pougy and Émilienne d'Alençon. Satine's desire to be 'a real actress' also reflects a popular idea expressed by the Parisienne in Uzanne's *Parisiennes de ce temps*:

> Mais venons-nous à prononcer ce mot: actrice, aussitôt un mouvement se produit, un sourire général se dessine, un espoir brille dans l'iris des yeux, une fièvre de désir électrise l'auditrice, et il n'est point de candidate à la vie indépendante qui ne se dise intérieurement, non sans passion: 'Une actrice … oh! Oui … être actrice! être adorée, fêtée, applaudie, recevoir les hommages, déchaîner les triomphes, sortir de l'existence terne et monotone, briller comme une étoile au firmament de la rampe, au zénith de la célébrité … Ah! certes! le rêve! L'idéal! … le bonheur!' (291–2)

> When one pronounces the word actress, there is a general movement, a smile, the eyes light up, a fever of desire electrifies the listener, and there is hardly a candidate for a life of independence who does not say to herself: 'An actress! Oh, to be an actress! To be adored, feted, applauded, to receive admiration, make triumphs, to leave a dull and monotonous existence and shine like a star behind the footlights, at the height of celebrity. Ah yes! That is the ideal happiness!' (144)

Satine's desire to escape her life as a music-hall performer at the Moulin Rouge and become a real actress finds expression in her rendition of

'One Day I'll Fly Away'. Her desire to be an actress is also, in part, the justification for her prostituting herself to the Duke.

Luhrmann's film is a screen onto which is projected a whole iconography of *la Parisienne* as courtesan. Fuller points out that in writing *Moulin Rouge!* Luhrmann and co-writer Craig Pearce took the Orphean myth and overlaid it 'with a mosaic of iconographic movie images and songs' (15). Luhrmann's film serves as a reminder of the capacity to continuously recycle stereotypes, and that 'no matter which genre, medium, or culture they hail from, all avatars (like melodramatic stereotypes and tunes) can be endlessly recycled at the ever-shifting point of consumption' (Kinder 8). One of these stereotypes or avatars is *la Parisienne*, a figure whose particularity already possesses a certain universality developed over the course of her history as myth, image and representation.

A Woman of Paris, *La Chamade* and *Moulin Rouge!* all take up motifs and tropes associated with the iconography of the Parisienne courtesan developed in nineteenth-century art, literature and visual culture. *A Woman of Paris* deals primarily with the notion of transformation signified through fashion: Marie's ambiguity, particularly in terms of her social status, derives from the obfuscation of her humble provincial origins by ostentatious displays of wealth, which also testify to the wealth of her benefactor. In *La Chamade* and *Moulin Rouge!*, too, conspicuous consumption forms part of the narrative texture of the films and depicts the Parisienne courtesan as, in part at least, a venal creature for whom luxury holds sway even over such 'higher' causes as love and morality. This depiction is treated differently in each film; however the motif of redemption is activated in each film to different ends. In Chaplin's film, Marie is ultimately redeemed through her guilt over the fate of Jean and is chastened by her experience as a courtesan and recast in the role of good woman through her return to the provinces. In Luhrmann's film, Satine's redemption comes through her death from consumption which ultimately spares her from making the archetypical choice between her wealthy suitor and her penniless lover. In *La Chamade*, redemption is achieved through the suspension of any moral judgement, driven largely by Sagan's own deliberate absence of ideology (Denuelle 191): Lucile is not spared the courtesan's choice and unashamedly chooses a life of luxury. These three different treatments demonstrate the possible variations within a single theme or motif of the Parisienne type.

As courtesans, Marie, Lucile and Satine fashion themselves as commodities in order to consume other commodities. Indeed the courtesan's subjectivity is expressed through her desire to become an object, to enter the world of use and exchange typical of the circulation of commodities. Courtesans achieve this circulation primarily through the use of luxury goods such as haute couture, and the fashionability of Satine, Lucile and Marie is foregrounded in each film, something which links them to the broader motif of the Parisienne type as an icon of fashion. Alongside fashionability, and yet inextricably tied up with it, these three courtesans are also ambiguous. Indeed, the ambiguity of the commodity, to be at once used and exchanged, is expressed in narrative terms in the ambiguity of the Parisienne courtesan: one does not know their origin or their true value. However their exchange is in part determined by the labour of their self-fashioning: Marie's clothing masks her humble origins; while the ambiguity of Deneuve's star persona, developed over several film roles and associated with the designer Yves Saint Laurent, overdetermines the character of Lucile. The case of Satine, however, represents a further turn of the screw in the ambiguity of the Parisienne courtesan insofar as her ambiguity stems from the fact that she is first and foremost a narrative construct of Christian, and enters the film by way of his desire or point of view. Indeed, the courtesan as a type is situated on the verge of two desires, her own desire to become a commodity, and the desire of the men who wish to possess her.

Parisienne iconography in cinema is frequently established by way of the star persona of certain actors, as is the case with Lucile in *La Chamade* due to the Parisienne iconographical profile of Deneuve, and this idea will be explored further in the next chapter in relation to four other stars who possess such a profile. This is not, however, the only point of convergence between the courtesan and the star. Indeed, Parisienne courtesans were among the first celebrities: not only were their images reproduced in visual art and literature, but their lives were often scrutinised in the popular press. Demimondaines like Cleo de Mérode and Blanche d'Antigny were popular nineteenth-century figures, whose images were reproduced and disseminated by way of new printing technologies. Garval points out that in 1900 Mérode 'was probably the most photographed woman in the world' (2) and argues that her 'postcard stardom is a key missing link in our understanding of modern celebrity's prehistory' (3). These celebrity courtesans often set the fashion of the day, and were much imitated in their style. Like courtesans, stars also function as commodities and play the commercial role of the seller of commodities, both directly through advertising and print media, and indirectly through their representation in cinema.

6
Star

An establishing shot of Paris cuts to the interior of an apartment. Brigitte (Brigitte Bardot) enters through a doorway carrying a breakfast tray, an apron tied around her waist, her blonde hair falling messily about her shoulders. As she turns to close the door it is revealed that she is wearing nothing beneath her apron. In another part of the city Judith (Charlotte Gainsbourg) arrives at a café, dressed in a man's shirt and an oversized military parka, a large canvas bag slung over her shoulder. Her hair is swept back in a loose chignon and she is wearing little, if any, make-up. She takes a seat and orders a Perrier with a wedge of lemon. In another café, on Boulevard Strasbourg – Saint-Denis, Angéla (Anna Karina), dressed in bright red stockings, a plaid skirt and white mackintosh, takes a sip of her *café-crème*, announces she is pressed for time and leaves. Returning from a weekend spent in Paris with her lover, Jeanne (Jeanne Moreau) checks her appearance in the hallstand mirror before entering her husband's drawing room.

Playful and coquettish Brigitte, bourgeois-bohemian Judith, gamine Angéla and cerebral and sensual Jeanne are four quintessential Parisiennes incarnated in cinema by four quintessentially Parisienne actresses in four Parisienne films: Brigitte Bardot in Michel Boisrond's *Une Parisienne* (1957); Charlotte Gainsbourg in Claude Berri's *L'un reste, l'autre part* (2004); Anna Karina in Jean-Luc Godard's *Une femme est une femme* (1961); and Jeanne Moreau in Louis Malle's *Les Amants* (1958), respectively. In each of the four scenes sketched above, the distinct star personae of Bardot, Gainsbourg, Karina and Moreau infect the Parisienne characters they play and, in turn, the characters infect the star personae of these actresses. This conflation of on- and off-screen identities creates a distinctly Parisienne iconographical profile for these stars, and each in her own way contributes to the reworking of the Parisienne type.

In the star theories of Edgar Morin and Ginette Vincendeau, a distinction is drawn between star and actor: while a star is always an actor, an actor is not necessarily always a star. For Morin, the star is 'more than an actor incarnating characters; he incarnates *himself in them*, and they become incarnate in him' (38). Morin also makes a distinction between who can be considered a star and who an actor: in order to be a star, an actor must in some way *play him or herself*. A character actor, whose roles change, often dramatically, with each successive appearance, is not necessarily a star, no matter how well known they are. Unlike an actor, a star possesses a certain persona which is not simply reducible to the sum of the roles he or she plays, but which is nonetheless infected by these roles (Morin 38).[1]

For Vincendeau, the star is more than the actor incarnating particular roles, and she uses the term 'persona' to indicate this difference. Vincendeau defines a star's persona with reference to three materials: performance, trade promotion and publicity, and commentaries and criticisms. The films, however, are always central. Vincendeau is less interested in the '"true" person behind the star' than in 'how the perceived authentic individual informs the star's image' (*Stars* xi). Similarly, the private lives of the stars are 'examined only in so far as they form part of their "persona"' (*Stars* xi).

As part of their star personae, Bardot, Moreau, Karina and Gainsbourg possess a Parisienne iconographical profile. This profile derives from film roles, and is supported by extra-cinematic media like fashion journals, interviews, press releases and red-carpet events. Primarily, however, an iconographical profile is the result of the cinematic image and its repetition within a particular cycle of films. The term 'iconographical profile' derives from an essay by Lawrence Alloway in which he argues that the primary subject matter of iconography in its initial stage is the physical world as it appears on film, which includes the actor or star (16).

The films set for consideration in this chapter belong to what might be called a cycle of Parisienne films. Not every Parisienne film features a star of the type outlined above; nor is every Parisienne character played by a star with a distinct Parisienne iconographical profile. In any Parisienne film there are three possible ways *la Parisienne* can appear on screen: played by an actor who is not a star; played by an actor who is a star but who does not possess a Parisienne iconographical profile; played by an actor who is a star and who also possesses a Parisienne iconographical profile. This chapter focuses on the Parisienne iconographical profiles of Bardot, Moreau, Karina and Gainsbourg. Certain studies have treated the star personae of Bardot, Moreau and Karina in a more general sense (Austin; Bazgan; Betz; Conway; Holmes; Leahy; Schwartz; Sellier; Vincendeau, 'Brigitte Bardot', 'The Star Reborn', *Brigitte Bardot*). This chapter builds upon these by focusing specifically on how these star personae relate to the Parisienne type. There has been, however, less critical or academic attention on the star persona of Charlotte Gainsbourg, which this chapter addresses. Significantly, these four stars are what Guy Austin calls 'modern' French stars; that is, they belong to a period of French cinema in which stars were becoming a distinct and influential phenomenon (3). Prior to the 1960s there was no star system in France comparable to that of Hollywood: 'This relative absence of a star system in France is due primarily to the distinctive nature of its production system and the less developed form of capitalism of which that in turn was a symptom' (Crisp 224–5). However, Austin argues that since its modernisation into a capitalist consumer society after the 1960s, France subsequently developed a star system of its own in which the power of stars began to influence the production and financing of films (6). French stars also began to be commodities in their own right and their images were used in extra-cinematic discourses such as advertising and fashion. The absence of a rigid studio system in France, however, meant that French stars had more control over the creation of their star personae, and they brought more of their own personalities to the characters they played.

'Viva Bardot! Viva Moreau!': the ingénue and the consummate professional

On a balmy night in a modest hall in a small Central American village seasoned music-hall performer Maria (Jeanne Moreau) takes to the stage with her new protégée, the slightly nervous and hesitant Maria (Brigitte Bardot), for their inaugural performance.[2] Midway through their song and dance number which extols the virtues of Paris and the city's women, Bardot's costume begins to irritate her. She pulls distractedly at her dress, at which point it tears. Mortified, she prepares to abandon the performance altogether, but a bemused Moreau commands she continue. In this scene from Louis Malle's star vehicle *Viva Maria!* (1965), which provides an apocryphal account of the origin of the art of striptease, the distinct star personae of Bardot and Moreau, the two *grandes demoiselles* of French cinema of the day, are put on display: the natural or innocent sex kitten incarnated by Bardot is juxtaposed with the cerebral and experienced seductress incarnated by Moreau.

In *Viva Maria!* Bardot and Moreau play to their star personae. In a 1966 review of the film, Richard Schickel writes: 'They are, of course, movie rarities – genuinely sexy sex symbols – but *Viva* carefully defines *la différence* between what each of them symbolizes ... and both girls edge their portrayals with knowing but unselfconscious satires of their public images' (8). Louis Malle himself remarks:

> They are both very, very sensitive, and they have sex appeal, though of a different kind. They feel always in danger, all the time they live on the edge of their nerves. I thought it would be funny to have Bardot and Moreau in the same picture. I wanted the chemistry between the trained actress and the film star, the sophisticated woman and the instinctive child. (qtd in Haining 142)

In this way, *Viva Maria!* can be considered first and foremost a star vehicle. Indeed Hugo Frey, in his book on Malle, describes it in just this way (46). In the trailer for the film, off-screen voices exclaim 'Viva Bardot! Viva Moreau!' before any reference to the film's title is made, foregrounding neither the film itself nor the director, but the two leading women. According to Morin, this is one of the most common indications that we are dealing not with directors or cinema as such but with the stars themselves: 'The names and faces of the stars devour all movie advertisements. The name of the film scarcely counts' (5). The fact that Bardot and Moreau share the common name Maria points to the fact that there is no need to distinguish the women at the level of *dramatis personae*. It is their distinct star personae, rather, which underscore their difference.

Both Bardot and Moreau have been characterised as modern women (Sellier 184; Vincendeau, *Stars* 115). However, their respective 'modernities' differ somewhat in their content. Bardot is usually associated with a new kind of femininity epitomised in Roger Vadim's *Et Dieu ... créa la femme* (1956), in which she is characterised as a more natural-looking, carefree and liberated woman (Vincendeau, *Stars* 115). Vincendeau remarks that Bardot 'rose to fame as the "scandalous" icon of a new hedonistic and sexually free lifestyle, her modernity anticipating the societal changes of the 1960s and 1970s' (*Brigitte Bardot* 1), and that in Bardot 'the mature sexual woman and the gamine merged: a cross between [Marilyn] Monroe and [Audrey] Hepburn, as it were, between the sexual know-how of the sex goddess and the charm of the adolescent' (*Stars* 93). Similarly, Leahy writes that Bardot 'represented a sexual freedom that ran contrary to dominant discourses on acceptable feminine behaviour' (71).

In contrast to Bardot, Moreau's modern woman is more subtle and cerebral. Vincendeau characterises Moreau's sexuality as 'mature' and 'existential' in contrast to Bardot's sex kitten, and claims that Moreau epitomised the modern liberated woman: her characters 'were modern because they inhabited the public sphere, leaving behind the domestic topography of earlier screen women' (*Stars* 125–6). Moreau's status as a modern woman is linked to her association with the New Wave. Her roles in Malle's *Ascenseur pour l'échafaud* (1957) and *Les Amants* (1958), as well as François Truffaut's *Jules et Jim* (1961), made her the embodiment of a new type of French femininity and sexuality, generally categorised as cerebral and sensual rather than purely physical. Paula Reed describes Moreau as 'an intellectual sex symbol' and 'the Nouvelle Vague incarnate' (*1960s* 24). For Vincendeau, too, Moreau is 'the archetypal New Wave star' (*Stars* 121). Like all the women associated with it, Moreau's persona reflected the New Wave ideology as described by Vincendeau: 'authenticity, modernity and sensuality' (*Stars* 117).

The differences between the star personae of Bardot and Moreau was already perceptible to critics prior to their pairing in *Viva Maria!* In a 1962 issue of *Cinémonde* Helene Mara writes:

Brigitte=Jeanne? Like twin sisters, they offer us the same portrait of the modern woman .... In the end they incarnate, each in her own way, both the eternal Eve, and the typically modern young woman of today. Each in her own way, that is to say Brigitte in a more elementary way. More innocent. More physical. Jeanne, with the weight of her reflections, of her intelligence. (qtd in Sellier 182)

The different star personae of Bardot and Moreau are particularly discernible in their respective Parisienne iconographical profiles: each embodies a different type of French femininity with a different set of predicates. This difference is evident in their respective pre-cinematic backgrounds, their mode of dress both on- and off-screen, and the amalgamation of their different film roles. *Viva Maria!* is interesting for its treatment of the type *la Parisienne*, particularly since it looks at the play of difference within the identity of this type. Identity is established by way of the nominal 'Maria' of the film's title, while difference is brought about by way of the star personae of the two actresses.

Pre-cinematic backgrounds

Before making films Bardot studied ballet and worked as a fashion model. According to Vincendeau, Bardot's background in ballet is responsible for her 'distinctive gait, poised, graceful, and sexy in equal measure' (*Brigitte Bardot* 8). This corporeal element is evident in a number of her film roles: she performs both choreographed numbers and impromptu dances in Boisrond's *Voulez-vous danser avec moi?* (1959) and *Cette sacrée gamine* (1956), *Et Dieu ... créa la femme*, *Une Parisienne* and Marc Allégret's *En Effeuillant la marguerite* (1956). Indeed, scenes depicting a dancing Bardot punctuate *Cette sacrée gamine*. The film features a dance sequence in which Brigitte Latour (Bardot) appears as a schoolgirl ballerina, a pirate, and a 'naked' bride, and concludes with a romantic duet. In an earlier scene, behind the bars of a crowded jail cell, Brigitte performs a wild, spontaneous dance, in which, with coquettish provocation, she noisily pops coloured balloons. The film concludes with Brigitte's accidental appearance on stage at a Parisian cabaret in an elaborate and farcical ruse to evade capture by a gang of criminals. *Voulez-vous danser avec moi?* also features an extended dance sequence in which Virginie Dandieu (Bardot) auditions for a position as a dance instructor. Rather than employing cuts or showing sections of the audition as another film may do for reasons of economy, the scene runs for the entire duration of her audition. Thus the sequence leaves the realm of narrative and enters into the pure spectacle of Bardot dancing.

Whereas Bardot began as a dancer, Moreau received her start in the theatre. On screen, this difference is often highlighted both by the roles they play, and by the way they are shot or framed. Typically, the films which established Bardot as a Parisienne feature at least one dance number and she is generally framed in a long shot, emphasising movement, physicality, and the totality of her body. In the case of Moreau, however, her bodily movements are secondary to her face and thoughts. She is rarely shown 'in action', and is predominantly framed in a close-up or a mid-shot.[3] Vincendeau writes that since *Ascenseur pour l'échafaud*, Moreau was 'at the centre of the shift in the representation of female eroticism from the body to the face' (*Stars* 125).

Moreau trained at the Paris Conservatoire drama school and had contracts with the Comédie-Française and the Théâtre National Populaire. She had a long career in popular French cinema before her involvement with the New Wave and auteur cinema. According to Sellier, the change in Moreau's image 'was prepared for by a very rich theatrical career' (184). For this reason Moreau was considered a real actress, in contrast with the more lightweight Bardot (Vincendeau, 'Brigitte Bardot' 122). Moreau's status as a 'real' actress is also reinforced by her choice of film roles. While Bardot mainly worked in mainstream cinema, especially comedies, Moreau worked with auteurs such as Malle, Truffaut, Orson Welles, Luis Buñuel, Michelangelo Antonioni and Jacques Demy, and claimed she 'never worried about box-office' (qtd in Vincendeau, 'Brigitte Bardot' 121). Bardot's and Moreau's respective distinct backgrounds are effectively utilised in *Viva Maria!*, with Moreau playing the consummate professional to Bardot's ingénue.

Fashion

The respective relationships Bardot and Moreau have to fashion and style again define the difference between their Parisienne iconographical profiles. Both in their own way are considered style icons and indeed appear in Paula Reed's *Fifty Fashion Looks that changed the 1950s* and *Fifty Fashion Looks that changed the 1960s*, both published in 2012. Bardot eschewed the perfectly groomed and classically feminine lines of haute couture, made famous by Christian Dior's New Look. With her preference for cheaper, simple fabrics and unkempt hair, Bardot forged a radical break from the fashion of the previous generation. In fact, in response to an offer from Coco Chanel to dress her, Bardot allegedly remarked: 'Couture is for grannies' (qtd in Steele, *Paris Fashion* 279). In contrast to Chanel's tailored outfits, Bardot preferred simple gingham dresses, striped sailor T-shirts, and jeans or Capri pants, and sparked an entire new trend in fashion which was, along with her hairstyle, much imitated (Vincendeau, *Brigitte Bardot* 1). In the 1990s and 2000s models Kate Moss, Claudia Schiffer, Lara Stone and Gemma Ward all 'explicitly imitated' the Bardot look (Vincendeau, *Stars* 47). In an article in *Life* magazine in August 1959, 'Bardolatrie in Paris: the Bébé Look', we read:

> In Paris this summer teen-age girls are pouting like bébés wearing little-girl dresses in a mass effort to look like actress Brigitte Bardot, who has made a fortune by looking like a wayward child. The young Parisiennes, piling bleached hair on top of their heads, letting it fall in all directions or securing it with a kerchief – all BB trademarks – are suffering from what the world would call a fad but the French nicely term '*bardolatrie*'. (14)

Conway remarks how Bardot 'sustained her visibility in the American press not as a film actress, but rather as an international fashion icon' (192–3), and that she significantly contributed to the trend for 'casually stylish and relatively inexpensive clothing that utterly transformed the way women dressed' (199). Bardot's looks have continually been a source of imitation. However, not simply a passive object in the circulation of commodities, Bardot actively 'subverted the power of couture not only through her championing of ready-to-wear clothes on and off screen, but through her creation of a radically new form of fashion. She wore blue jeans or simple dresses, and her long, dishevelled bleached-blonde hair was copied then as today' (Church-Gibson 99). In the realm of fashion this subversion is typical of the Parisienne type, to which the earliest physiologies attest. In *Les Parisiennes*, Arsène Houssaye writes: 'La Parisienne n'est pas à la mode, elle est la mode' (268) (*La Parisienne* is not in fashion, she is fashion). From a 'follower of fashion', Bardot 'graduate[d] to trailblazer and, in this respect, the most imitated star in the world' (Vincendeau *Brigitte Bardot* 12).

While the more relaxed and androgynous Bardot eschewed haute couture, the more classically feminine Moreau embraced it. Coco Chanel provided Moreau's costumes in *Les Amants* and Pierre Cardin provided her costumes for *Viva Maria!*, *La Baie des anges* (Jacques Demy 1963) and *The Yellow Rolls Royce* (Anthony Asquith 1964), as well as designing outfits for her off-screen. In her biography of Moreau, Marianne Gray writes: 'Always clad in Cardin, she was the ultimate, elegant *Parisienne*' (58). In contrast to Bardot's wild, 'natural' hair, Moreau's hair is neat and controlled, much like her handling of the accidental striptease in *Viva Maria!* Moreau, like Bardot, is considered a style icon and there is an entry dedicated to her in *Fifty Fashion Looks that Changed the 1960s* under the title 'Jeanne Moreau: The face of the Nouvelle Vague'. Ironically, for Reed it was not Moreau's 'signature' look worked out through her association with Chanel and Cardin that is the most enduring aspect of her fashionability, but rather two exceptions to this rule: her appearance as Cathérine in *Jules et Jim*, and as Maria in *Viva Maria!*: 'Women everywhere were suddenly wearing grandmother specs, long scarves, gaiters, boots, knickerbockers and poor boy hats. Her style influence endured, sending yet more women on the road to ringletted and ruffled romanticism after she made the look famous in *Viva Maria!*' (24). This is something Moreau has in common with another cinematic Parisienne, Audrey Hepburn, whose association with couture is less memorable and less imitated than the simple, existential look of Capri pants, ballet pumps and turtleneck sweaters worn in Stanley Donen's *Funny Face* (1956).

Amalgamation of film roles

The respective Parisienne films of Bardot and Moreau, and the way in which the amalgamation of these film roles has contributed to a specific Parisienne iconographical profile, also define the difference between the two stars.

Bardot's persona is characterised as Parisienne predominantly due to the amalgamation of film roles in which she plays the Parisienne type. In *Cette sacrée gamine* Bardot plays Brigitte Latour, a naughty schoolgirl who becomes involved with Parisian cabaret singer, Jean Clary (Jean Bretonnière). According to Vincendeau, the film 'consecrated Bardot as a combination of naughty schoolgirl, sex kitten and romantic ingénue' (*Brigitte Bardot* 23). In another of her Parisienne films, *En Effeuillant la marguerite*, Bardot plays Agnès Dumont, a rebellious provincial youth who, having fled to Paris, finds herself entering an amateur striptease contest. In Boisrond's second Bardot vehicle, *Voulez-vous danser avec moi?*, Bardot plays Virginie Dandieu, who secures a post as an instructor at a Parisian dance school in order to clear her husband of murder.

In addition to these more 'lightweight' ventures which served to establish Bardot's star persona, two later films used this persona in a more self-referential way, both affirming and interrogating it: Malle's *Vie privée* (1962) and Godard's *Le Mépris* (1963). Both Malle and Godard cast Bardot 'as a means to deconstruct mass celebrity' (Vincendeau, *Brigitte Bardot* 98). In *Vie privée*, Bardot plays fictional film star Jill, a character based on Bardot herself. Like Bardot and the Parisienne type, Jill is a style icon whose look is much imitated. The film contains scenes set in the streets of Paris depicting young women dressed in clothing inspired by the Bardot look. In *Le Mépris*, Bardot plays Camille, a Parisienne involved in a *ménage à trois* with her screenwriter husband and a rich film producer. Godard's treatment of Bardot is interesting because while she remains an object of desire for the male characters in the film she is also given an elusive inner life captured through a series of ponderous close-ups and mid-shots set to George Delarue's elegiac music. In *Le Mépris*, Godard elevates Bardot 'to the status of an international, exportable, *cinephile* icon', lifting her out of the popular sphere, which previously had a monopoly on her image (Vincendeau, *Brigitte Bardot* 106).

It was Boisrond's appropriately titled *Une Parisienne*, however, which deliberately connected Bardot's burgeoning star persona with the Parisienne type. In a key scene, Brigitte carries a breakfast tray to her husband in bed. She turns to close the bedroom door and we see she is wearing only panties beneath her apron. Thus her turn, performed for a pragmatic reason, enacts an impromptu or accidental striptease of the kind we later see in *Viva Maria!* The scene concludes with a dance number in which she playfully unties her apron strings, a further metaphor for her persona which, according to Simone de Beauvoir, 'challenges certain taboos accepted by the preceding age' (58). Her dance here recalls the famous mambo scene in *Et Dieu ... créa la femme* in which Bardot performs a spontaneous erotic dance to exotic rhythmic music. The scene is bookended with exterior shots of Paris which connects the imagery of the city with the character of Brigitte. The final shot superimposes multiple reflections of Brigitte over an exterior shot of Paris, visually inscribing her image(s) on the city landscape. That the character of Boisrond's film is also named Brigitte further points to the conflation of star and character.

In contrast to Bardot's innocent, natural and almost adolescent sexuality, Moreau is a direct descendant of the *filles d'Eve* or the daughters of Eve: introverted, seductive and dangerous. In the 1960s, Oriana Fallaci referred to Moreau as a femme fatale, and in the late 1990s Molly Haskell called her 'La Belle Dame sans Merci' (Vincendeau, *Stars* 121). This image of Moreau is derived not only from her New Wave films but also films like Buñuel's *Le Journal d'une femme de chambre* (1964); Welles's *The Trial* (1962), in which she also plays a striptease artist, and Joseph Losey's *Eva* (1962). Vincendeau remarks: 'Deadly female sexuality is an important streak of Moreau's work' (*Stars* 127). In *Jules et Jim*, Cathérine (Moreau) kills herself and her lover Jim; in *Ascenseur pour l'échafaud*, Florence (Moreau) convinces her lover to murder her husband; and in *La Mariée était en noir* Julie (Moreau) seduces and then murders the men responsible for the death of her husband. Moreau's appeal endured throughout these films despite the fact that, at the time, she was considered among the film-producer set to be unphotogenic (Gray 25). Moreau is also often cast in the role of prostitute or kept woman: 'The archetype of the prostitute – an avatar of the sexualised, threatening woman –

has consistently informed Jeanne Moreau's star image. She has played prostitutes, strippers or madams in numerous films' (Austin 35).

In *Viva Maria!*, the sequence depicting the two Marias' inaugural performance emphasises the distinct star personae of Bardot and Moreau. Both constitute different aspects of Parisienne iconography. At the same time as the star personae of Moreau and Bardot enhance the Parisienne-ness of the characters of Maria and Maria, the fact that Moreau and Bardot have been immortalised on screen as the founders of striptease reciprocally enhances their status as Parisiennes. Indeed, Malle's account of the origin of striptease is not dissimilar from other versions which describe the invention of the art form. Jon Stratton provides an account which situates the origins of striptease in late nineteenth-century Paris: 'On 9 February 1893, at the Moulin Rouge in Paris, an artist's model named Mona entertained the students at the Four Arts Ball by gradually taking her clothes off. She was fined a hundred francs, but within a year a professional striptease was taking place at another Parisian music hall with the title "Le Coucher d'Yvette"' (100). Acknowledging that the origins of striptease are highly contested, and various dates and situations have been proposed from ancient Babylonia to twentieth-century America, Anne Cheng provides another account which also situates the art form's origins in late nineteenth-century Paris. She writes that *The People's Almanac* 'credits the origin of the striptease in France to an act in 1890s in Paris in which a woman slowly removed her clothes in a vain search for a flea crawling on her body. At around the same time, venues such as the *Moulin Rouge* and the *Folies Bergère* were pioneering semi-nude dancing and tableaux vivants' (6–7). These originary myths locate the key moment in the history of striptease in late nineteenth-century Paris and identify the art as a French, or more specifically, Parisian, development.

Ostensibly a film about a small revolution in Central America, *Viva Maria!* is above all an homage to *la Parisienne* and the film's two Parisienne stars; the song and dance numbers they perform are testament to this. The song accompanying the striptease sequence is a celebration of the women of Paris, extolling the virtues of the city, the women's accoutrements and the variations in the type:

On a chanté la douceur des tropiques ...
Oui mais Paris c'est tellement plus beau

Jolis bas noirs et blanches jarretelles
Trottins, cousettes aux coquins retroussis
Grandes cocottes aux frivoles dentelles
C'est tout cela qui fait notre Paris.

(One has sung of the calmness of the tropics ...
Yes, but Paris is really much more beautiful

Pretty black stockings and white suspenders
Errand girls, seamstresses with their cheeky turn-ups
Grand cocottes in frivolous lace
It's all of this that makes our Paris.)

The costumes and hairstyles worn by Moreau and Bardot for their inaugural performance bear a close resemblance to the Parisienne of Degas's 1878 pastel portrait, *Café-Concert Singer*. The painting depicts a chanteuse in a red gown with a fur-trimmed neckline. She wears a black choker with a small medallion and her hair is piled up on her head.

In a second song-and-dance number, a chorus line of men sing: 'les p'tites femmes, les p'tites femmes de Paris'. This song underlines the difference between the two star personae of Moreau and Bardot, and this difference is metonymically encapsulated by reference to their hair: 'Mais blondes ou brunes à Paris font mieux' (Whether blonde or brunette they're better in Paris). Bardot enunciates the word 'blonde', underscoring the way her 'long blonde hair ... became a key part of her erotic iconography' (Vincendeau, *Brigitte Bardot* 46). Moreau enunciates the word 'brunette', emphasising her difference from Bardot and aligning herself with the intellectual brunettes of the French New Wave.

Bardot's and Moreau's stardom has been associated with New Wave cinema, although their star personae have also extended beyond this movement. Another star who has a Parisienne iconographical profile and who was much more closely associated with the New Wave is Anna Karina. Indeed. Genevieve Sellier argues that Moreau and Karina 'can be considered the two opposing poles' of the New Wave 'galaxy': Moreau 'manages to impose herself as the "star" of the New Wave', while Karina 'plays the unexportable model of a lone creator' (150). Sellier is referring to Karina as the creation and property of Godard; however, while Karina's stardom is generally considered to be confined to Godard's New Wave films, it was not as unexportable as Sellier claims, at least in the textual, if not in the media and economic sense. Indeed, Pierre Koralnik's 1967 film, *Anna*, imports Karina's star persona from the New Wave and uses it to create a star vehicle which is the culmination of the persona formed during her Godard period.

'Laquelle est la vraie?': Anna Karina in *Anna*

Anna Karina's biography follows a narrative trajectory typical of the Parisienne type. Born Hanne Karin Blarke Bayer in Copenhagen in 1940, Karina can be counted among Parisiennes who, born outside Paris, come to the French capital to reinvent themselves. Karina's career began in Denmark where she worked alternately as a cabaret singer and a model in commercials and short films. In 1958, aged 17, she moved to Paris and worked as a model for fashion designer Pierre Cardin, among others. In the offices of French magazine *Elle*, Karina met Coco Chanel, who advised her to change her name (Brody 78).

While working as a fashion and television model, Karina caught the attention of Jean-Luc Godard, who at the time was a film critic for *Cahiers du Cinéma*. Godard offered her a role in his first feature film, *À bout de souffle* (1960). Karina declined the role but was subsequently cast in Godard's *Le Petit soldat* (1960) (Brody 77–8). However, due to *Le Petit soldat* being banned in France, it was Karina's next film with Godard, *Une Femme est une femme* (1961), which first drew the public's attention to the actress and laid the groundwork for her Parisienne iconographical profile. Karina won the Best Actress award at the 1961 Berlin Film festival for *Une Femme est une femme*, in which she plays Angéla, a striptease artist living in working-class Strasbourg – Saint-Denis.

Karina's work with Godard has often been characterised as an artist/muse collaboration, although Karina herself, in *Russh* magazine, describes it as a Pygmalion-like scenario (Gardiner). Critics have shared this view of the relationship: 'Karina had almost no experience as an actress. Not only did Godard make use of her occasionally faulty French, but he made her hesitations and her awkwardness an essential element of her performance' (Brody 91). Thus Godard took aspects of Karina the actress and used them to create the characters she incarnated. In particular, her awkwardness contributed to the gaucheness of the gamine and childlike Parisienne type that she came to typify.

In the films Karina made with Godard, the director repeatedly cast her in Parisienne roles: Angéla in *Une Femme est une femme*, Odile in *Bande à part* (1964), Natacha von Braun in *Alphaville* (1965), Nana in *Vivre sa vie* (1962), Marianne Renoir in *Pierrot le fou* (1965) and Paula Nelson in *Made in U.S.A.* (1966). The amalgamation of these screen roles established Karina's Parisienne iconographical profile, primarily by blurring the line between character and actress. Critics have remarked of Karina's films with Godard that they are equally about the actress herself as they are about the fictitious character she portrays. Jean-Louis Bory's review of *Vivre sa vie* describes the film as 'Godard's film about Karina' (qtd in Sellier 65). Sellier cites several critics who agree that *Vivre sa vie* is Godard's 'loving homage to his actress' (64–5). Brody describes *Une Femme est une femme* as 'autobiographical', and goes on to remark that the subject of the film was 'Godard's own effort to make a film starring Anna Karina about their life together' (110). Describing a scene from *Le Petit soldat* in which Veronica (Karina) is being photographed by her lover Bruno (Michel Subor), Karina remarks: 'It's a declaration of love. Jean-Luc took the place of the photographer and directed my gestures, the hair like this, the hands like that, the head at an angle' (qtd in Brody 91). This blurring of character and actress in Karina's Godard films often took place at the level of dramatis personae. In *Une Femme est une femme* Karina's character is called Angéla, a deliberate conjunction of Anna and *ange* or angel. In *Pierrot le fou*, Karina plays Marianne Renoir, again a variation on Anna, which also denotes the figure of the French republic and links Karina both to the French nation and French womanhood, and to Pierre-Auguste Renoir's conception of French femininity. In *Vivre sa vie*, Karina plays aspiring actress Nana who turns to prostitution after losing her job in a record store. The reference is to Zola's infamous courtesan, but the name is also an anagram of Anna.

Icon of style

On a cold July day in 2009, young women dressed in A-line skirts, red stockings, ballet flats and trench coats, sporting blunt fringes and wing-tipped eyeliner, spill out of Melbourne's Forum Theater onto Flinders Street. They are there as part of the Melbourne International Film Festival's retrospective on Anna Karina. Fifty years after the release of *Une Femme est une femme*, these young women are testament to the enduring appeal of Karina's personal style.

The clothing Karina wore in the films she made with Godard, often taken from her own wardrobe, established the actress as an icon of style. New Wave actresses 'embodied the "young fashion" that was becoming a major commercial force, relayed by women's magazines … . But where Bardot "sexed-up" youth fashion, Karina prefigured the 1960s skinny adolescent look *à la* Twiggy' (Vincendeau *Stars* 119). The Karina look of the New Wave period continues to inspire fashion and style today. English model, contributing editor at British *Vogue* and trendsetter Alexa Chung has in recent years explicitly imitated the Karina look. In her pop-culture fashion book *It* (2013), Chung cites Karina as one of her formative style icons. The September–October 2008 issue of *Russh* magazine features Karina in the regular feature 'Beauty Icon', which opens with the line: 'New Wave belle Anna Karina is a timeless brunette beauty with impeccably chic credentials' (Chung 112). The spread features photographs of Karina alongside make-up items intended to help the reader achieve her look. There are also many blogs and websites dedicated to demonstrating how to imitate the Karina look. The New Wave Film website (newwavefilm.com) includes a page titled 'French New Wave Fashion: Anna Karina' which includes an 'Anna Karina Style Cheat Sheet' and tips on how to achieve her look through a choice of outfits, make-up and hairstyling, alongside many photographs of the actress and even 'mood boards'. One such mood board is revealing in that it juxtaposes variations on the clothing Karina wore in her New Wave films with items signifying Paris and Frenchness (the Eiffel tower and the beret) on the one hand, and intellectualism (coffee and cigarettes, the pile of books and the film magazine) on the other, making Karina, in Betz's words, an 'iconic art film star' (97). A cardboard suitcase signifies both Karina's retrospective appeal and her cosmopolitanism, and the overall colour scheme of the mood board, the red, white and blue of the tricolour, mirrors the palate of Karina's Godard-era films.

Anna Karina's style has also influenced fashion designers. The Agnès B Autumn/Winter 2008 Collection was inspired by Karina's wardrobe for her Godard films. The collection featured A-line plaid skirts, cardigans, ballet flats and sailor hats; the models even wore their hair styled like Karina's, either shoulder-length to long hair with a fringe, or the short Louise Brooks-style bob Karina sported in *Vivre sa vie*. Her style was also celebrated on the cover of a 2008 issue of *Mean* magazine, which features a fashion spread in which actress Kate Beckinsale is carefully dressed and posed to resemble Anna Karina from the famous Roller Girl Sequence of Koralnik's *Anna*. The cover of *Mean* magazine draws on an image of Karina not usually considered iconic, but which, decades after her Godard years, is beginning to be recognised as such.

Anna *(1967)*

Pierre Koralnik's 1967 film *Anna* plays on Karina's pre-established star persona and both augments and transforms her Parisienne iconographical profile established through her work with Godard. In this way, like *Viva Maria!* for Bardot and Moreau, *Anna* can be considered a star vehicle for Karina. Koralnik's film deliberately blurs the line between star and character, most notably by using the actress's name as the film's title.

Anna tells the story of Serge (Jean-Claude Brialy), a young executive and photographer working in an advertising agency on the Champs-Elysées. While on a shoot at a train station, he inadvertently photographs a young woman (Karina) who accidentally wanders into the frame after momentarily losing her glasses. Later, in the darkroom, the image of the woman captures Serge's attention; however without her glasses, he fails to recognise her as the colourist who works in the same agency. Transfixed by the mysterious woman – or, rather, by her *image* – Serge devotes himself to finding her. He blows up the photograph and has it pasted all over Paris.

The darkroom scene in *Anna* is prefigured by another famous darkroom scene from Stanley Donen's *Funny Face* (1956). Indeed, Koralnik's film owes a debt to Donen's musical, made some ten years earlier.

In Donen's film, fashion photographer Dick Avery (Fred Astaire) inadvertently photographs Jo Stockton (Audrey Hepburn) in a Greenwich Village bookshop. Dick enlarges the photograph of Jo's face, reduced here to its essential component parts (eyes, nose, lips, eyebrows) and, like Serge, immediately falls for the image. There is also a visual similarity in the way in which both Dick and Serge are compelled to isolate the face of the woman in the crowded photograph, crop it, blow it up, and then wash out the tones of the face so that it is reduced to the outlines of features against a stark white background. The process is one of abstraction: the pigmentation of the skin is erased and the colour of flesh and blood neutralised, removing the subject from the realm of the human and placing it into the realm of deities.

While *Anna* is significant in terms of its treatment of the star persona of Karina, it is also significant in terms of its treatment of the figure of *la Parisienne*. After having spent the previous few days searching the streets of Paris for the woman in the photograph, he encounters Anna who, seeing his perplexed and exhausted state, remarks: 'C'est cette femme transparente qui vous tue' (it's that unknown woman who is killing you). Unbeknownst to Serge, the mystery woman for whom he is searching is standing right in front of him. Obsessed by her image, he is incapable of recognising her in the flesh. A prose poem of Baudelaire's entitled 'Laquelle est la vraie?' deals with the dilemma of the poet when faced with the reality of the woman he has idealised. The poet does not recognise this 'true' woman as the ideal of his fantasy. The poem opens with the following lines: 'J'ai connu une certaine Bénédicta, qui remplissait l'atmosphère d'idéal, et dont les yeux répandaient le désir de la grandeur, de la beauté, de la gloire et de tout ce qui fait croire à l'immortalité' (*Selected Poems* 175) (I knew a certain Bénédicta, who filled the air with the Ideal, and whose eyes spread everywhere the desire for greatness, for beauty, for glory and for everything that makes one believe in immortality). When later confronted with the real Bénédicta, the poet refuses to relinquish his idéal, preferring instead to 'reste[r] attaché, pour toujours peut-être, à la fosse de l'idéal' (176) (remain attached, perhaps forever, to the grave of the ideal). In this way, Koralnik's film draws on a Baudelairean conception of love that is only possible in the modern city, and which, as Walter Benjamin remarks, 'was spared, rather than denied fulfilment' (*Illuminations* 170). At the centre of this conception is the mythological figure of *la Parisienne*, at once real and ideal. The film does not end with Anna and Serge coming together; rather the final shot shows Anna on a train leaving Paris. Indeed, in one scene, late in the film, Serge and Anna pass each other on escalators moving in opposite directions in a Paris Metro station. Their eyes meet, but the expected moment of recognition does not take place. *Anna* is based around this fundamental idea of misrecognition central to the mythology of *la Parisienne*, and of the impossibility of capturing her. As Houssaye remarks: 'Qui pourrait bien peindre la Parisienne? Son grand art est de ne jamais se ressembler à elle-même' (273) (Who could accurately render *la Parisienne*? Her great art is to never resemble herself).

Misrecognition is also a concept that can be applied to critics' initial reception of Karina as the mere construct of Godard. Indeed, Sellier's remark that Godard fashioned Karina and was largely responsible for the development of her star persona contradicts both the notion of *la Parisienne* as self-fashioning and as active muse. Even Karina's own remark about the Pygmalion-like nature of her relationship with the director is misleading in this respect. It is not so much the case that Karina was Godard's actress but rather that Godard was *her* director, insofar as he did not fashion or mould her but rather put to use those traits of her personality developed before their initial collaboration, tailoring roles to fit her idiosyncrasies rather than shaping her to fit the roles. Further, the notion of the 'unexportability' of Karina's star persona also appears to contradict the subsequent use and development of this persona in films like Koralnik's *Anna* and the later Godard/Karina collaboration *Made in U.S.A.* Karina's enduring legacy as a Parisienne – her personal style – was less a construct of Godard's than facilitated by him and the demands of New Wave film production, most importantly the ethos of naturalism and the budgetary restraints which meant dispensing with costume designers. This allowed Karina to develop as a star more on her own terms with a distinctive acting style and look.

Karina, as well as Bardot and Moreau, developed their star personae and Parisienne profiles during the period of French cinema dating from the mid-1950s to the late 1960s. However, *la Parisienne* as star continues to evolve in contemporary cinema, evidenced in the star persona and iconographical profile of a more recent Parisienne actor, singer and style icon: Charlotte Gainsbourg.

Chez les bobos: Charlotte Gainsbourg

A tall, young woman enters a Parisian café dressed in the casual chic clothing of the bourgeois bohemian, or 'bobo'. The woman is Judith from Claude Berri's 2004 film *L'un reste, l'autre part*, but it could equally be French actress and singer Charlotte Gainsbourg arriving at a café for an interview. Indeed this is how one reporter describes Gainsbourg: 'Tall, lean, with straight brown hair and large, irregular features, plainly dressed in jeans and a baggy khaki jacket, she has a kind of understated geeky chic' (Johnston 5).

The Parisienne-ness of Charlotte Gainsbourg's star persona, her Parisienne iconographical profile, is constructed along the following interrelated lines: her successive film roles (both Parisienne and non-Parisienne), her significance as a style icon, her role as a muse to fashion designer Nicolas Ghesquière, her *jolie laide* appearance, her bohemian parentage and her role in advertising fashion and beauty products. Taken together, these various traits form a unified image of Gainsbourg as the quintessential Parisienne type, and align her with historical precursors from both cinema and the arts. In spite of the fact that Gainsbourg's films are quite diverse in their subject matter, the characters she plays generally conform to the same type and represent an amalgamation of the actress's traits. Even where the films deal with historical rather than contemporary content (like *Jane Eyre* (1996) and *The Golden Door* (2006)), Gainsbourg still appears to play herself.

Gainsbourg's star persona was beginning to be formed from a very young age, and was established both via association with her famous parents (French singer Serge Gainsbourg and British-born actress Jane Birkin) and in her early film roles. In terms of the development of her Parisienne profile, however, I would argue that the most important period began in 2001 with Yvan Attal's *Ma Femme est une actrice*, which features Gainsbourg for the first time as a fully developed and recognisable star with a specific profile. 2007 was a watershed year, when she was invited to guest-edit *Vogue Paris*, something which can be considered confirmation of her Parisienne status.

In *Ma Femme est une actrice*, the protagonist Charlotte incarnates *la Parisienne* in several ways, foremost of which is her look. Charlotte's chic appearance is typical of the bobo or bourgeois bohemian Parisienne of the late twentieth and early twenty-first centuries. Not only is Gainsbourg's appearance typical of this look, but she is considered one of its most famous exponents (Murphy). The look consists primarily of dishevelled hair, minimal natural-look make-up, and a 'uniform' of jeans, a man's shirt and a trench coat, all connoting a casual air. Indeed, Simone Girner notes how in *Ma Femme est une actrice* Gainsbourg 'wears clothes picked from her own closet' (99). This is not something new to Gainsbourg or to the Parisienne type in cinema. New Wave directors had Parisienne actresses like Jean Seberg and Anna Karina wear their own clothes, for two main reasons: on the one hand, budgetary constraints did not allow for wardrobe in the traditional sense; and on the other New Wave filmmakers desired a heightened level of naturalism in the image previously absent from the tradition of quality in French cinema. The quest for this naturalness also resulted in a simplicity of dress, when compared with the designer gowns frequently used in the cinema of the preceding decade. This relative simplicity of dress was described by Uzanne during the Belle Époque as a keystone of the grace of *la Parisienne* (*The Modern Parisienne* 77). In Attal's film, the use of Gainsbourg's personal wardrobe is a deliberate narrative device which seeks to erase the distinction between real life and cinema, between fiction and biography, and between character and celebrity. *Ma Femme est une actrice* is a 'deliberate choreography of the couple's celebrity status, a calculated mix of autobiographical accuracy and outrageous fiction' (A. Smith 185). In the opening scene of the film, husband and wife Charlotte and Yvan (played by real-life partners Gainsbourg and Attal) stroll home through Paris after dining out. Dressed in a trench coat, the collar carelessly turned up, flared jeans and a grey V-neck sweater, hair worn in a loose chignon, and a satchel slung over her shoulder, the willowy actress epitomises the effortlessly chic Parisienne. Three young fans stop to ask Charlotte for her autograph and pose for a photograph with her. Charlotte graciously obliges while a nonplussed Yvan looks on.

Alongside this blurring of art and life, Gainsbourg's star persona as it is used in the film also exemplifies other typically Parisienne tropes. First,

Charlotte, like many Parisiennes, is an actress/performer. Second, she is cosmopolitan, a bilingual actress who works in English-language and French-language cinemas and moves between Paris and London. Third, Charlotte is involved in a *ménage à trois*, a typical Parisienne narrative trope best exemplified in Henri Becque's 1885 play *La Parisienne*, which follows the intrigues of a *ménage à trois* between a charming, seductive Parisienne, her petit-bourgeois husband and her passionate lover. Variations on the *ménage à trois* motif are found in many Parisienne films in which the Parisienne character is either having an affair or must choose between two men: Billy Wilder's *Sabrina* (1954), Ernst Lubitsch's *Design for Living* (1933), Godard's *Une femme est une femme* (1961), Truffaut's *Jules et Jim* (1961), Chaplin's *A Woman of Paris* (1923) and Cavalier's *La Chamade* (1968) are examples of this.

Film roles

The accumulation of Gainsbourg's film roles contributes to her Parisienne iconographical profile in two ways. First, successive roles in Parisienne films in which she plays a Parisienne type build up and establish her identification with the type: films such as *L'un reste, l'autre part*, Eric Lartigau's *Prête-moi ta main* (2006), Attal's *Ils se marièrent et eurent beaucoup d'enfants* (2004) and *Ma Femme est une actrice* fall into this category. Secondly, her roles in art-house and international films add a cosmopolitan and bohemian element to her star persona which further links her to the Parisienne type: films such as Lars Von Trier's *Antichrist* (2009), *Melancholia* (2011), and most recently, *Nymphomaniac Volume 1* and *Nymphomaniac Volume 2* (both 2013); Andrew Birkin's *The Cement Garden* (1993); Alejandro González Iñárritu's *21 Grams* (2003); Michel Gondry's *The Science of Sleep* (2006); Dominik Moll's *Lemming* (2006); Emanuele Crialese's *The Golden Door* (2006); Todd Haynes's *I'm Not There* (2007); and Dawn O'Neill's *The Tree* (2010) fall into this category. In addition to Attal's *Ma Femme est une actrice*, Gainsbourg has appeared in other films in which she plays a character named Charlotte, demonstrating an ongoing predilection for blurring the line between character and actor in her films. These include Elie Chouraqui's *Paroles et Musique* (1984), Claude Miller's *L'Effrontée* (1985) and Serge Gainsbourg's *Charlotte Forever* (1986).

Jolie laide

The individuality or uniqueness of Gainsbourg's face always comes through in her film roles, somewhat overpowering the character: 'The thing about Gainsbourg is that whatever the role, however wonderfully she acts, she's not physically a chameleon: it's still always her face, her features that you're looking at, her father's jaw, the boyish smile, the quirky look' (Chrisafis 10). Another feature of the Parisienne-ness of Gainsbourg's star persona is that she is considered *jolie laide*, which loosely translates as 'ugly pretty'. In 1868, Louise de Taillac remarked: 'Of all women, Parisiennes are not the prettiest, this is well-known; and yet they are the most seductive women in the world' (qtd in De Young, 'Women in Black' 252). In a 2009 edition of *Vogue*, Sarah Mower says about Gainsbourg and her half-sister Lou Doillon: 'They have *je ne sais quoi*. They are *bien dans leur peau*. They invented chic. They have mystique ... . And sometimes they're *jolie laide* into the bargain, a quality we rest-of-the-worlders can't for the life of us understand but that turns out in the flesh to be yet more annoyingly attractive than conventional prettiness' (194). Mower identifies *jolie laide* as particular to the Parisienne type, and goes on to detail how Gainsbourg and Doillon epitomise this: 'Charlotte and Lou have the chiselled cheekbones, strong noses, and style conviction that give them each the kind of *jolie laide* magnetism uniquely bankable in Paris' (194). Natasha Fraser-Cavassoni describes Charlotte Gainsbourg as 'an unconventional beauty' (3), and Joe Zee and Maggie Bullock refer to her 'odd, haunting beauty' (205). Writing for *The New York Times*, Daphne Merkin remarks: 'Today's version of an iconic *jolie laide* is the French actress Charlotte Gainsbourg, whose complex gamine charm has pedigreed status' (42). Gainsbourg herself confirmed these observations when in *Harper's Bazaar* she referred to her 'funny looks' (qtd in Mistry 129). The idea of the *jolie laide* indeed goes back as far as the first sociological studies of *la Parisienne* as a type. In *Parisienne*s *de ce temps* Uzanne remarks: 'La gigolette est presque toujours jeune, souvent jolie, ou bien elle montre cette affriolante laideur de beaucoup de Parisiennes qui est pire que la beauté' (362), 'The *gigolette* is almost always young, and often pretty; or else she has the fascinating ugliness which in many Parisiennes is a more deadly bait than beauty' (*The Modern Parisienne* 179–80).

Icon of style

Charlotte Gainsbourg is often described in both critical work and the popular fashion press as a style icon, and her look is alternately labelled 'chic' (Menkes 48), 'Parisian chic' (Fressange 15), 'utilitarian chic' (Zee and Bullock 201), 'understated cool' (Zee and Bullock 210) and 'a study in understated elegance' (Murphy). Zee and Bullock describe Gainsbourg as a 'fashion muse to indie-leaning women around the globe' (205). Writing on how French women are renowned for a certain *je ne sais quoi* when it comes to their clothing, Georgina Safe notes that Gainsbourg, alongside her mother Jane Birkin and half-sister Lou Doillon, belongs to a category of Parisian women who 'shrug up the sleeves of their blazers and trench coats and wear them over casual T-shirts with jeans ... in a fascinating melange of "I just threw this on" and sophisticated sex appeal' (4). Gainsbourg's signature look conforms to the global ideal of what constitutes the chic Parisienne: 'She is very beautiful in the way that American women always want French women to be beautiful: no makeup, slightly careless, incredibly thin' (Larocca).

The trench coat marked the Gainsbourg of the early 2000s as distinctly *Parisienne*. In a feature in a 2004 edition of *Harper's Bazaar*, entitled 'The Allure of the Trench', Suzy Menkes writes: 'The one piece that every woman can wear anywhere is the trench. Seasonless, timeless and eternally chic, it is epitomized here by style icons Charlotte Rampling and Charlotte Gainsbourg' (153). The trench is considered de rigueur for the Parisienne, and was established as such through cinema, the fashion press and style guides. Throughout the history of cinema, the Parisienne type is often depicted in a trench coat: Nelly (Michèle Morgan) in Marcel Carné's *Le Quai des brumes* (1938), Thérèse (Marie Dubois) in François Truffaut's *Tirez sur le pianist* (1960), Patricia (Jean Seberg) in Godard's *À bout de souffle* (1960), Paula (Anna Karina) in Godard's *Made in U.S.A.* (1966), Geneviève (Cathérine Deneuve) in Jacques Demy's *Les Parapluies de Cherbourg* (1964) and Eva Grace (Kylie Minogue) in Leos Carax's *Holy Motors* (2012) are just a few examples. In the fashion press, including recent style guides, the trench is considered the quintessential item of the Parisienne wardrobe. In *Paris Street Style*, Isabelle Thomas and Frédérique

Veysset write: 'After Lauren Bacall popularized the tight-belted trench coat, Jane Birkin and Charlotte Gainsbourg gave it contemporary chic by wearing it casually with sneakers and jeans' (52).

Gainsbourg has also been credited with transforming the look of *la Parisienne* and influencing the fashion of a generation. In a three-page feature on Gainsbourg's wardrobe in *Vogue Paris*, we read: 'C'est parce que sa garde-robe a transformé l'image de la Parisienne que Vogue lui a demandé d'ouvrir les portes de son dressing' (141) (Since her wardrobe has transformed the image of *la Parisienne*, *Vogue* asked her to open the doors of her dressing room). In a feature article in *The New York Times*, Tim Murphy notes that Gainsbourg is better known for her style or look than for anything else, for either her film roles or her music: 'Her clean-scrubbed, slouchy daytime look has almost single-handedly redefined everyday French style for a generation of young Parisian women. Her look, which she has cultivated since her late teens … typifies an artfully rumpled yuppie-hipster hybrid that has taken hold in France: the bourgeois-bohemian, or le bobo'. Gainsbourg's much-imitated look has been prescribed by style guides and fashion magazines for those wanting to embody the sartorial elegance of *la Parisienne*. In 2010, French fashion magazine *Grazia* published an online style feature entitled 'Charlotte Gainsbourg: Le Chic Parisien' amongst a gallery of six French style icons including Juliette Greco, Jane Birkin, Vanessa Paradis, Cathérine Deneuve and Brigitte Bardot. The magazine praised Gainsbourg's look for its absence of affectation. In 2012, *Grazia* also posted an online gallery of Gainsbourg under the headline 'Les idées mode à piquer à Charlotte Gainsbourg' (Fashion ideas to steal from Charlotte Gainsbourg). The accompanying text reads:

> Icône mode de toute une génération, Charlotte Gainsbourg sait incarner l'image de la Parisienne rive gauche en transformant des basiques, comme le jean flare et le trench burberry, en pièces cultes. Simple et naturelle, elle dompte la mode avec élégance. (Grazia.fr 2012)
>
> (Fashion icon of an entire generation, Charlotte Gainsbourg knows how to incarnate the image of *la Parisienne rive gauche* in transforming basics, like flared jeans and a Burberry trench, into cult pieces. Simple and natural, she tempers fashion with elegance.)

Gainsbourg's status as style icon is also founded on her minimal use of make-up and her unkempt hair, both recognisable features of the bobo look. Fashion magazine features and style websites frequently advocate this look made famous by Gainsbourg; however there are precedents in the history of the Parisienne type. Bardot is one, but Gainsbourg's look can also be traced to the more bohemian Parisiennes of the Left Bank such as Juliette Gréco:

> There is of course another Parisian woman – the bohemian – who pre-dates the pre-war Left Bank of Hemingway, let alone that of the post-war Existentialists. She can be traced back to the stories of Offenbach, which inspired Puccini's opera *La Bohème*. A particular style for the bohemians – black turtlenecks and uncoiffed, long hair ... emerged in Paris in the post-war years ... . The stylish chanteuse Juliette Greco ... became an alternative fashion icon. (Church-Gibson 96–7)

Gainsbourg's predilection for an everyday uniform also aligns her with the sartorial restraint of *la Parisienne bohème* and the Parisiennes of the post-war existential movement who wore head-to-toe black as part of their anti-fashion statement. Mairi Mackenzie describes this phenomenon as follows: 'Usually educated, white and middle class, Existentialists rejected materialism and thus (theoretically) fashion. However, this anti-fashion stance became a trend all of its own and the uniform adopted eventually filtered into the fashion system' (92). Of her own predilection for the uniform as a concept, Gainsbourg has remarked: 'I find it reassuring to put on the same clothes every day' (qtd in Mower 194) and 'I dress in a practical way ... I always wear the same things' (qtd in Buck 288). Like the Left Bank Parisiennes of which she is a descendant, Gainsbourg's own uniform has become a fashion statement in its own right, in spite of its initial eschewal of fashion as such.

Not all of Gainsbourg's fashion profile is constructed from her own personal wardrobe. In extra-cinematic discourse, she has also been described as the muse of fashion designer Nicolas Ghesquière, creative director of the Paris fashion house Balenciaga from 1997 to 2012. Gainsbourg is currently working with Ghesquière in his new appointment with Louis Vuitton and has appeared in fashion advertisements for the brand. In terms of a film star promoting French fashion, Gainsbourg is a particularly interesting case: she has a long-standing association with Ghesquière, yet the designer has never designed costumes for her film roles. This is in contrast to other cinematic fashion designer/muse relationships such as Cathérine Deneuve and Yves Saint Laurent, Audrey Hepburn and Givenchy and Jeanne Moreau and Pierre Cardin, in which the couturier designed for the actress both on- and off-screen. Gainsbourg instead relies on Ghesquière for her off-screen film events. This highlights the way in which film and fashion converge in the off-screen spectacle of red-carpet events such as award ceremonies (the Oscars and the Césars), film festivals (most notably, Cannes) and film premières. In spite of this association with a designer label, however, and of her role as the face of Balenciaga and subsequently Louis Vuitton, Gainsbourg as a style icon is not best known for her association with haute couture. Rather, it is her everyday uniform that has made her a style icon.

Advertising

As a Parisienne, Charlotte Gainsbourg fulfils the same commercial function as her nineteenth-century predecessors: 'Ubiquitous in fashion plates, journal illustrations and posters, namely the mass media images of the nineteenth century, the greater part of the representations of the Parisienne had commercial functions' (Iskin 185).The Parisienne type, associated with consumer culture since the nineteenth century, has been used extensively in advertising campaigns, and even appeared as the mascot for the Paris World's Fair in 1900. Since the World's Fair was primarily a showcase of French industry, *la Parisienne* became the official mascot of French commodities. With the advent of fashion media and, later, cinema, *la Parisienne* frequently became the purveyor of a certain style or look, either originating in the fashion industry or later taken up by it. These looks have been commercialised, usually as supplementary features in fashion magazines.

Gainsbourg's Parisienne iconographical profile has been used to sell commodities both directly and indirectly. The most direct instance was when she lent her face to Balenciaga for their fragrances 'Balenciaga Paris' and 'L'essence'. The advertising campaigns for both fragrances read: 'As worn by Charlotte Gainsbourg'. As the worldwide face of the Balenciaga fragrance Gainsbourg was established as a global image of French femininity. More indirectly, through associated film press and fashion-magazine supplements, Gainsbourg became the purveyor of a range of commodities associated with the Parisienne-ness of her star persona. A 2007 edition of *Vogue Paris* devoted to Gainsbourg outlines precise details of her personal life, including wardrobe items, perfume, musical tastes, favourite brand of tea (Mariages Frères) and scented candles (Diptyque). As Edgar Morin remarks: the star 'is not only a tutelary genius who guarantees the excellence of a product. In effect, she invites us to use *her* cigarettes, *her* favourite toothpaste, i.e., to identify ourselves with her ... . Hence we can understand that the star's greatest effectiveness functions in relation to merchandise already infused with erotic magic' (169). When taken in the context of star studies, these considerations on Gainsbourg lead to a somewhat contradictory conclusion. If, as Murphy remarked, Gainsbourg is more famous for what she does off screen than on, this leads us away from stardom as Vincendeau defined it and towards what she calls celebrity. In stardom, the films are paramount, whereas in celebrity an image is cultivated by other means. For Vincendeau, for example, Brigitte Bardot's star status is worked out primarily in extra-filmic discourse, her film roles being secondary or even inconsequential. In this sense, Gainsbourg too may be more a celebrity than a star; that is, in Vincendeau's words, a female star whose celebrity is 'always far in excess than that of her films' (*Brigitte Bardot* 3).

In each case presented in this chapter, the personal style of the actress began as a statement outside the general fashion trends of the time: Bardot's gingham dresses and St Tropez look; Moreau's boyish Cathérine in *Jules et Jim* and her Romanticism in *Viva Maria!* which broke with the more austere haute couture of her earlier films; Karina's personal wardrobe from her New Wave films; and Gainsbourg's casual chic or bobo look. The self-fashioning aspect of these Parisienne stars was in part facilitated by the absence of a rigorous star system in France during the 1950s and 1960s, which allowed these actors to take a more active role in the development of their personae.

By the time of Gainsbourg's emergence as a star, stardom had already began to cross the threshold to celebrity, a process that is already evident in Bardot's persona; that is, towards a star whose fame is far more than her film roles: 'Bardot's initial construction as a star through the press and in particular photography anticipated the celebrity phenomenon by several decades. She therefore straddles both classic film stardom, whose heyday in France precisely coincided with the time of her full emergence in the mid-1950s, and the celebrity culture of today. (Vincendeau, *Brigitte Bardot* 12). Indeed, Gainsbourg and Bardot are somewhat comparable cases: both mixed lightweight romantic comedies with more serious art films, and their film projects do not appear to directly affect their celebrity status. A bad film review did nothing to lessen Bardot's celebrity, and Gainsbourg's personal style would probably remain influential regardless of the way her films are received or whether they are seen at all. This is in spite of the fact that Gainsbourg, unlike Bardot, is a critically recognised acting talent, received the Best Actress award at Cannes for her role in von Trier's *Antichrist*, and makes films in several countries. In the context of French cinema, Gainsbourg, like Bardot, Moreau and Karina, was not a box-office star: her stardom emerged more from extra-filmic discourse such as promotion and the fashion press, with her films taking a more secondary role even if they received critical recognition. From this it also may be possible to conclude that French female stars are more carefully constructed than their male counterparts, and that they rely more heavily on extra-cinematic discourses to achieve a certain level of exposure. Thus the Parisienne star treads the fine line between stardom and celebrity, something which links her to the very first Parisiennes who were best known for their style and exploits.

What Gainsbourg shares with French actresses like Bardot, Moreau and Karina is a Parisienne iconographical profile that draws on a mythology deeply ingrained in French cultural life. It is this mythology which overdetermines Gainsbourg's star persona and which may account for that *je ne sais quoi* journalists, critics and fashion editorials attribute to the French star. For Morin, the true test of a star is that we are always aware of watching *them* in their films, and not just a *character*: there is what Morin calls a 'reciprocal interpenetration' of actor and role in the creation of a star persona, but we cannot overcome the awareness that it is Gainsbourg – or Bardot or Moreau or Karina, for that matter – that we are watching.

Notes

1 While this chapter does not explicitly engage with Richard Dyer's work on stars, it must be acknowledged that Dyer is generally credited with having founded star studies. Dyer's seminal book, *Stars* (1979), was a major influence on Vincendeau, particularly his tripartite analysis of the star as a 'social phenomenon', 'image' and 'sign'.
2 I will refer to the two Marias by the actresses' names, Moreau and Bardot, both for the sake of clarity, and to emphasise the conflation of the actors with the characters they play.
3 The exception to this rule is the running race in Truffaut's *Jules et Jim*. The exceptions in Bardot's case are her two New Wave films, Louis Malle's *Vie privée* (1962) and Jean-Luc Godard's *Le mépris* (1963), in which Bardot is treated somewhat differently than in her earlier films and is shot in a more Moreau-esque fashion.

Conclusion: 'Look, let's start all over again. What's she like?'

'Look, let's start all over again, shall we!? What's she like?' This remark, made by Adam to Henri in Vincente Minnelli's *An American in Paris*, concludes the sequence in which Henri attempts to describe Parisienne Lise. To the question 'Who or what is *la Parisienne*?', we might be inclined to remark along with Adam: 'Look, let's start all over again!' Indeed, contemporary bourgeois bohemian bilingual actress Charlotte, who divides her time between Paris and London in *Ma Femme est une actrice*, seems to have little in common with the elusive and classically elegant kept woman Lucile in *La Chamade*, or with the androgynous *parigote* and café-concert performer Clara in *Le Jour se lève*. Similarly, Greenwich Village bookstore assistant Jo Stockton in *Funny Face* resembles neither street urchin Michelle of the 1980s Parisian underworld in *Frantic*, nor the resplendent Polish princess Elena Sorokowska from Belle Époque Paris in *Elena et les hommes*.

We get no direct answer to Adam's question from Henri about the true nature and identity of Lise. While Minnelli's film appears to leave Adam's question hanging, a clue is provided later in the film, during the *American in Paris* ballet sequence. Each of the ballet's sequences evokes an artist's work, with sets inspired by the famous canvases of Renoir, Cézanne, Rousseau, Dufy, Toulouse-Lautrec and Utrillo. Indeed, the ballet provides a clue not only to the mystery of Lise specifically, but of *la Parisienne* in general. One sequence opens in an enchanted flower market in the city, bathed in the warm glow of the afternoon sun. The scene, filled with a profusion of flowers and awash with brilliant colours, radiates a cheerful festive gaiety and ease. The lightness of tone, brightness of colour and rose tint recall the paintings of Renoir with their soft, feathery brushstrokes of radiant colour and shimmering palette. Against this Renoir-inspired backdrop, Lise enters the flower market right of screen. She resembles a figure straight out of a Renoir painting, and wears a diaphanous, dusty, pastel-blue dress which traces the contours of her figure and features delicate flower details which fall loosely about her. Holding a vivid red rose, Lise performs a *pas de deux* in the classical ballet style with Jerry (Gene Kelly). Her soft, harmonious, dreamy dress and graceful dance, the abundance of flowers and the joyful palette of the scene create a certain air of fantasy discernible in Renoir's canvases.

In a later sequence, we are presented with a scene of Parisian nightlife. Inside the smoky atmosphere of a bustling café-concert late at night, revellers are seated around tables on bentwood chairs. The scene's lurid, gaudy and intense colour, gloomy ambience and turbulent spectacle and festivity create what the film's script describes as 'a complete Lautrec environment' (qtd in Schwartz, *It's So French!* 38). The scene is populated by the iconic figures of Toulouse-Lautrec's posters and paintings, including the woman clown Cha-u-Kao, troubadour Aristide Bruant, chanteuse Yvette Guilbert, Alsatian laundress-cum-dancer la Goulue and Valentin-le-Désossé. In the midst of the vitality of the sequence, Lise appears on stage in a line of cancan dancers. Her blackstockinged, high-kicking leg emerges from beneath the billowing, multi-layered, full skirt of vivid orange and canary yellow fabric. She is dressed in a resplendent dress featuring a black bodice with enormous sequined cream-coloured 'gigot' sleeves ballooning out from her shoulders, and a voluminous skirt which fans out from her tiny waist. The gown is accessorised with long, black opera gloves and a cream bonnet lavishly adorned with a large, vibrant orange rosette and black feathers. Lise resembles music-hall dancer Jane Avril, 'La Mélinite', as she is represented in Toulouse-Lautrec's colour lithographic poster, *Jane Avril* (1893).

Despite the fact that the setting of *An American in Paris* is contemporaneous with its production, the ballet sequence evokes fin-de-siècle Paris. Schwartz argues this is because the film owes a 'genealogical debt' (*It's So French!* 38) to the art and mass culture of the epoch. *An American in Paris*, according to Schwartz, makes 'explicit both the importance of visual culture in late-nineteenth-century Paris and its connection to contemporary film culture of the 1950s. Paris and

Hollywood formed an axis of cultural circulation in which the former served as the cultural crucible for the latter' (*It's So French!* 34). The purpose of the sequence, which may otherwise be dismissed as gratuitous, with character and narrative taking a 'backseat' to the 'goal of creating stunning visual effects' (Schwartz, *It's So French!* 36), is in fact an iconographical retelling of the narrative in which Jerry first meets Lise, courts, loses, finds and loses her again. Indeed, for much of the sequence Lise remains elusive to Jerry and, in a key transition in the Renoir-inspired sequence, Jerry suddenly finds himself holding a mass of flowers where he had only a moment earlier held Lise. This transition is key because it demonstrates visually and literally the difficulty of grasping *la Parisienne*.

The *American in Paris* ballet sequence establishes visually a connection between Lise and the nineteenth-century figure of *la Parisienne*. Iconography, as it has been employed in this book, is less about defining or interpreting than about recognising certain types and the motifs with which they are associated. Indeed, association is the main mental operation of iconography. In Minnelli's film, Adam does not pose his question in strictly ontological terms, but rather uses the comparative hinge 'like', suggesting that what is required are not definitions as such but synonyms or traits; or, in iconographical terms, *motifs*. The answer the ballet sequence provides is indeed couched in these terms: Lise is *like* a woman from a Renoir canvas or from an advertising poster by Toulouse-Lautrec. In other words, her identity is ultimately displaced, both temporally and spatially. In order to understand who or what Lise is like, we need to familiarise ourselves with these women from nineteenth-century French painting, and by casting Lise in the role both of the central figure of a Renoir canvas and nineteenth-century Parisienne music-hall star Jane Avril as imagined by Toulouse-Lautrec, the sequence reveals her iconographical prefigurations. This leaves one possible and overarching definition of *la Parisienne*, which might be expressed as follows: *difficult to define or grasp, yet possessing a recognisable chain of associations, or iconography.*

It is now possible to offer the following provisional definition of *la Parisienne*: a type of which atypicality is the dominant feature; a type whose identity is continuously displaced or deferred, simultaneously reaching back to her earliest manifestations in the nineteenth century and forward to future manifestations which will both affirm and rework the iconography of the type. The further turn of the screw for the difficulty of defining *la Parisienne* as a type is that this difficulty is not in spite of her iconography but is in fact built into it. This apparent contradiction is accounted for within iconography itself as a methodology, the two aspects of which are stability and mutability. Since a type is only type because of recognisable motifs, certain motifs must be established which have both universal, and particular or historical validity. The universality of the type appears through an accumulation of its particulars, and this is primarily why there is such slippage between the concept of *la Parisienne* and its associated categories, and her physical embodiment in the photographed, written or painted world. What sets the Parisienne type apart, however, is that while variations on a type or genre are permitted and even welcomed within iconography as such (types may evolve historically, incidentally, or even deliberately without ceasing to be types), variability and elusiveness form an integral part of the Parisienne iconography and are not things external to it. In other words, a type in the usual sense is at all times self-identical, and this forms the basis of the recognition necessary for iconography; *la Parisienne*, on the other hand, is that type which, in Houssaye's words, 'never resembles herself' (273), whose typology and thus iconography is always in question.

One of the ways iconography may respond to its dual imperatives of stability and mutability is by constructing a cycle of films featuring a certain type, and one of the goals of this book was to go some way towards constructing what might be called a cycle of Parisienne films. This cycle, like the type *la Parisienne* itself, is never complete, but is continuously evolving. Each of the films considered in detail in this thesis constitutes part of this cycle of Parisienne films. To these films can also be added films discussed peripherally in each chapter. However, the cycle, even as it stands today, is far from limited to these films, and there are many which have not received mention here that could easily have found a place; the same can also be said of actresses. The iconographical concept of a cycle of films not only demonstrates the way films can be grouped non-traditionally – that is, not only according to genre, director, nation or film movement – but also the way future scholarship on the type can add to a cycle by considering other films in different combinations.

The nature of a book is such that it calls for structure, progression and, at times, an almost linear narrative structure. The need to adopt this structure does not imply however, that the type *la Parisienne* in cinema is a linearly developing type; it is, rather, a network of multiple intersections viewed in retrospect. For this reason, too, a comprehensive and chronological Parisienne filmography has not been provided, not only because such a list may be soon rendered incomplete, but also because the lifeblood of iconography flows in part due to the pleasure of recognition and may be prematurely curtailed by pre-empting the discovery of the type in films not discussed here. The task here, rather, is to provide the motifs by which future recognitions, even if they come from the past, are made possible.

Films cited

2 ou 3 choses que je sais d'elle. Dir. Jean-Luc Godard. 1967. Madman Entertainment, 2006. DVD.
8 femmes. Dir. François Ozon. 2001. Magna Pacific, 2001. DVD.
21 Grams. Dir. Alejandro González Iñárritu. 2003. Reel DVD, 2010. DVD.
À bout de souffle. Dir. Jean-Luc Godard. 1960. Universal, 2007. DVD.
Algiers. Dir. John Cromwell. 1938. Alpha Video, 2002. DVD.
Alphaville, une étrange aventure de Lemmy Caution. Dir. Jean-Luc Godard. 1965. Universal, 2007. DVD.
Les Amants. Dir. Louis Malle. 1958. Aztec International Entertainment, 2005. DVD.
An American in Paris. Dir. Vincente Minnelli. 1951. Turner Entertainment, 2003. DVD.
Anna. Dir. Pierre Koralnik. 1967. Mercury, 2009. DVD.
Antichrist. Dir. Lars Von Trier. 2009. Criterion Collection, 2010. DVD.
Arch of Triumph. Dir. Lewis Milestone. 1948. Olive Films, 2014. DVD.
Ascenseur pour l'échafaud. Dir. Louis Malle. 1957. Aztec International Entertainment, 2006. DVD.
The Asphalt Jungle. Dir. John Huston. 1950. Warner Home Video, 2004. DVD.
La Baie des anges. Dir. Jacques Demy. 1963. Arte France Développement, 2008. DVD.
Bande à part. Dir. Jean-Luc Godard. Anouchka Films/Orsay Films. 1964. Film.
Bande de filles. Dir. Céline Sciamma. 2014. Pyramid Distribution. Film.
La Bandera. Dir. Julien Duvivier. 1935. Vanguard Cinema, 2003. DVD.
Belle de jour. Dir. Luis Buñuel. 1967. Optimum Releasing, 2007. DVD.
La Bête humaine. Dir. Jean Renoir. 1938. Criterion collection, 2006. DVD.
The Big Sleep. Dir. Howard Hawks. 1946. Warner Home Video, 2000. DVD.
Bob le flambeur. Dir. Jean-Pierre Melville. 1955. Studio Canal Image, 2002. DVD.
Breakfast at Tiffany's. Dir. Blake Edwards. 1961. Paramount Home Entertainment, 2006. DVD.
Brigitte et Brigitte. Dir. Luc Moullet. 1966. Facets Video, 2006. DVD.
Camille Claudel 1915. Dir. Bruno Dumont. 2013. Rialto, 2013. DVD.

FILMS CITED

Can-Can. Dir. Walter Lang. 1960. Twentieth Century Fox Home Entertainment, 2007. DVD.
Le Carrosse d'or. Dir. Jean Renoir. 1952. Madman, 2009. DVD.
Casablanca. Dir. Michael Curtiz. 1942. Warner Home Video, 2003. DVD.
Casque d'or. Dir. Jacques Becker. 1952. Universal Studios, 2009. DVD.
The Cement Garden. Dir. Andrew Birkin. 1993. New Yorker Video, 2000. DVD.
Cette sacrée gamine. Dir. Michel Boisrond. 1956. Universal Pictures, 2008. DVD.
La Chamade. Dir. Alain Cavalier. 1968. Shock, 2006. DVD.
Charade. Dir. Stanley Donen. 1963. MRA Entertainment, 2001. DVD.
Charlotte et Véronique ou Tous les garçons s'appellent Patrick. Dir. Jean-Luc Godard. 1957. Criterion Collection, 2004. DVD.
Charlotte Forever. Dir. Serge Gainsbourg. 1985. LCJ Editions, 2005. DVD.
Chaos. Dir. Coline Serreau. 2001. New Yorker Video, 2003. DVD.
Cléo de cinq à sept. Dir. Agnès Varda. 1962. Criterion Collection, 2007. DVD.
Daddy Long Legs. Dir. Jean Negulesco. 1955. Twentieth Century Fox Home Entertainment, 2007. DVD.
Design for Living. Dir. Ernst Lubitsch. 1933. Criterion Collection, 2011. DVD.
Detour. Dir. Edgar G. Ulmer. 1945. Warner Home Video, 2000. DVD.
Les Demoiselles de Rochefort. Dir. Jacques Demy. 1966. Arte France Développement, 2008. DVD.
Diary of a Chambermaid. Dir. Jean Renoir. 1946. Olive Films, 2013. DVD.
Double Indemnity. Dir. Billy Wilder. 1944. Madman Entertainment, 2006. DVD.
Du Rififi chez les hommes. Dir. Jules Dassin. 1955. Madman Entertainment, 2001. DVD.
L'Effrontée. Dir. Claude Miller. 1985. Wellspring, 2003. DVD.
Elena et les hommes. Dir. Jean Renoir. 1956. Madman Entertainment, 2010. DVD.
En Effeuillant la marguerite. Dir. Marc Allégret. 1956. Home Vision Entertainment, 2001. DVD.
Et Dieu … créa la femme. Dir. Roger Vadim. 1956. Criterion Collection, 2000. DVD.
Eva. Dir. Joseph Losey. 1962. Madman Entertainment, 2010. DVD.
Le Fabuleux destin d'Amélie Poulain. Dir. Jean-Pierre Jeunet. 2001. Magna Pacific, 2002. DVD.
Fallen Angel. Dir. Otto Preminger. 1945. Madman Entertainment, 2009. DVD.
Une Femme est une femme. Dir. Jean-Luc Godard. 1961. Criterion Collection, 2004. DVD.
Frantic. Dir. Roman Polanski. 1988. Warner Home Video, 2000. DVD.
French Cancan. Dir. Jean Renoir. 1955. Criterion collection, 2004. DVD.
Funny Face. Dir. Stanley Donen. 1956. Paramount Home Entertainment, 2009. DVD.

FILMS CITED 187

Gentlemen Prefer Blondes. Dir. Howard Hawks. 1953. Twentieth Century Fox Home Entertainment, 2006. DVD.
Gigi. Dir. Vincente Minnelli. 1958. Warner Home Video, 2000. DVD.
Gigola. Dir. Laure Charpentier. 2010. QC Cinema, 2010. DVD.
Gilda. Dir. Charles Vidor. 1946. Columbia Tristar Home Video, 1999. DVD.
The Golden Door. Dir. Emanuele Crialese. 2006. Studio Canal, 2007. DVD.
Goodbye Again. Dir. Anatole Litvak. 1961. Shock, 2013. DVD.
Holy Motors. Dir. Leos Carax. 2012. Artificial Eye, 2013. DVD.
Hôtel du nord. Dir. Marcel Carné. 1938. René Chateau, 1994. VHS.
How to Steal a Million. Dir. William Wyler. 1966. Twentieth Century Fox Home Entertainment, 2006. DVD.
Human Desire. Dir. Fritz Lang. 1958. Columbia Tri-Star Home Video, 2004. DVD.
Ils se marièrent et eurent beaucoup d'enfants. Dir. Yvan Attal. 2004. Kino International, 2005. DVD.
I'm Not There. Dir. Todd Haynes. 2007. Icon Home Entertainment, 2008. DVD.
Irma la Douce. Dir. Billy Wilder. 1963. Twentieth Century Fox Home Entertainment, 2006. DVD.
Jane Eyre. Dir. Franco Zeffirelli. 1996. Echo Bridge Home Entertainment, 2011. DVD.
Le Jour se lève. Dir. Marcel Carné. 1939. Janus Films, 2006. DVD.
Le Journal d'une femme de chambre. Dir. Luis Buñuel. 1964. Criterion collection, 2001. DVD.
Jules et Jim. Dir. François Truffaut. 1961. Umbrella, 2003. DVD.
Klimt. Dir. Raúl Ruiz. 2006. Koch Lorber Films, 2007. DVD.
The Last Time I Saw Paris. Dir. Richard Brooks. 1954 MRA Entertainment, 2001. DVD.
Laura. Dir. Otto Preminger. 1944. 20th Century Fox Home Entertainment, 2004. DVD.
Lemming. Dir. Dominik Moll. 2006. Strand Releasing Home Video, 2006. DVD.
Les Girls. Dir. George Cukor. 1957. Warner Home Video, 2003. DVD.
Lola. Dir. Jacques Demy. 1961. Arte France Développement, 2008. DVD.
The Long Night. Dir. Anatole Litvak. 1947. Kino Video, 2000. DVD.
Madame Bovary. Dir. Jean Renoir. 1933. Studio Canal, 2005. DVD.
Made in U.S.A. Dir. Jean-Luc Godard. 1966. Warner Home Video, 2005. DVD.
Ma Femme est une actrice. Dir. Yvan Attal. 2001. Twentieth Century Fox Home Entertainment, 2004. DVD.
The Maltese Falcon. Dir. John Huston. 1941. Warner Home Video, 2006. DVD.
La Mariée était en noir. Dir. François Truffaut. 1968. MGM Home Entertainment, 2001. DVD.
Masculin féminin. Dir. Jean-Luc Godard. 1966. Madman, 2006. DVD.
Melancholia. Dir. Lars Von Trier. 2011. Magnolia Home Entertainment, 2012. DVD.

Le Mépris. Dir. Jean-Luc Godard. 1963. Universal, 2007. DVD.
Midnight in Paris. Dir. Woody Allen. 2011. Hopscotch Entertainment, 2012. DVD.
Model Shop. Dir. Jacques Demy. 1969. Sony Pictures Home Entertainment, 2009. DVD.
Moulin Rouge. Dir. John Huston. 1952. Magna Pacific, 2002. DVD.
Moulin Rouge! Dir. Baz Lurhmann. 2002. Twentieth Century Fox Home Entertainment, 2008. DVD.
Nana. Dir. Jean Renoir. 1926. Lions Gate Entertainment, 2007. DVD.
Napoléon. Dir. Abel Gance. 1927. Manga Films, 2004. DVD.
Nathalie Granger. Dir. Marguerite Duras. 1972. Blaq Out, 2008. DVD.
A New Kind of Love. Dir. Melville Shavelson. 1963. Paramount Home Entertainment, 2005. DVD.
Nymphomaniac: Volume 1. Dir. Lars Von Trier. 2013. Paramount Pictures, 2014. DVD.
Nymphomaniac: Volume 2. Dir. Lars Von Trier. 2013. Paramount Pictures, 2014. DVD.
Out of the Past. Dir. Jacques Tourneur. 1947. Turner Entertainment, 2004. DVD.
Pandora's Box. Dir. G.W. Pabst. 1929. Criterion Collection, 2006. DVD.
Les Parapluies de Cherbourg. Dir. Jacques Demy. 1964. Koch Vision, 2004. DVD.
Paris. Dir. Edmund Goulding. 1926. MGM. Film.
Une Parisienne. Dir. Michel Boisrond. 1957. C'est la Vie, 2003. DVD.
Paris When It Sizzles. Dir. Richard Quine. 1963. Paramount Home Entertainment, 2009. DVD.
Paroles et Musique. Dir. Elie Chouraqui. 1984. Somerville House, 2008. DVD.
Pépé le Moko. Dir. Julien Duvivier. 1937. Janus Films, 2006. DVD.
Le Petit soldat. Dir. Jean-Luc Godard. 1960. Universal, 2007. DVD.
Pièges. Dir. Robert Siodmak. 1939. Spéva Films. Film.
Pierrot le fou. Dir. Jean-Luc Godard. 1965. Fox Lorber Home Video, 1999. DVD.
La Piscine. Dir. Jacques Deray. 1969. Park Circus, 2011. DVD.
Le Plaisir. Dir. Max Ophüls. 1952. Madman, 2009. DVD.
The Postman Always Rings Twice. Dir. Tay Garnett. 1946. Warner Home Video, 2005. DVD.
Prête-moi ta main. Dir. Eric Lartigau. 2006. Lionsgate, 2009. DVD.
Le Quai des brumes. Dir. Marcel Carné. 1938. Criterion Collection, 2004. DVD.
The Rage of Paris. Dir. Henry Koster. 1938. Alpha Video, 2005. DVD.
La Règle du jeu. Dir. Jean Renoir. 1939. Criterion collection, 2004. DVD.
Reunion in France. Dir. Jules Dassin. 1942. Warner Bros. Entertainment, 2010. DVD.
Rich, Young and Pretty. Dir. Norman Taurog. 1951. Warner Archives, 2009. DVD.

Sabrina. Dir. Billy Wilder. 1954. Paramount Home Entertainment, 2009. DVD.
Sagan. Dir. Diane Kurys. 2008. Universal Studios Home Entertainment, 2009. DVD.
The Science of Sleep. Dir. Michel Gondry. 2006. Madman, 2007. DVD.
Silk Stockings. Dir. Rouben Mamoulian. 1957. Warner Home Video, 2003. DVD.
La Sirène du Mississippi. Dir. François Truffaut. 1969. Shock, 2010. DVD.
Tirez sur le pianiste. Dir. François Truffaut. 1960. Umbrella Entertainment, 2004. DVD.
Touchez pas au grisbi. 1954. Dir. Jacques Becker. Madman, 2010. DVD.
The Tree. Dir. Dawn O'Neill. 2010. Universal Pictures, 2011. DVD.
The Trial. Dir. Orson Welles. 1962. Universal Studios, 2009. DVD.
Trop belle pour toi. Dir. Bertrand Blier. 1989. Umbrella Entertainment, 2006. DVD.
L'un reste, l'autre part. Dir. Claude Berri. 2004. Madman Entertainment, 2008. DVD.
Vie privée. Dir. Louis Malle. 1962. MGM Warner, 1993. VHS.
Viva Maria! Dir. Louis Malle. 1965. Fox Video, 2005. DVD.
Vivre sa vie. Dir. Jean-Luc Godard. 1962. Madman Entertainment, 2006. DVD.
Voulez-vous danser avec moi? Michel Boisrond. 1959. Universal Pictures, 2008. DVD.
A Woman of Paris. Dir. Charles Chaplin. 1923. Paramount Home Entertainment, 2010. DVD.
The Women. Dir. George Cukor. 1939. Warner Home Video, 2002. DVD.
The Yellow Rolls Royce. Dir. Anthony Asquith. 1964. Warner Home Video, 2009. DVD.

References

Allen, Virginia M. *The Femme Fatale: Erotic Icon*. Troy, NY: Whitson, 1983. Print.
Alloway, Lawrence. 'Lawrence Alloway on the Iconography of the Movies.' 1963. *Movie Reader*. Ed. Ian Cameron. New York: Praeger, 1972. 16–18. Print.
Andrew, Dudley. 'Breathless: Old as New.' *Breathless*. Ed. Andrew. New Brunswick, NJ: U of Rutgers P, 1987. 10. Print.
— *Mists of Regret: Culture and Sensibility in Classic French Film*. Princeton, NJ: U of Princeton P, 1995. Print.
Andrew, Dudley, and Ungar, Steven. *Popular Front Paris and the Poetics of Culture*. Cambridge, MA: Harvard UP, 2005. Print.
Armes, Roy. *French Cinema*. New York: Oxford UP, 1985. Print.
Aronovich, Ricardo. 'Entretien avec Ricardo Aronovich: ouvrir des possibilités au métier en scène.' By Michel Ciment. *Positif* Apr. 2006: 16–20. Print.
Austin, Guy. *Stars in Modern French Film*. London: Arnold, 2003. Print.
Bade, Patrick. *Femme Fatale: Images of Evil and Fascinating Women*. London: Ash & Grant, 1979. Print.
Banville, Théodore de. 'Le Génie des Parisiennes.' *Conte pour les Femmes*. Paris: G. Charpentier, 1881.
— *Les Parisiennes de Paris*. 1886. Paris: Dodo Press, 2008. Print.
'Bardolatrie in Paris: The Bébé Look.' *Life* 47, 10 Aug. 1959, 14–15. Print.
Barthes, Roland. *Mythologies*. Trans. Annette Lavers. London: HarperCollins, 1973. Print.
Baudelaire, Charles. *Œuvres complètes*. Paris: Seuil, 1968. Print.
— *Selected Poems*. Trans. Carol Clark. London: Penguin, 1995. Print.
— 'The Painter of Modern Life.' Trans. P.E. Charvet. *Baudelaire: Selected Writings on Art and Literature*. Ed. Robert Baldick and Betty Radice. London: Penguin, 2006. 390–435. Print.
Baudouin. *75 Parisiennes*. Paris: CF + Snoeck, 2012. Print.
Bayles, Janette. 'Gendered configurations of colonial and metropolitan space in *Pépé le Moko*.' *Australian Journal of French Studies* 36.1 (1999): 39–57. Print.

Bazgan, Nicoleta. 'Female bodies in Paris: iconic urban femininity and Parisian journeys.' *Studies in French Cinema* 10.2 (2010): 95–109. Print.
'Beauty Icon: Anna Karina.' *Russh* Sept.–Oct. 2008: 112. Print.
Beauvoir, Simone de. Trans. Bernard Fretchman. *Brigitte Bardot and the Lolita Syndrome*. London: Four Square, 1962. Print.
Becque, Henry. 'La Parisienne.' *Œuvres complètes*. 1885. Paris: G. Grès, 1924–26. *Gallica, Bibliothèque numérique*. 1–122. Web. 15 Mar. 2013. http://gallica.bnf.fr/ark:/12148/bpt6k209967c. Accessed 28 Oct. 2016.
Benjamin, Walter. *Illuminations*. Trans. Harry Zohn. New York: Schocken, 1968. Print.
— *The Arcades Project*. Trans. Howard Eiland and Kevin McLaughlin. Cambridge, MA: Belknap, 1999. Print.
— *The Writer of Modern Life: Essays on Charles Baudelaire*. Trans. Howard Eiland, Edmund Jephcott, Rodney Livingston and Harry Zohn. Ed. Michael W. Jennings. Cambridge, MA: Harvard UP, 2006. Print.
Bergala, Alain. *Godard au travail: les années 60*. Paris: Cahiers du Cinéma, 2006. Print.
— *Brune, blonde: la chevelure féminine dans l'art et le cinéma*. Paris: Skira Flammarion, 2010. Print.
— 'Foreword.' In *Brune/Blonde, l'exposition virtuelle*. La Cinémathèque française: Marion Langlois Online Publishing, n.d. Web. 17 Dec. 2013.
Bergan, Ronald. *Jean Renoir: Projections of Paradise*. New York: Overlook, 1992. Print.
Bergoffen, Deborah B. *The Philosophy of Simone de Beauvoir: Gendered Phenomenologies, Erotic Generosities*. Albany: State U of New York P. 1997. Print.
Berlanstein, Lenard R. *Daughters of Eve: A Cultural History of French Theater Women from the Old Regime to the Fin de Siècle*. Cambridge, MA: Harvard UP, 2001. Print.
Bernstein, Richard. *Fragile Glory: A Portrait of France and the French*. New York: Bodley Head, 1991. Print.
Bertin, Célia. *Jean Renoir: A Life in Pictures*. Trans. Mireille Muellner and Leonard Muellner. Baltimore, MD: Johns Hopkins UP, 1991. Print.
Betz, Mark. *Beyond the Subtitle: Remapping European Art Cinema*. Minneapolis: U of Minnesota P, 2009. Print.
Borde, Raymond, and Étienne Chaumeton. *A Panorama of American Film Noir 1941–1953*. 1955. Trans. Paul Hammond. San Francisco, CA: City Lights Books, 2002. Print.
Bouquet, Carole. 'Elegance.' Trans. Louise Lalaurie Rogers. In *Parisiennes: A Celebration of French Women*. Ed. Bouquet. Paris: Flammarion, 2007. 174. Print.
Bourget, Jean-Loup. 'En relisant Panofsky.' *Positif* 259 (1982): 38–43. Print.
Braudy, Leo. "Renoir at home: interview with Jean Renoir." *Film Quarterly* 50.1 (1996): 2–8. *Jstor*. Web. 19 May 2014.
'Breathless.' *Marie Claire Australia* Mar. 2014: 118–29. Print.

Brody, Richard. *Everything is Cinema: the Working Life of Jean-Luc Godard*. New York: Henry Holt, 2008. Print.
Bruzzi, Stella. *Undressing Cinema: Clothing and Identity in the Movies*. London: Routledge, 1997. Print.
Buck, Joan Juliet. 'The Most Private Star.' *Vogue* 10 (2006): 287–8. *ProQuest*. Web. 2 May. 2014.
Campbell, Russell. *Marked Women: Prostitutes and Prostitution in the Cinema*. Madison: Wisconsin UP, 2006. Print.
Caputo, Davide. *Polanski and Perception: The Psychology of Seeing and the Cinema of Roman Polanski*. Bristol: Intellect, 2012. Print.
Carter, Michael. *Fashion Classics from Carlyle to Barthes*. Oxford: Berg, 2006. Print.
Cavell, Stanley. 'Types; Cycles as Genres.' *Film Theory and Criticism: Introductory Readings*. Ed. Gerald Mast and Marshall Cohen. 2nd ed. New York: Oxford UP, 1979. 311–17. Print.
Chadwick, Whitney. *Amazons in the Drawing Room: The Art of Romaine Brooks*. Berkeley: U of California P, 2000. Print.
Chapier, Henry. 'Cinema and Fashion: A Parallel Destiny.' Trans. Sally Norman and Caroline Bouché. *French Elegance in the Cinema*. Ed. Madeleine Delpierre, Marianne de Fleury and Dominique Lebrun. Paris: Société de l'histoire du costume, 1988. 7–8. Print.
Cheng, Anne Anlin. 'Skin deep: Josephine Baker and the colonial fetish.' *Camera Obscura* 23.69 (2008): 34–79. *Art & Architecture Complete*. Web. 4 Dec. 2011.
Chrisafis, Angelique. 'G2: "I Prefer to Anticipate the Bad Side rather than Get a Slap in the Face Later": France's most Self-Critical Film Star, Charlotte Gainsbourg has Grown Up Surrounded by Controversy. as She Collaborates with Lars Von Trier Once again, in Melancholia, She Talks to Angelique Chrisafis.' *Guardian*: 10. 29 Sept. 2011. *ProQuest*. Web. 24 Mar. 2014.
Chung, Alexa. *It*. London: Penguin, 2013. Print.
Church-Gibson, Pamela. 'New Stars, New Fashions and the Female Audience: Cinema, Consumption and Cities 1953–1966.' *Fashion's World Cities*. Ed. Christopher Breward and David Gilbert. Oxford: Berg, 2006. 89–106. Print.
Clayson, Hollis. *Painted Love: Prostitution in French Art of the Impressionist Era*. New Haven, CT: Yale UP, 1991. Print.
Cocteau, Jean. *Thomas l'imposteur*. 1923. *Jean Cocteau: Œuvres romanesques complètes*. Paris, Gallimard, 2006. 372–432. Print.
Colette. *Chéri*. Paris: Fayard, 1920. Print.
— *Chéri*. Trans. Roger Senhouse. London: Vintage, 2001. Print.
— *La vagabonde*. Paris: Fayard, 1936. Print.
— *Gigi*. Paris: J. Ferenczi & Fils, 1945. Print.
Conway, Kelley. 'Brigitte Bardot: From International Star to Fashion Icon.' *New Constellations*. New Brunswick; NJ: Rutgers UP, 2012. 183. Web.
Craik, Jennifer. *Fashion: The Key Concepts*. Oxford: Berg, 2009. Print.

REFERENCES

Crisp, Colin. *Genre, Myth, and Convention in the French Cinema, 1929–1939*. Bloomington: Indiana UP, 2002. Print.

Cronin, Paul. *Roman Polanski: Interviews*. Jackson: U of Mississippi P, 2005. Print.

Cronin, Vincent. *Paris on the Eve*. London: Collins, 1989. Print.

Davis, Colin. 'Jean Renoir's *Elena et les hommes* (1956) and the shadow of imperialism.' *Studies in French Cinema* 11.1 (2011): 17–29. Print.

de Baecque, Antoine, and Serge Toubiana. *Truffaut*. Trans. Catherine Temerson. Berkeley: U of California P, 2000. Print.

DeJean, Joan. *The Essence of Style: How the French Invented High Fashion, Fine Food, Chic Cafés, Style, Sophistication, and Glamour*. New York: Free Press, 2005. Print.

Delord, Taxile. *Physiologie de la Parisienne*. Paris: Aubert, 1841. *Gallica, Bibliothèque numérique*. Web. 7 Apr. 2011. http://gallica.bnf.fr/ark:/12148/btv1b85303146. Accessed 4 Nov. 2016.

Denuelle, Sabine. *La Parisienne dans l'art*. Paris: Citadelles & Mazenod, 2011. Print.

De Young, Justine. 'Fashion and Intimate Portraits.' *Impressionism, Fashion, and Modernity*. Ed. Gloria Groom. New Haven, CT: Yale UP, 2012. 107–23. Print.

— 'Women in Black: Fashion, Modernity and Modernism in Paris, 1860–1890.' Order No. 3355748. Northwestern University, 2009. Ann Arbor: *ProQuest*. Web. 21 Aug. 2014.

Doan, Laura L. *Fashioning Sapphism: The Origins of a Modern English Lesbian Culture*. New York: Columbia UP, 2001. Print.

Dubreuil, Maroussia. 'Woody Allen's Paris: Reconstructing the Past.' Trans. Alexandra Keens. *Paris by Hollywood*. Ed. Antoine de Baecque. Paris: Flammarion, 2012. 246–59. Print.

Dumas *fils*, Alexandre. *La Dame aux camélias*. Paris: Michel Lévy, 1852. *Gallica, Bibliothèque numérique*. Web. 3 Mar. 2014. http://gallica.bnf.fr/ark:/12148/bpt6k6572546p. Accessed 4 Nov. 2016.

— *The Lady of the Camellias*. Trans. Liesl Schillinger. New York: Penguin, 2013. Print.

Durgnat, Raymond. *Jean Renoir*. Los Angeles: California UP: 1974. Print.

Ďurovičová, Natasa, and Kathleen Newman. *World Cinemas, Transnational Perspectives*. New York: Routledge, 2009. Print.

Eliot, T.S. *Collected Poems 1909–1962*. London: Faber, 2002. Print.

Elliott, Bridget, and Jo-Ann Wallace. 'Fleurs du mal or second-hand roses?: Natalie Barney, Romaine Brooks, and the "originality of the avant-garde".' *Feminist Review* 40 (1992): 6. *ProQuest*. Web. 23 Aug. 2012.

Ezra, Elizabeth, and Terry Rowden. *Transnational Cinema: The Film Reader*. New York: Routledge, 2006. Print.

Faulkner, William. *The Wild Palms*. 1939. London: Vintage Random House, 2000. Print.

— *Requiem for a Nun*. New York: Random House, 1951. Print.

Felski, Rita. *The Gender of Modernity*. Cambridge, MA: Harvard UP, 1995. Print.
Ferrari, Jean-Christophe. 'The Parisienne: Object of American Desire.' Trans. Alexandra Keens. *Paris by Hollywood*. Ed. Antoine de Baecque. Paris: Flammarion, 2012. 70–83. Print.
Fizdale, Robert, and Arthur Gold. *Misia: The Life of Misia Sert*. London: Macmillan, 1980. Print.
Flaubert, Gustave. *L'Éducation sentimentale*. Paris: Gallimard, 2010. Print.
— *Sentimental Education*. Trans. Robert Baldick. Harmondsworth: Penguin, 1961. Print.
Forth, Christopher E. *The Dreyfus Affair and the Crisis of French Manhood*. Baltimore, MD: Johns Hopkins UP, 2006. Print.
Fox, James. 'Even for Paris, This Was Impressive.' *Vanity Fair* Feb. 2014: 103. Print.
Fraser-Cavassoni, Natasha. 'Charlotte Gainsbourg is Not a Style Icon; and if You Ask Her, nor is She an Actress Or an Artist. But Judging from Her Provocative Body of Work, She's all that and More.' *WSJ: the Magazine from the Wall Street Journal* 03 2012 ProQuest. Web. 2 Mar. 2014.
'French New Wave Fashion: Anna Karina.' *New Wave Film*, n.p. Web. 31 Jan. 2014.
Fressange, Inès de la. *Parisian Chic*. Trans. Louise Rogers Lalaurie. Paris: Flammarion, 2011. Print.
Frey, Hugo. *Louis Malle*. Manchester: Manchester UP, 2004. Print.
Friedberg, Anne, American Council of Learned Societies, and NetLibrary, Inc. *Window Shopping: Cinema and the Postmodern*. Berkeley: U of California P, 1993. Web.
Fuller, Graham. 'Strictly red.' *Sight & Sound* 11.6 (2001): 14–16. Print.
Garb, Tamar. *Bodies of Modernity: Figure and Flesh in Fin-de Siècle France*. New York: Thames & Hudson, 1998. Print.
— '"Painting the "Parisienne": James Tissot and the Making of the Modern Woman.' *Seductive Surfaces: The Art of Tissot*. Ed. Katharine Jordan Lochnan. New Haven, CT: Yale UP, 1999. 95–120. Print.
Garcia, Patricia. 'Alexa Chung Has It: Her New Book and Her Best Style Moments of 2013.' *Vogue*. Condé Nast Digital, 29 Oct. 2013. Web. 5 Apr. 2014.
Gardiner, Josh. 'Anna Karina.' *Russh*. Switzer Media, n.d. Web. 12 June 2014. http://www.russhmagazine.com/arts-music/artists/profile-anna-karina. Accessed 4 Nov. 2016.
Garval, Michael D. *Cléo de Mérode and the Rise of Modern Celebrity Culture*. Farnham: Ashgate, 2012. Print.
Gautier, Théophile. *Mademoiselle de Maupin*. Paris: Charpentier, 1876. *Gallica, Bibliothèque numérique*. Web. 30 May 2012. http://gallica.bnf.fr/ark:/12148/bpt6k804300. Accessed 4 Nov. 2016.
Gendarme, Jean-Baptiste. Foreword. *75 Parisiennes*. Paris: CF + Snoeck, 2012. iii–iv. Print.

Gilbert, David. 'World Cities of Fashion.' *The Fashion Reader: Second Edition.* Ed. Linda Welters and Abby Lillethun. Oxford: Berg, 2011. 237–42. Print.

Girner, Simone. 'People are Talking about: Personal Best.' *Vogue* 1 July 2002: 99. *ProQuest.* Web. 5 Mar. 2014.

Godley, Chris, and Meg Hemphill. 'Costume Designs of Midnight in Paris.' 13 June 2011. *Hollywood Reporter.* Web. 10 May 2014.

Grant, Barry Keith. *Film Genre: From Iconography to Ideology.* London: Wallflower, 2007. Print.

Gray, Marianne. *La Moreau: A Biography of Jeanne Moreau.* New York: Donald I. Fine, 1996. Print.

Groom, Gloria, ed. *Impressionism, Fashion, and Modernity.* New Haven, CT: Yale UP, 2012. Print.

Gruber, Helmut. 'Jean Gabin: doomed worker-hero of a doomed France.' *International Labor and Working Class History* 59 (2001): 15–35. *ProQuest.* Web. 12 Oct. 2012.

Haining, Peter. *The Legend of Brigitte Bardot.* London: W.H. Allen, 1983. Print.

Hanson, Helen, and Catherine O'Rawe. *The Femme Fatale: Images, Histories, Contexts.* London: Palgrave Macmillan, 2010. Print.

Harris, Sue. 'Renoir's Paris: the city as film set.' *South Central Review* 28.3 (Fall): 84–102. *Project Muse.* Web. 19 May 2014.

Harvey, David. *Paris, Capital of Modernity.* New York: Routledge, 2006. Print.

Hayward, Susan. *French National Cinema.* 2nd ed. New York: Routledge, 2005. Print.

— 'Design at Work: Renoir's Costume Dramas of the 1950s.' *A Companion to Jean Renoir.* Ed. Alastair Phillips and Ginette Vincendeau. Oxford: Wiley-Blackwell, 2013. 88–105. Print.

Hérail, René James, and Edwin A. Lovatt. *Dictionary of Modern Colloquial French.* London: Routledge, 1984. Print.

Higonnet, Patrice. *Paris: Capital of the World.* Trans. Arthur Goldhammer. Cambridge, MA: Harvard UP, 2002. Print.

Hillier, Jim, and Alastair Phillips. *100 Film Noirs.* London: Palgrave Macmillan, 2009. Print.

Holmes, Diana. '"A Girl of Today": Brigitte Bardot.' *Stardom in Postwar France.* Ed. Holmes and John Gaffney. New York: Berghahn Books, 2011. 40–66. Print.

Horwath, Alexander. 'A Walking Contradiction (Partly Truth and Partly Fiction).' *The Last Great American Picture Show: New Hollywood Cinema in the 1970s.* Ed. Horwath, Thomas Elsaesser and Noel King. Amsterdam: Amsterdam UP, 2004. 83–106. Print.

Houssaye, Arsène. *Les Parisiennes.* Paris: E. Dentu, 1869. Boston: Elibron Classics, 2006. Print.

Humphrey, Claire. 'Parisienne femininity and the politics of embodiment.' *French Cultural Studies* 23.3 (2012): 256–65. Web. *Sage Premier.* 6 Apr. 2013.

Hussey, Andrew. *Paris: A Secret History*. London: Bloomsbury, 2006. Print.
'Les idées mode à piquer à Charlotte Gainsbourg.' *Grazia.fr*. 4 May 2012. Web. 8 Mar 2014.
Iskin, Ruth E. *Modern Women and Parisian Consumer Culture in Impressionist Painting*. Cambridge: Cambridge UP, 2007. Print.
'Jean Seberg.' *Vogue* Oct. 1990: 362–75. Print.
Johnson, Julie. 'A Contested City: Gwen John, Suzanne Valadon, and Women Artists in Fin-de-Siècle Paris.' *City Limits: Perspectives on the Historical European City*. Ed. Glenn Clark, Judith Owens and Greg T. Smith. Montreal: McGill-Queen's UP, 2010. Print.
Johnston, Sheila. 'Stepping Out of Serge's Shadow: Charlotte Gainsbourg Talks to Sheila Johnston about Her Famous Parents, and Taking Her Own Path to Fame.' *Daily Telegraph*: 5. 16 June 2007. ProQuest. Web. 25 Aug. 2014.
Kavanagh, Julie. Introduction. Alexandre Dumas Fils. *The Lady of the Camellias*. Trans. Liesl Schillinger. New York: Penguin, 2013. Print.
Kinder, Marsha. 'Moulin Rouge.' *Film Quarterly* 55.3 (2002): 52–9. ProQuest. Web. 31 Dec. 2013.
King, Ross. *The Judgment of Paris: The Revolutionary Decade That Gave the World Impressionism*. New York: Walker, 2006. Print.
Kinsman, Jane. *Paris in the Late 19th Century*. Canberra: National Gallery of Australia, 1996. Print.
Lamy, Marie-Noëlle. *The Cambridge French–English Thesaurus*. Cambridge: Cambridge UP, 1998. Print.
Larocca, Amy. '62 Minutes With Charlotte Gainsbourg; Born to Fame, or at Least Experience, the Singer, Actress, and Fashion Muse Is Just Glad to See Her Kids Again, At Last.' *New York* 17 May 2010. Academic OneFile. Web. 29 Dec. 2012.
Lathers, Marie. *Bodies of Art: French Literary Realism and the Artist's Model*. Lincoln: U of Nebraska Press, 2001. Print.
Leahy, Sarah. 'The matter of myth: Brigitte Bardot, stardom and sex.' *Studies in French Cinema* 3.2 (2003): 71–81. Web.
Levin, Thomas Y. 'Iconology at the movies: Panofsky's film theory.' *Yale Journal of Criticism* 9.1 (1996): 27–55. Project Muse. Web. 22 May 2013.
Levy, Gayle A. *Refiguring the Muse*. New York: Peter Lang, 1999. Print.
Lussier, Suzanne. *Art Deco Fashion*. Boston: Bulfinch Press, 2003. Print.
Mackenzie, Mairi. *Isms: Understanding Fashion*. New York: Rizzoli, 2010. Print.
Macnab, Geoffrey. 'Gold leaf and shadow-play.' *Sight & Sound* 16.9 (2006): 30–4. EBSCOhost. Web. 9 Dec. 2012.
Mac Orlan, Pierre. *Le Quai des brumes*. Paris: Gallimard, 1927. Print.
Mancoff, Debra N. *Fashion in Impressionist Paris*. London: Merrell, 2012. Print.
Marie, Michel. *The French New Wave: An Artistic School*. Trans. Richard Neupert. Oxford: Blackwell, 2003. Print.

Marguerite, Victor. *La Garçonne*. Paris: Flammarion, 1922. Print.
Marshall, Nancy Rose. 'Parisiennes.' *James Tissot: Victorian Life/Modern Love.* Ed. Malcolm Warner. New Haven, CT: Yale UP, 1999. 147–50. Print.
Maupassant, Guy de. 'La Parure.' 1884. *Contes et nouvelles*. Vol. I. Paris: Gallimard, 1974. 1198–206. Print.
Maurois, André. *Femmes de Paris*. Paris: Plon, 1954. Print.
— *Women of Paris*. Trans. Norman Denny. London: André Deutsch, 1958. Print.
Mazierska, Ewa. *Roman Polanski: The Cinema of a Cultural Traveller*. London: I.B. Tauris, 2007. Print.
Menkes, Suzy. 'The Allure of the Trench.' *Harper's Bazaar* 05 2004: 153, 155, 157–8, 161. *ProQuest*. Web. 21 Nov. 2013.
Menon, Elizabeth Kolbinger. 'Images of Pleasure and Vice: Women of the Fringe.' *Montmartre and the Making of Mass Culture*. Ed. Gabriel P. Weisberg. Piscataway, NJ: Rutgers UP, 2001. 37–71. Print.
— *Evil by Design: The Creation and Marketing of the Femme Fatale*. Urbana: U of Illinois P, 2006. Print.
Mercer, John, and Martin Shingler. *Melodrama: Genre, Style and Sensibility*. London: Wallflower, 2004. Print.
Merimée, Prosper. *Carmen*. 1845. Trans. Richard Griffin. Cammeray, NSW: Southern Cross Books, 1984. Print.
Merkin, Daphne. 'The Unfairest of Them All.' *New York Times* 16 Oct. 2005: 42(L). *Academic OneFile*. Web. 21 Feb. 2014.
Middleton, William. 'Catherine the Great.' *Harper's Bazaar* 03 2000: 342–3. *ProQuest*. Web. 19 Nov. 2013.
Mistry, Meenal. 'Bazaar Movies: Charlotte Gainsbourg.' *Harper's Bazaar* 11 2011: 129. *ProQuest*. Web. 14 Oct. 2013.
Montorgueil, Georges, *La Parisienne peinte par elle-même*. Paris: L. Conquet, 1897. *Gallica, Bibliothèque numérique*. Web. 28 May 2011. http://gallica.bnf.fr/ark:/12148/bpt6k123293b. Accessed 4 Nov. 2016.
Morin, Edgar. *The Stars*. Trans. Richard Howard. New York: Grove, 1960. Print.
Moseley, Rachel. 'Dress, Class and Audrey Hepburn: The Significance of the Cinderella Story.' *Fashioning Film Stars, Dress, Culture, Identity*. Ed. Moseley. London: BFI, 2005. 109–20. Print.
— 'Introduction.' *Fashioning Film Stars, Dress, Culture, Identity*. Ed. Moseley. London: BFI, 2005. 1–8. Print.
Mower, Sarah. 'Skinny Genes.' *Vogue* Apr. 2009: 194. *Academic OneFile*. Web. 21 Aug. 2013.
Mulvey, Laura. *Visual and Other Pleasures*. Basingstoke: Palgrave: 1989. Print.
Munich, Adrienne. 'Fashion Shows.' Introduction. *Fashion in Film*. Ed. Munich. Bloomington: Indiana UP, 2011. 1–14. Print.
Murphy, Tim. 'Indifference and Whispers Prove Alluring.' *New York Times*, late edition (East Coast). 10 Nov. 2011. *ProQuest*. Web. 4 Feb. 2014.

Nacache, Jacqueline. *Hollywood: L'ellipse et l'infilmé*. Paris: L'Harmattan, 2001. Print.
Neale, Steve. *Genre and Hollywood*. London: Routledge, 2000. Print.
Nelmes, Jill. *An Introduction to Film Studies*. New York: Routledge, 2003. Print.
Nelson, Brian. Introduction. *The Ladies' Paradise*. By Émile Zola. Trans. Nelson. Oxford: Oxford UP, 1998. vii–xxiii. Print.
Nowell-Smith, Geoffrey. 'Theatre of complicity.' *Sight & Sound* 15.4 (2005): 36–40. *Art & Architecture Complete*. Web. 10 June 2014.
Ossman, Susan. 'Cosmopolitan Content.' *Moving Matters: Paths of Serial Migration*. Stanford, CA: Stanford UP, 2013. 19–35. Print.
Owens, Mitchell. 'A Muse with a Vision of Her Own, Built on Crystal.' *New York Times*, late edition (East Coast). 3 Jan. 1999. *ProQuest*. Web. 25 Feb. 2014.
Panofsky, Erwin. 'Introductory.' *Studies in Iconology: Humanistic Themes in the Art of the Renaissance*. Oxford: Westview Press, 1972. Print.
— 'Style and Medium in the Motion Pictures.' 1934. Rev. ed. 1947. *Film Theory and Criticism: Introductory Readings*. Ed. Gerald Mast and Marshall Cohen. 2nd ed. New York: Oxford UP, 1979: 243–63. Print.
Parisiennes: A Celebration of French Women. Paris: Flammarion, 2007. Print.
Parsons, Deborah L. *Streetwalking the Metropolis: Women, the City, and Modernity*. Oxford: Oxford UP, 2000. Print.
Philippe, Claude-Jean. *Jean Renoir, une vie en œuvres*. Mesnil-sur-l'Estrée: Gramet, 2005. Print.
Phillips, Lynn. 'Crossing the Line.' *New York Times* 17 Apr. 2011: 56(L). *Academic OneFile*. Web. 27 Sept. 2012.
Pouillard, Veronique. 'In the Shadow of Paris? French Haute Couture and Belgian Fashion Between the Wars.' *Producing Fashion: Commerce, Culture, and Consumers*. Ed. Regina Lee Blaszczyk. Philadelphia: Pennsylvania UP, 2008. 62–81. Print.
Pullar, Ellen. '"A star who is not like the others": Arletty's publicity persona during the 1930s.' *Studies in French Cinema* 12.1 (2012): 7–19. *Film & Television Literature Index with Full Text*. Web. 22 Dec. 2013.
Rearick, Charles. *Paris Dreams, Paris Memories: The City and Its Mystique*. Stanford, CA: Stanford UP, 2011. Print.
Reed, Paula. *Fifty Fashion Looks That Changed the 1950s*. London: Conran Octopus, 2012. Print.
— *Fifty Fashion Looks That Changed the 1960s*. London: Conran Octopus, 2012. Print.
Renoir, Jean. *Renoir: My Father*. Trans. Randolph and Dorothy Weaver. London: Reprint Society, 1964. Print.
Rétaillaud-Bajac, Emmanuelle.'"Entrechic" et "chien": les séductions de la Parisienne, de Jean-Jacques Rousseau à Yves Saint Laurent.' *Genre, sexualité & societé* 10 (2013): n.p. *DOAJ*. Web. 8 Apr. 2014.
Reyes, Raquel A.G. *Love, Passion and Patriotism: Sexuality and the Philippine*

Propaganda. Movement, 1882–1892. Seattle: U of Washington P, 2008. Print.
Richardson, Joanna. *The Courtesans: the Demimonde in Nineteenth-Century France.* London: Weidenfeld & Nicolson, 1967. Print.
Roberts, Mary Louise. *Civilization without Sexes: Reconstructing Gender in Postwar France, 1917–1927.* Chicago: U of Chicago P, 1994. Print.
Roberts, Randy W. 'John Wayne Goes to War.' *Hollywood's America: Twentieth-century America Through Film.* Ed. Steven Mintz and Randy W. Roberts. 4th rev. ed. Oxford: Wiley-Blackwell, 2010. 144–62. Print.
Rocamora, Agnès. *Fashioning the City: Paris, Fashion and the Media.* London: I.B. Tauris, 2009. Print.
Ross, Kristin. *Fast Cars, Clean Bodies: Decolonization and the Reordering of French Culture.* Cambridge, MA: MIT Press, 1995. Print.
Rounding, Virginia. *Grandes Horizontales: The Lives and Legends of Marie Duplessis, Cora Pearl, La Paiva and La Présidente.* London: Bloomsbury, 2003. Print.
Ruiz, Raúl. 'Note d'intention.' *Une fantaisie 'à la manière' de Schnitzler.* Apr. 2006. *Le Cinéma de Raoul Ruiz.* Web. 8 Apr. 2014. http://www.lecinemaderaoulruiz.com/raoul-ruiz-cineaste/klimt. Accessed 10 Nov. 2016.
Safe, Georgina. 'Try On Everything Under the Sun.' *Sydney Morning Herald* (Sydney, Australia). 10 Jan. 2012: 4. *Academic OneFile.* Web. 23 Apr. 2014.
Sagan, Françoise. *La Chamade.* Paris: Julliard, 1965. Print.
— *La Chamade.* Trans. John Murray. Harmondsworth: Penguin, 1968. Print.
Sarris, Andrew. 'Pop Go the Movies!' 1964. *The Primal Screen.* New York: Simon & Schuster, 1973. 69–76. Print.
Schickel, Richard. 'Two Sexpots in a Fine, Old- Fashioned Fantasy.' Review of *Viva Maria! Life* 60, 28 Jan. 1966, 8. Print.
Schilt, Thibaut. *François Ozon.* Urbana: Illinois UP, 2011. Print.
Schlossman, Beryl. 'The night of the poet: Baudelaire, Benjamin, and the woman in the street.' *Modern Language Notes* 119.5 (2004): 1013–32. *ProQuest.* Web. 17 Aug. 2013.
Schwartz, Vanessa R. *Spectacular Realities: Early Mass Culture in Fin-de-siècle France.* Berkeley: U of California P, 1998. Print.
— *It's So French! Hollywood, Paris and the Making of Cosmopolitan Film Culture.* Chicago: U of Chicago P, 2007. Print.
— *Paris, 1900: 'Cancan' Films.* Ed. Antoine de Baecque. Paris: Flammarion, 2012. 110–31. Print.
Sellier, Geneviève. *Masculine Singular: French New Wave Cinema.* Trans. Kristin Ross. Durham, NC: Duke UP, 2008. Print.
Sheridan, Jayne. *Fashion, Media, Promotion: The New Black Magic.* Oxford: Wiley-Blackwell, 2010. Print.
Simon, Marie. *Fashion in Art: The Second Empire and Impressionism.* London: Zwemmer, 1995. Print.
Smith, Alison. 'Men in Unfamiliar Places: A Response to Phil Powrie.' *Studies in French Cinema: UK Perspectives, 1985–2010.* Ed. Will Higbee and Sarah Leahy. Bristol: Intellect, 2011. 177–90. Print.

Smith, Dina M. 'Global Cinderella: Sabrina (1954), Hollywood, and postwar internationalism.' *Cinema Journal* 41.4 (2002): 27–51. *ProQuest*. Web. 22 May. 2012.

Smith, Steve. 'Godard and film noir: a reading of À *bout de souffle*.' *Nottingham French Studies* 32.1 (1993): 65–73. Print.

Solomon-Godeau, Abigail. 'The Other Side of Venus: The Visual Economy of Feminine Display.' *The Sex of Things: Gender and Consumption in Historical Perspective*. Ed. Victoria de Grazia and Elle Furlough. Berkeley: U of California P, 1996. 113–50. Print.

Søndergaard, Sidsel Maria. *Women in Impressionism: From Mythical Feminine to Modern Woman*. Milan: Skira, 2006. Print.

Spicer, Andrew. Introduction. *European Film Noir*. Ed. Spicer. Manchester: Manchester UP, 2007. 1–22. Print.

Steele, Valerie. *Paris Fashion: A Cultural History*. Rev. ed. New York: Berg, 1998. Print.

— 'Femme fatale: fashion and visual culture in fin-de-siècle Paris.' *Fashion Theory* 8.3 (2004): 315–28. Print.

— 'Édouard Manet: *Nana*.' *Impressionism, Fashion and Modernity*. Ed. Gloria Groom. New Haven, CT: Yale UP, 2012. 124–33. Print.

Stewart, Janet. 'Filming Vienna 1900: the poetics of cinema and the politics of ornament in Raúl Ruiz's *Klimt*.' *Journal of Austrian Studies* 46.2 (2013): 49–79. *Project Muse*. Web. 17 Dec. 2013.

Stratton, Jon. *The Desirable Body: Cultural Fetishism and the Erotics of Consumption*. Manchester, Manchester UP, 1996. Print.

Street, Sarah. *Costume and Cinema: Dress Codes in Popular Film*. London: Wallflower, 2001. Print.

Tétart-Vittu, Françoise. 'Édouard Manet: *The Parisienne*.' *Impressionism, Fashion, and Modernity*. Ed. Gloria Groom. New Haven, CT: Yale UP, 2012. 78–83. Print.

Thomas, Isabelle, and Frédérique Veysset. *Paris Street Style: A Guide to Effortless Chic*. Trans. Anthony Roberts. New York: Abrams Image, 2013. Print.

Tiersten, Lisa. *Marianne in the Market: Envisioning Consumer Society in Fin-de-Siècle France*. Berkeley: U of California Press, 2001. Print.

Tinterow, Gary. 'Édouard Manet: *Young Lady in 1866*.' *Impressionism, Fashion, and Modernity*. Ed. Gloria Groom. New Haven, CT: Yale UP, 2012. 26–31. Print.

Turim, Maureen. 'Poetic Realism as Psychoanalytical and Ideological Operation: Marcel Carné's *Le Jour se lève* (1939).' *French Film: Texts and Contexts*. Ed. Susan Hayward and Ginette Vincendeau. London: Routledge, 2002. 63–77. Print.

Turk, Edward B. *Child of Paradise: Marcel Carné and the Golden Age of French Cinema*. Cambridge, MA: Harvard UP, 1989. Print.

Uzanne, Louis Octave. *Parisiennes de ce temps en leurs divers milieux, états et conditions: études pour servir à l'histoire des femmes, de la société, de la galanterie française, des moeurs contemporaines et de l'égoïsme masculin*

... Paris: Mercure de France, 1910. *Gallica, Bibliothèque numérique*. Web. 7 Feb. 2011. http://gallica.bnf.fr/ark:/12148/bpt6k828380. Accessed 4 Nov. 2016.
— *The Modern Parisienne*. London: Heinemann, 1912. Print.
Vezin, Annette, and Luc Vezin. *The 20th Century Muse*. Trans. Toula Ballas. New York: Harry N. Abrams, 2003. Print.
Vincendeau, Ginette. *Pépé le Moko*. London: BFI, 1998. Print.
— 'Brigitte Bardot.' *World Cinema: Critical Approaches*. Ed. Hill and Church Gibson. New York: Oxford UP, 2000. 112–16. Print.
— *Stars and Stardom in French Cinema*. London: Continuum, 2000. Print.
— 'French Film Noir.' *European Film Noir*. Ed. Andrew Spicer. Manchester: Manchester UP, 2007. 23–54. Print.
— 'The star reborn.' *Sight & Sound* 19.5 (2009): 17–24. *Art & Architecture Complete*. Web. 1 Mar. 2014.
---- *Brigitte Bardot*. Basingstoke: Palgrave Macmillan, 2013. Print.
Viviani, Christian. 'Audrey Hepburn: Parisian Icon.' Trans. Alexandra Keens. *Paris by Hollywood*. Ed. Antoine de Baecque. Paris: Flammarion, 2012. 166–81. Print.
Vogue Paris. No. 883. Dec. 2007–Jan. 2008. Print.
Waldron, Darren. '"Une mine d'or inépuisable": the queer pleasures of François Ozon's *8 femmes/8 Women* (2002).' *Studies in French Cinema* 10.1 (2010): 69–82. Print.
Weiner, Susan. 'When a prostitute becomes an orphan: Pierre Mac Orlan's *Le Quai des brumes* (1927) in the service of poetic realism.' *Studies in French Cinema* 6.2 (2006): 129–40. Print.
Welch, Ellen R. *A Taste for the Foreign: Worldly Knowledge and Literary Pleasure in Early Modern French Fiction*. Lanham, MD: Delaware UP, 2011. Print.
Whiteley, Nigel. *Art and Pluralism: Lawrence Alloway's Cultural Criticism*. Liverpool: Liverpool UP, 2012. Print.
Wilde, Oscar. 'The Decay of Lying.' *Oscar Wilde – The Major Works*. Ed. Isobel Murray. Oxford: Oxford UP, 2000. 215–39. Print.
Williamson, Judith. *Decoding Advertisements: Ideology and Meaning in Advertising*. London: Marion Boyars, 1978. Print.
Wiser, William. *The Crazy Years: Paris in the Twenties*. London: Thames & Hudson, 1983. Print.
Wolff, Janet. 'The invisible flâneuse: women and the literature of modernity.' *Theory, Culture & Society* 2.3 1985: 37–46. Print.
Wollen, Peter, et al. *In Black and White: Dress from the 1920s to Today*. Columbus: Wexner Center for the Arts, Ohio State University, 1992. Print.
Young, Caroline. *Classic Hollywood Style*. London: Frances Lincoln, 2012. Print.
Zee, Joe, and Maggie Bullock. *The ELLEments of Personal Style: 25 Modern Fashion Icons on How to Dress, Shop, and Live*. New York: Gotham Books, 2010. Print.

Zola, Émile. *Nana*. Paris: G. Charpentier, 1880. *Gallica, Bibliothèque numérique*. Web. 7 Nov. 2013. http://gallica.bnf.fr/ark:/12148/bpt6k623380z. Accessed 4 Nov. 2016.

— *Nana*. Trans. George Holden. London: Penguin, 1972. Print.

— *L'œuvre*. 1885. Paris: Bibliothèque-Charpe

Index

Allen, Woody
   Midnight in Paris 20, 22, 23, 25, 40–6
Alloway, Lawrence 10–11, 151
D'Antigny, Blanche 143, 144
Arletty 105–6
Attal, Yvan
   Ma Femme est une actrice 170
Avedon, Richard 80–1

Balzac, Honore de
   Illusions perdues 108
Banville, Théodore de 18, 25–6, 47, 55
Bardot, Brigitte 14, 152–62, 178
Baudelaire, Charles 19, 57–9, 86, 95, 97, 116
Baudouin
   75 Parisiennes 6–7
Beauvoir, Simone de 119n
Becque, Henri 171
Bellanger, Marguerite 31
Benjamin, Walter 4, 50–1, 55, 57, 58, 59–60, 83, 95, 121, 167–8
Béraud, Jean 139
Bergman, Ingrid 32–3
Boisrond, Michel
   Une Parisienne 160
Bonnemains, Marguerite de 31
Bourget, Jean-Loup 8–9
Boutet, Henri 22

Carné, Marcel
   Le Jour se lève 95, 102–8
   Le Quai des brumes 95, 96, 108–12
Caron, Leslie 1–3, 83
Cavalier, Alain
   La Chamade 120, 123–4, 133–40, 147–9
Chanel, Coco 41–2, 111
Chaplin, Charles
   A Woman of Paris 120, 123–4, 126–32, 147–9
Charpentier, Marguerite 31–2
Colette 131
Crawford, Joan 78–9

Darrieux, Danielle 137–8
Dassin, Jules
   Du Rififi chez les hommes 95, 100–2
   Reunion in France 78–9, 93
Degas, Edgar 162
Delord, Taxile 42–3, 48–9, 72–3
Demy, Jacques
   Lola 55, 68
   Model Shop 54–60
Deneuve, Cathérine 135–7, 138–9
Doillon, Lou 172
Donen, Stanley
   Funny Face 76, 80–2, 93, 94, 166–7
Dumas, Alexandre 60, 125–6, 132, 140–2

Duvivier, Julien
   Pépé le moko 50–4

Eliot, T. S. 44, 45

Faulkner, William 44, 135
Flaubert, Gustave 19, 21
Fréhel 53–4

Gainsbourg, Charlotte 169–78
Gautier, Théophile 97, 105–6
Givenchy, Hubert de 76–7, 94
Godard, Jean-Luc
   À bout de souffle 90–2, 95, 112–14, 118
   and Karina 163–4, 168
   Le Mépris 159
Gréco, Juliette 175
Godebska, Misia 26–31

Haussmann, Georges-Eugène 4
Hawks, Howard
   Gentlemen Prefer Blondes 143–4, 145
Hayworth, Rita 145
Head, Edith 80
Hepburn, Audrey 60–8, 76–7, 80–2, 94
Houssaye, Arsène 39, 43, 73, 84, 89, 158

Japonisme 37–8

Karina, Anna 163–8
Koralnik, Pierre
   Anna 166–8

Luhrmann, Baz
   Moulin Rouge! 120, 124, 140–9

Malle, Louis
   Viva Maria! 152–3, 161–2
Maupassant, Guy de 27–8
Mérode, Cléo de 34–5, 36

Minnelli, Vincente
   An American in Paris 1–3, 180–2
   Gigi 82–4, 93, 129
Monroe, Marilyn 143
Montorgueil, Georges 5, 22
Moreau, Jeanne 152–62
Morgan, Michèle 108–9, 110–11
Morin, Edgar 151, 177
Moss, Kate 47
Mulvey, Laura 12–13

Ophüls, Max
   Madame de... 137–8
Ozon, François
   8 femmes 87–90, 93

Panofsky, Erwin
   theory of iconography 7–10
Poetic Realism 102–4, 117
Polanski, Roman
   Frantic 84–6, 93
Préchac, Jean de 42, 48

Renoir, Pierre-Auguste 28
Renoir, Jean
   Elena et les hommes 22–3, 24, 26–34, 46
Ruiz, Raúl
   Klimt 20, 23, 24–5, 34–9, 46

Sagan, Françoise 133–4
Saint Laurent, Yves 47, 69–70
Schwartz, Vanessa
   Frenchness films 62–3
Sciamma, Céline
   Bande de filles 15
Seberg, Jean 90–2, 114–15
Simmel, Georg 82, 121

Tissot, James 130
Toulouse-Lautrec, Henri de 86, 181, 182
Truffaut, François
   La Sirène du Mississippi 138–9

Uzanne, Louis Octave 2–3, 23, 29–30, 37, 47, 48, 72, 74, 75, 81, 90, 128, 130–1, 146, 172

Vidor, Charles
 Gilda 145
Vincendeau, Ginette 14, 52, 53, 78, 100, 102, 135, 151, 154, 177, 178

Wilde, Oscar 19
Wilder, Billy
 Sabrina 60–8, 76

Zola, Émile
 Nana 19–20, 101, 122, 132, 140

EU authorised representative for GPSR:
Easy Access System Europe, Mustamäe tee 50,
10621 Tallinn, Estonia
gpsr.requests@easproject.com

www.ingramcontent.com/pod-product-compliance
Lightning Source LLC
Chambersburg PA
CBHW082105250426
43673CB00067B/1842